Handbook on Radio and Television Audience Research

Graham Mytton

BBC World Service Training Trust

UNESCO

unicef
United Nations Children's Fund

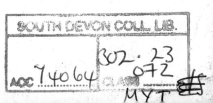

BBC World Service Training Trust, Bush House, London WC2B 4PH, United Kingdom
UNESCO, 7, Place de Fontenoy, 75352 Paris 07 SP, France
UNICEF, Unicef House, 3 UN Plaza, New York, NY 10017, United States of America

Printed in the United Kingdom
Design by Peter Cope FCSD
Cover illustration by Stewart Walton

Preface	6

1 Introduction	10
Exercise	*12*
Why Audience Research?	13

2 History of Audience Research	15

3 Audience Measurement or Quantitative Research	18
3.1 Sampling:	19
Theory and Practice	19
Samples and Censuses	20
Defining the 'Universe'	20
Selecting a Representative Sample	21
The Sampling Frame	22
Exercise	*23*
Random or Probability Samples	24
Stratified Random Samples	25
Random Sampling Within a Survey	27
Quota Samples	30
Telephone Samples	31
Snowball Samples	32
Sampling and Statistical Theory:	32
Exercise	*36*
3.2 The Questionnaire: The Art of Asking Questions	37
Designing a Questionnaire	37
Questions to Ask Before Designing Questions	41
Not All Questions are Answerable!	43
Types of Question	44
Exercise	*48*
Comment	*49*
Making Questions Work	51
The Order of Questions	53
Checking or Testing the Reliability of Questions	54
Social and Cultural Acceptability and Self Portrayal	54
Validity	55
3.3 Pilot Testing	55

3.4	The Interview	56
	The Role of the Interviewer	56
	Checking Interviewers	59
3.5	Checking and Editing of Questionnaires	60
	Back Checking	60
3.6	Some Common Problems Encountered in Field Research and Some Solutions	61
3.7	Translation of Questionnaires into Different Languages	64
3.8	Audience and Media Measurement Research Methods in Use Today	65
	Self-completion Diaries	66
	Television and Radio Audience Meters	69
	Personal Interviews	72
3.9	Research Among Specific Target Groups	78
3.10	Survey Research for Small Stations	79
3.11	Other Methods of Audience Measurement Research	79
	Exercise	*81*
	Comment	*81*

4	**Audience Opinion and Reaction**	**82**
4.1	Panels	82
	Exercise	*82*
	Exercise	*86*
4.2	Postal Self-completion Questionnaires	86
4.3	On-air Questionnaires for Radio Stations	89
4.4	Appreciation Indices	91
4.5	Other Measures	93

5	**Qualitative Research**	**94**
5.1	Focus Groups, Sometimes Known as Group Discussions	95
	Role Play	101
	Photo Sorting	101
	Collages	101
	Personification	101
	Picture or Scene Completion	102
	Word Association	102
	Product and Service Mapping	102
	Sentence Completion	103
	Obituaries	103

Examples of Focus Groups Used in Audience Research ... 103

5.2　In-depth Interviews ... 105

5.3　Participant Observation ... 106

5.4　Reliability and Validity in Qualitative Research ... 108

Exercise ... *109*

5.5　Analysis and Reporting Qualitative Research ... 110

6　Desk Research ... **111**

**7　Listeners' Viewers' and Readers' Letters, Phone Calls
and other Personal Communications from the Audience** ... **112**

8　Research to Improve and Test Effectiveness ... **114**

Hall Tests – or Similar Ways of Pretesting Advertising etc ... 116

Research into the Effectiveness of Advertising and Other Media Messages ... 117

9　Data Analysis ... **124**

9.1　Interpretation and Terminology ... 125

9.2　Ratings and Gross Rating Points ... 126

Exercise ... *128*

Comment ... *128*

9.3　Amount of Listening or Viewing, and Share ... 130

9.4　Reach ... 132

10 Readership Research ... **138**

Exercise ... *138*

11 Adapting Audience Research to Different Cultures ... **140**

12 How Research is Used ... **143**

12.1　Meeting the Challenge of Competition ... 143

12.2　Understanding Audiences ... 146

12.3　Strategic Research – Seeing the Big Picture ... 149

Exercise ... *153*

Appendices ... **155**

Bibliography ... **183**

Glossary of Terms ... **185**

References ... **189**

Preface

This manual is a substantially revised and updated version of an earlier book by me published in 1993 by UNESCO and UNICEF, *A Handbook on Television and Radio Audience Research*. The purpose of that book was to provide an outline of how radio and television audience research is done, how it is used and what its purposes are. In that book I attempted to show readers how to go about doing audience research, but also to show those involved in broadcasting, who might never actually do research themselves, how to understand research so that they may be better able to use it in their work.

There were several reasons for this revision. First, broadcasting is changing very fast and there was much in the old book that was simply out of date.

Second, research is changing. New methods of audience measurement are being developed. Advances in other areas need to be reflected.

Third, I have had the chance over the past five years to use the book in training broadcasters, researchers and communicators as well as college and university students taking broader communications studies courses. I have learned a lot from them both about what was missing and also what needed further elaboration or explanation. I have included new sections on aspects of audience research that were previously omitted. I have used new examples of audience research questionnaires and have included up to date audience and media data from a number of countries.

Fourth, while this manual remains focused mainly on radio and television, I have, where appropriate, included references to research into other communication channels, including printed media. Many of the methods described are used in other kinds of social and market research.

The original idea for this book came in 1990 from Morten Giersing of UNICEF when he worked for UNESCO. He and others had noted the lack of suitable published works on audience research and how to do it. Most of what existed fell into two broad categories. First there were the mostly empirical studies done mainly in the developed world. Much of this work is dominated by the demands of advertisers. There was also a fair amount of material about research in the non-commercial public service sector. This was also mostly from the richer industrialised countries.

Second there was a large and growing body of mostly theoretical and critical studies produced by academic scholars. A lot of this is very far removed from the practical day-to-day problems and issues facing radio and television broadcasters and others who use these and other modern communications media.

There is a growing interest in audience research in developing countries. It is being seen less as an expensive luxury and more as an essential tool in developing better broadcasting and better-targeted advertising and advocacy. With the rapid changes in communications technology, the growth of deregulation and the changes in consumer behaviour, audience and other forms of market research become ever more vital. There is also a growing interest in using the techniques of market research in improving the effectiveness of development activity. This book, like the first edition, is intended to be relevant to all situations, covering as it does all appropriate methods and techniques. There is, however, a deliberate emphasis on the needs of less developed media markets.

The first edition of this book has been used in training courses and workshops run by UNICEF, the Commonwealth Broadcasting Association, the European Broadcasting Union and others. I have been involved in many of these. This has enabled me to note areas in the book that need expansion or improvement. The first edition has been translated into several languages including Vietnamese, Lao, Russian and Chinese. It is hoped that this edition may also soon appear in other languages. It has also been used in post-graduate University teaching. I hope that this new edition will, like the last, be of use not only to broadcasters, advertisers and development officials who seek to use the media more effectively and efficiently but also to academic bodies interested in knowing how research is done in the broadcasting industry.

Many people have assisted me and provided helpful advice, either for the first or the second edition, or for both. I cannot mention them all, but I would especially like to thank many European audience researchers who gave advice and offered material. They include Claude Geertz formerly of RTBF Belgium, Jaroslav Kostál formerly of Czech Radio, Heikki Kasari of Yleisradio Finland, Peter Diem and Judith Stelmach of ORF Austria, Matthias Steinmann of SRG Switzerland, Laura Martinez formerly of Catalan TV and Radio, Silvano Minitti of RAI Italy, Valentina Zlobina of the Voice of Russia, Kersti Raudam of Estonian Television, Lina Trochalitou of ERT Greece, Robert Towler of ITC UK, Peter Jenkins of RAJAR UK, Carole Paplorey of TV5 France, Oliver Zöllner of Deutsche Welle Germany, Viera Štefancová and Ivan Kralik of Slovakia Television, and Wim Bekkers of NOS The Netherlands. Audience researchers from other parts of the world have also been of great assistance. They include Edwin Sinjwala and the late Tobias Sumaili of ZNBC Zambia, Jurgens Brand formerly of NBC Namibia, Daan Van Vuuren of SABC South Africa, B Kurana and BS Chandrasekhar of Doordarshan India, Maude Blankson-Mills of GBC Ghana, Chen Ruoyu of CCTV China, Nobuko Shiraishi of NHK Japan, Nandana Karunanayake of SLBC Sri Lanka, Rosemary Whewell of the former NZBC New Zealand, Dennis List of ABC Australia, and Philip Savage and Barry Kiefl of CBC Canada.

Robert Fortner of Calvin College, Michigan provided useful comments for the first edition. Peter Menneer, a former BBC colleague and now a leading independent audience research consultant has read and commented very helpfully on the second edition. I am especially indebted to him for assistance on statistical analyses. Frank Gray of FEBC made some vital last moment corrections.

There has been a large input from the BBC. I have drawn extensively from the world-wide knowledge and experiences of my former colleagues in audience research at the

BBC World Service. I was in charge of audience research there between 1982 and 1998 during which time we ran audience research projects of all kinds and in every continent. BBC audience and marketing research staff, both past and present, including David Ostry, Myra Hunt, Hugh Hope-Stone, Shirley Kennedy, Ruth Grimley, Clare Sumpner, Colin Wilding, Allen Cooper, Robert Kitching, Melissa Baker, Satu Salmi and Liz Fuller have in various ways and at various times been very helpful in providing material and analyses of data for me. Tim Ward, Cheryl Chaundy and Michael Gilsenan have been patiently helpful in giving assistance with handling, copying and moving about computer files. Another colleague, Carol Forrester who compiles and collects data about broadcasters and their audiences all over the world for the BBC World Service has always been immensely helpful. She is one of those very special colleagues who never seem to refuse a request for information, however hard to find. Carol's counterpart in the BBC's domestic services, Andrew Hemming is cast in much the same mould and has also been a great help in finding up-to-date and, above all, accurate data for me to use or refer to.

My former assistant, Marie Dziedzic, gave much essential support in the production of both editions. Caroline Thomson, Deputy Managing Director of the BBC World Service and Gwyneth Henderson, Head of BBC World Service Training have been enthusiastic supporters of this second edition and I am delighted that the BBC is a co-publisher of it. Melanie Lowndes and David Bradshaw of the BBC's legal department helped to make a publishing agreement with UNICEF and UNESCO possible.

Without Morten Giersing's encouragement, first when he worked at UNESCO and then at UNICEF, the work would never have been started. Andrew Claypole of UNICEF has enthusiastically supported the project for a new edition. I hope that the result will not disappoint them nor UNICEF, the main sponsor.

Janet, my wife, has put up with my long absences from home, running courses and workshops around the world. More recently she has put up with my long absences in my study struggling to finish this new edition on time. She has checked the final manuscript. I hope we will see a little more of each other now that the work is completed.

I am indebted to many people and organisations for permission to include material. The extract from *Yes Prime Minister* is reproduced by kind permission of BBC Worldwide. The extract from *The Manual for Culturally Adapted Research* is reproduced by kind permission of the author, Professor Scarlett Epstein. Professor Epstein has also given helpful advice for this edition. Some sections of this new edition originally appeared in a module published by Leicester University for their MA in Communications Studies, by Distance Learning. This was produced as a supplement to the first edition of this book. This second edition now brings the material together in one volume.

I am grateful to all these people for their help and encouragement. But any weaknesses or faults that remain are my responsibility. My only remaining wish is that the book is useful, especially in promoting better broadcasting and better use of all forms of communication by those bodies which seek to improve the lot of their fellow men and women.

I am indebted to Peter Cope for the layout and design of this book. I believe that it is now a more attractive and easier to use manual than its predecessor was. I am especially grateful for all the work he has done to make the various charts, tables and facsimiles of questionnaires etc. attractive and readable.

One of the outcomes I would be most happy to see is the development of international networks of people involved in audience and communications research. This already exists in Europe and, to some extent, in other developed countries. It is my hope and intention to do what I can to assist the development of such networks throughout the world. I will be involved in The Commonwealth Broadcasting Association's plans to include an audience research section on its Internet web site. It does not exist yet, but it will be in place very soon. The home page for the CBA is http://www.oneworld.org/cba/index.htm. Soon there will be a link from this to an audience research page or pages and, it is hoped, to other similar sites.

This new version of the manual includes training exercises and projects that, I hope, will help the student to learn through both practice and investigation. I would like to hear from anyone using the book who may have queries or comments and I am prepared to give advice when needed.

The book is intended to help make broadcasting and communication around the world more effective and worthwhile. It has been an exciting project to produce something that will, I fervently hope, be of real practical value in not only helping broadcasters do their work better but also in showing the value and use of audience and market research to all those who use the media, whether in development and advocacy for the public good or for advertising in the commercial world.

Graham Mytton
Roffeys
Coldharbour
Dorking
RH5 6HE
UK
Fax: +44 1306 712958
Email: gmytton@gn.apc.org

Introduction

Radio and television are 20th century phenomena. The years between 1900 and 2000 have probably seen more changes in technology than any previous century. The electronic media have played a major role in those changes and in all parts of the world now feature as an important part of the daily lives of most people. Many of the major differences that we find in the world of the year 2000, when compared to a century ago, are the direct result of the arrival and development during that period of what we call the mass media.

Radio reaches almost everyone everywhere. It is true that some people still have no regular access to it but the number is shrinking. Television also has grown rapidly in recent years, reaching many people in some of the very poorest parts of the world.[1] The printed press is also important but its impact and reach is more varied and is, in some communities and areas, rather restricted on account of high levels of illiteracy.

The world's population in mid 1998 was estimated to be 5,926 million.[2] At the same time it was estimated that there were 2,400 million radio receivers and 1,300 million television sets. That is one radio set for every two and a half people and one television for every four and a half. However, radio sets are very unevenly distributed. While there are more radios than people in rich countries like Australia, France, the United Kingdom, Sweden, Canada and the United States, we find that in poor countries like Bhutan, Bangladesh, Guinea Bissau and Burkina Faso, there is only about one radio set or fewer for every ten people. There are 22 other countries that have a similarly low level of radio ownership.[3]

There are even greater disparities in access to television. While in some of the richer countries most households have more than one set, there are 27 countries where there is only one television set for every one hundred or more people.

There are also great disparities in the development of the two media at the programme and transmission end. The inhabitants of even quite small United States cities usually have more than 20 television and 40 radio stations or channels to chose from, even if they have no cable or satellite connection. If they have these, their range of choice may extend to several hundred channels. In many West European countries the number of television and radio channels has increased considerably over the past twenty years as both media have been deregulated; that is to say, they are no longer monopolies of the state or public sector. Commercial and other independent operators have been licensed to own and run stations. The same process has also happened rapidly in East and Central Europe where formerly under communist rule there was a total state monopoly.

There are several countries in other parts of the world where there is only a single state-owned television channel and perhaps two or three state radio stations, usually enjoying a total monopoly. These are mostly less developed, poorer countries. In some of them, private stations have been licensed in recent years, but these tend to be confined to the major cities. Although there are often private newspapers and other independent print media in Africa and Asia, in most countries the electronic media have tended to be organised as a state monopoly. Now, even this is changing. In the 1980s in Africa, there were only six radio or television stations on the whole continent not owned by the state. Since about 1990 however we have seen the beginnings of the end of state monopoly in countries as diverse as Sierra Leone, Burkina Faso, Ivory Coast, Tanzania, Mozambique, Malawi, Gabon, Mali and South Africa. The process has been slow and, at the time of writing, most African and Asian people still have relatively little choice in the domestic radio and TV services available to them.

Historically, the organisation of radio and television has followed two broad patterns or models. In most of Europe broadcasting began in the nineteen twenties as an activity organised by the state. Radio was run either as a public service more or less independently of the government or directly by the government as an instrument of the state. Thus, in Britain, the Scandinavian countries, the Netherlands, Switzerland and a few others, broadcasting was legislated for as a public service provided for by a non-governmental agency, independent of political authority, but established by the state. In the communist countries and also in France and some other European states, broadcasting was run as a department of the government.[4]

On the other hand, in the United States from the very beginning, radio, and later television also, was organised as a commercial profit-making activity. The government was involved in the granting of licences to broadcast but in not much else.[5]

The rest of the world adopted one or other of these two alternative but very different approaches to the regulation and organisation of broadcasting. Most of Latin America chose to take the US road. Most of Africa and Asia, formerly under European colonial rule, followed the European model. Thus it was that in the whole of Africa the colonial powers, mostly France and Britain, bequeathed broadcasting systems to the newly independent states that came directly or indirectly under state control. It was the same in India, Pakistan, Sri Lanka, Malaysia, Vietnam, Laos and most other ex-British and ex-French territories.

Broadcasting in most countries is now being diversified. Those countries in Europe, Asia and Africa that formerly had state or public service monopolies have mostly now permitted independent broadcasters. Many of these operate on a commercial basis, relying on the sale of advertising and the commercial sponsorship of programmes. Some are community-based and funded by a mixture of public funds, advertising and voluntary contributions. Some seek to serve a religious purpose. There are also a few which have a partisan political purpose but these are relatively rare.

Exercise

> *How many domestic – that is based in your country – radio and television stations are available to you where you live? How many are available in the capital city and how many in other towns and cities? And how many are available to people in the rural areas? How many of these stations are privately owned and how many belong to public bodies like the government or local authorities? Are there any community-based stations independent of both government and commercial organisations? Are there any religious or politically motivated stations? Distinguish between television and radio and consider why there might be more in one category than another. Try to discover the reasons for both the number and the range of ownership of radio and television in your country? What are the laws governing the ownership of radio and television stations?*

The two electronic media play a major role in world information. Pictures and reports of events and people from different parts of the globe are carried everywhere and at great speed. During the 1991 war in the Arabian/Persian Gulf, television viewers were able to see pictures of the bombing of Baghdad on television screens or hear radio reports of air raids as they happened. Immediacy of certain kinds of information has come to be normal and expected. However, it does not mean necessarily that we are, as a result, better informed than we were before this era of more rapid global communication. Indeed the main impact of the modern mass media may be less in the rapid dissemination of information and more in the wider dissemination of certain ways of seeing the world.

The electronic media may be doing rather more than merely giving information. Some see them as having an unwelcome influence. They are thought to enhance the power of the already powerful. They are criticised for lowering cultural standards and of blurring the distinctive richness of many world cultures. Critics see them as promoting false values. They are seen as being dominated by powerful nations or multinational companies and as weakening further the already weak.

There are others who see the modern electronic mass media as leading to greater violence, immorality and disrespect for tradition. They are often blamed for the supposed increase in crime. Many other ills of modern society have been blamed on television – rather less on radio.

At the same time, others view the electronic media as having mostly beneficial effects. It is argued that they make democracy possible by widely disseminating the kinds of information people need when exercising democratic choices. They cut across social and economic barriers and provide equal access to educational and other information by which people can improve their own personal circumstances.

It is not at all easy to decide who is right in this debate. Have the modern mass media had mostly beneficial or harmful effects? Put this way the question is probably unanswerable. The fact is that modern life as most of the world knows it could not be imagined without electronic mass communication. The systems of mass communication found in the world today form part of the way in which world societies function. One might as well ask, 'Is modern society beneficial or harmful?' A more interesting set of questions arises instead if we think about the media with these facts in mind: What role do they play in different societies? How much are they used, for what purpose and by whom? What are the consequences when the media change in some way?

Why Audience Research?

The questions 'Who is listening?' or 'Who is watching?' are surely not unwarranted or even remarkable questions to ask. Certainly the broadcasters need to know something about the people who are watching or listening. In all kinds of human communication activity we think about the person or persons with whom we are communicating. A teacher speaks in a different manner and about different things to schoolchildren in their first year from those in their sixth year. If we speak to someone who does not speak our own language very well we try to make allowances for this fact. We use different ways of addressing members of our own family, the local shopkeeper, the police, subordinates and superiors. Every time we speak, write a letter, make a phone call or write a book like this one, we need to make an effort to consider with whom we are communicating. If we don't know, we do a little research. When we meet someone for the first time we tend to ask questions that might, in various ways, help us to continue to communicate by modifying in some way, if necessary, the way in which we communicate. Have we met before? Have we certain things in common? Do we share similar interests? What can we ascertain about the other person's attitudes, knowledge or personality that would help us communicate better?

Radio and television broadcasting are peculiar forms of communication. Most of the communicating is one-directional. Broadcasts are transmitted and the broadcaster may assume that what is being broadcast is being watched or listened to. Why is this assumption made and is it always justified?

Let us consider this a little further. It is a fact that a good deal of broadcasting activity in the world goes on without much effort being made to find out what is really happening at the other end! If you made a speech in a large hall full of people and slowly everyone got up and walked out, what would you do? Or consider what you would do if everyone started talking, ignoring what you were saying? You would change what you were saying, attempt to attract everyone's interest and attention, or perhaps you would stop speaking altogether in sheer embarrassment! You would certainly soon feel very foolish if you continued to speak without changing anything unless you were extraordinarily thick-skinned! And yet, a not inconsiderable amount of radio and television broadcasting in the world is like this, especially in countries where there is a state monopoly or very little competition. Broadcasting continues inexorably but no one seems to attempt to find out anything about viewers and listeners. However, there is evidence now that many broadcasters are themselves waking up to the realities

13

of how broadcasting really works. They are beginning to take notice of their audiences, how they actually behave, what they are interested in and so on.

Audience research is more than a matter of knowing if anyone is listening or viewing, important though this undoubtedly is. By audience research we mean the various methods and techniques used to find out about the audience. It covers a wide range of information gathering exercises. For whom is a programme intended? Are they listening or viewing? Do radio broadcasters, living in the cities, know what time to broadcast to farmers? They might think they do but experience shows that without research they can get it wrong. If programmes are aimed at children, are children actually watching or listening? If educational programmes are made and transmitted, are they meeting a need perceived by the broadcaster but not by the intended audience? If the broadcasts meet an audience need, are they made in such a way that will attract the intended audience? Are they available to listen or watch at the time allocated? Do they know about the programmes? What is their experience of using the programmes?

Broadcasting is one of a range of goods and services available to the public but unlike most other goods and services, no selling takes place. If you are selling soft drinks, you can easily find out on a yearly, monthly or even daily basis how many cans or bottles are being sold. If you are running a hospital, you can find out from your records how many people have been admitted over a given period of time. If you are running a bus service you can add up the tickets you have sold and count the miles that have been travelled. Newspaper proprietors can count their sales. But broadcasters have no such easily obtained evidence of consumption or use. That does not mean it is not needed. Nor does it mean that it cannot be obtained.

The major radio and television stations in the less developed countries as well as in many industrialised countries are often funded out of taxation or licence revenue. In this case they are expected to provide a public service, serving the interests of the whole of the tax or licence-paying public. But how can a public service broadcasting station receiving public funds show that it is providing an adequate and appreciated public service unless it does audience research? Part of a public service station's purpose will usually be to serve certain minority interests. This also needs to be researched so that it can be established that these requirements are being met satisfactorily.

Research is essential when the main source of funds for broadcasting is advertising and programme sponsorship. How much should different time slots cost the advertisers? How many people and what kinds of people are listening or viewing at different times and to which programmes? Which is the best time to advertise if one wants to reach housewives? What is the channel listened to most by professional people?

History of Audience Research

2

There was a time when, in the developed industrialised countries where broadcasting began in the 1920s, audience research was not at all widespread. Broadcasters in the early days of radio in Europe and the United States knew remarkably little about their listeners. What they thought they knew was based on very unreliable and misleading methods.

In the very early days of radio in the United States, there was no systematic audience research. Very often it was the personal likes and dislikes of a prospective commercial sponsor – most US broadcasting was and is paid for by advertising – which determined what went on air. An advertiser might sponsor a programme from personal tastes and preferences.[6] But advertisers soon began to realise that they needed information that was independent of their views and opinions or those of the owners of the radio stations.

The first form of measurement used in the United States to guide programming was obtained by counting the number of letters elicited by programmes. Other 'measurements' used by broadcasters in the early days were no more reliable. Some radio station managers used to draw a circle on a map with a hundred-mile radius around the station and determine the number of people who lived within that circle. But such a procedure is entirely meaningless so far as measuring the audience was concerned. Differences in transmitter power, local geography, station programming, wavelengths, and numerous other factors are known to influence the size of the populations habitually reached by each station.

15

Broadcasting also began in Europe in the 1920s. In Britain, radio broadcasting began in 1922, first as a service for the purchasers of the new wireless sets provided by a consortium of manufacturers. This was very soon turned into a public corporation, the BBC, with a Royal Charter to provide radio transmissions of information, education and entertainment as a public service monopoly. In Britain there was no commercial broadcasting on television until 1955 and no commercial radio until 1973. The BBC had no audience research for more than ten years after its establishment in 1922. Moreover, audience research did not begin without an argument about whether it was really necessary.

> "I cannot help feeling more and more strongly that we are fundamentally ignorant as to how our various programmes are received, and what is their relative popularity. It must be a source of considerable disquiet to many people besides myself to think that it is quite possible that a very great deal of our money and time and effort may be expended on broadcasting into a void. (Val Gielgud, BBC Productions Director, 1930)

> "I do not share Gielgud's view on the democratic issue. However complete and effective any survey we launch might be, I should still be convinced that our policy and programme building should be based first and last upon our conviction as to what should and should not be broadcast. As far as meeting

public demand is concerned, I believe that the right way is to provide for a more conscious differentiation of objectives within our daily programme. (Charles Siepmann, BBC Director of Talks, 1930).

These two points of view are not actually impossible to reconcile. Audience research does not aim to tell programme makers what to do. Gielgud's views were actually shared by many programme makers who felt the need to have some more reliable information on the growing audience. This information would help them to do their jobs better. It would also help those in management allocate resources better to meet their public service obligations. Siepmann's remarks seem to have been more in the nature of a caution against over-reliance on quantitative audience research. According to Robert Silvey, the founder of audience research in the BBC, Siepmann became a firm supporter from the early days.[8]

Audience research was formally established within the BBC in 1936. Its role has, from the outset, included serving as an instrument of public accountability as well as providing an information system for programme makers and management. There have been several special studies on particular contemporary broadcasting issues which help the corporation decide on major policy issues. This function has been especially important in recent years, as the broadcasting scene has changed so rapidly in the UK. In the United States the process was completely different. American radio was, from the beginning, guided by one fundamental principle: people are attracted to listen if they get programmes they want. All American audience measurement has derived from this basic marketing principle. Through it, the broadcasters attempt to furnish people with the programmes that sufficiently large numbers of people will want to hear, not with programmes which someone thinks they ought to listen to. The determination of the programme preferences and desires of the general public, or of target audiences within it, is a major requirement of radio and TV audience research in any broadcasting system run on commercial lines.

However, this principle is modified by an uneven consideration given to those preferences and desires. This is because two different market principles are involved in commercial broadcasting. Indeed this is also true of other communications activities that rely, at least in part, on advertising, like, for example, newspaper and magazine publishing. There are two markets involved. Readers, listeners and viewers choose what they read, listen to or watch. Advertisers also choose where they will place their advertisements. Programmes or newspapers that appeal to large numbers of people with spending power are more likely to attract advertising and sponsorship than those which reach smaller numbers of people, or people with less spending power. Programmes or publications for the old, the poor and for minorities may be less likely to receive commercial backing. In the broadcasting world this is the fundamental difference between public service and commercial broadcasting and it is reflected in the outlook and approach of audience research.

Some people in broadcasting, especially in public service or state-run radio or television, are suspicious of research, especially research using the methods of market research. Their view is one I frequently encounter. "How can anything which helps those who are interested only in selling more soft drinks, cosmetics or baby food possibly be of interest or value to those of us who are keen to use broadcasting for the real benefit of people?" It is a profoundly short-sighted view. Whatever we may think about the activities of commercial firms that seek to maximise their sales and profits, sometimes perhaps unscrupulously, we have to recognise that the techniques they employ do actually work. Advertising clearly brings results, otherwise very large sums of money would not be spent on it. It doesn't always work in the way intended. Indeed many expensive campaigns fail to achieve the intended results. The sums spent on advertising in the rich industrial countries are very large indeed. And because some advertising is seen to fail, large sums are spent on research designed to discover the most effective means of advertising. Can these methods not be also used for more general human benefit? The same techniques can of course be used to improve and make more effective any kind of communication. If the need is to improve broadcasting to farmers, or broadcasts to improve public health, infant nutrition, adult education, or anything else, research can help. Just as it can maximise the effectiveness of advertising cosmetics, it can also do the same for more worthwhile communications activities.

Audience research can be used as a means of maximising the effectiveness of public advocacy campaigns, and of improving and enhancing education and information for effective democracy and good government. Audience research is a means of providing essential information to aid the creative process of programme making. It can be used as a means of maximising the efficient and cost-effective use of limited resources. And it can be used to test if the objectives of any educational or information campaign have been successful.

The objective may be a simple one; to increase awareness of a consumer brand – a new soft drink or a washing powder, or to make people aware of the dangers in drinking water from polluted sources. In these cases, messages via the media can be shown to increase awareness. It becomes a little more complicated and difficult to test the effectiveness of advertising or educational promotion in changing peoples' attitudes and behaviour.

Audience Measurement or Quantitative Research

This is the core activity of any broadcasting audience research and the one into which most effort is put. It is why it occupies the largest section of this book. How can we find out how many listen to or watch which services, which programmes and at what times? How do we know what kinds of people are reached by this or that programme or service?

The single most common kind of research activity so far as TV and radio are concerned is audience measurement. It is not difficult to see why this is so. Broadcasting is unique among the range of services and goods available to the public. It is the only one for which we have no readily available information about the users or 'customers'. When you listen to a radio station or watch a TV channel, nothing material is actually consumed. No physical transaction takes place. Sometimes we use the word 'consumers' about viewers or listeners to make an analogy with goods like food, drink and so on. These products are actually consumed; something physical disappears and is no more! Broadcasting is not quite like that! We can get some idea of how much beer is drunk or rice is eaten by looking at production or sales figures. We can find out how many people go to the cinema by looking at how many tickets are sold. But there is no similar way of telling how many people watch a TV programme or listen to something on radio. With the printed media we are in a kind of halfway position. Newspapers and magazines are bought and usually thrown away within a short period (although practices can vary greatly). Something is more obviously 'consumed'. But this is measurable easily only in a very partial way. We can usually obtain sales figures for magazines and newspapers and independent bodies often audit these so that the figures can be regarded as reliable. However, because a single newspaper or magazine can be read by more than one person, sales figures tell us nothing much about readership. This is why readership surveys are carried out in most major press markets in the world.

TV and radio audience measurement has to rely entirely on some kind of survey instrument, for no sales transaction takes place, except in the case of the new and still very limited examples of subscription and pay-per-view television channels. Quantitative research of one kind or another is essential if we want to measure audiences for TV and radio, as we know them at present. I shall describe how this is done.

Later I will describe the measures that are commonly used in audience research, especially such terms as *Reach, Share* and *Ratings*. We will also see how advertisers and broadcasters use these terms.

When I ran the audience research department of the BBC World Service I was often asked, "How do you know how many listeners the BBC has?" My colleagues in the department that dealt with domestic radio and television services were asked similar questions. There are well-established methods by which we can calculate how many listen to or watch BBC and other programmes at different times and on different days of the week. When audience measurement is carried out according to certain principles

3

it is usually possible to make reasonably accurate estimates of the numbers of listeners or viewers to different services and programmes. It is also possible to work out the times that they listen or watch and the number of minutes or hours spent watching or listening, and the kinds of programmes that attract the most listening. Research can normally provide information about the kinds of people who form the audience for different programmes at various times in the day. Research of this kind carried out over a period of time can plot trends in audience behaviour. It can show whether new programmes have increased or decreased audience size, whether new services have achieved their audience target objectives or whether there are any significant long term trends.

How is this done? The principles of audience measurement are not complex or difficult to understand. What we do is select a sample of the population and ask appropriate questions designed to collect data about their television viewing or radio listening. There are various ways of doing this but before describing them, let us look in some detail at the principle and practice of sampling. How can a sample represent everyone?

3.1   Sampling

All branches of social, market and opinion research share the same principles of sampling that we use in audience measurement. Those principles are also used in every day life. Experience tells us that we can draw conclusions from a few chance observations. In a market we might buy and taste an orange to see if it is ripe and sweet before buying a quantity. The farmer opens a few cobs of maize to see if a whole field is ready to harvest.

It is important to choose our samples with some care. We might pick the one orange out of a whole pile that was not sweet. The farmer would be foolish to select a couple of maize cobs from a corner of the field where the maize was obviously more ready than the rest.

Theory and Practice

The principle of sampling is to remove bias as far as possible so that the sample we select is as representative of the whole as we can make it. It does not mean that it will always tell us the whole story; there are always going to be some differences between the characteristics of the sample and those of the population or universe from which it was drawn. We can reduce the magnitude and likelihood of the differences, or bias, by increasing the size of the sample. Thus the more oranges we taste, the more maize cobs the farmer opens, the more certain we can be that the qualities represented by the sample are true of the whole lot; in other words, that the unsampled items will be the same.

The problem is that increasing the sample doesn't increase reliability by the same proportion. Interviewing 200 people selected at random from an area containing many thousands of people does not give us information twice as reliable as interviewing 100 people. To double the reliability of a sample you have to quadruple its size. So our sample would have to be 400 to be twice as reliable as a sample of 100.[9]

The point to remember is that a lot of valuable social research is based on a law of statistical regularity which states that a small group chosen at random from a large group will share much the same characteristics. This is an important principle.

Samples and Censuses

Sometimes it is necessary to contact everyone and not to sample. Most countries have censuses of their entire populations. Many countries have a census every ten years. The main reason for a comprehensive count of everyone within a defined geographical area is to record reliable information on a given date. But it is a very expensive activity and is really necessary only when it is a matter of accurately counting whole populations.

The acquisition of this information then assists the sampling of the population between censuses. Indeed, one of the most important aids to good sample survey research, including radio and television audience measurement, is an up-to-date and reliable census with detailed information on population size and distribution, age and sex composition, educational level, type of dwelling and other similar data. You can more easily take a sample and, above all, check that your sample really does reflect the population as a whole, or the section of it that you propose to select, when you have access to these important demographic criteria.

Public opinion polls are a well-known example of the use of sampling to find out about the population as a whole. In a general election, everyone of voting age should be able to record his or her vote. But it is not necessary to have an election to know about public opinion. Between elections we can find out the state of political opinion by selecting and interviewing a sample representative of the electorate as a whole, This is done regularly in most democratic countries. The electorate as a whole is the 'universe' which the sample will be designed to represent.

Defining the 'Universe'

The universe is defined as the population we wish to describe through taking a sample. It may be the entire population, but this is unusual. In social and market research we tend usually not to sample the whole population. Often we sample people in various smaller 'universes' or populations. Sometimes they may be clearly and relatively easily defined. They may be, for example, adults aged 15 and over. They could be children of school age, adults in towns with more than 20,000 inhabitants, or all women in a village aged 15 and over. Such definitions are straightforward and it is usually easy to determine who is included and who is excluded in the population under study. Some populations or universes for study are less well defined and may be constantly changing. Just think, for example, of the following examples. The homeless population of London, the unemployed of Los Angeles, the rural poor of Sudan, Afghan refugees, the displaced forest peoples in Brazil. Obviously some decisions have to be taken by the researcher to help define these shifting populations precisely enough to make sampling possible. In each case the universe for study needs to be carefully and precisely defined.

Most audience research involves whole populations of adults and children down to a certain defined age. Sometimes, for practical reasons or because of the requirements of the research, the universe will be confined to urban areas. Sometimes only rural areas will be covered. Sometimes only one or two regions may be selected.

Selecting a Representative Sample

In audience research we are most often involved in selecting samples of the whole adult population. We are going to look at the process of selection of such a sample. The task is to find a method as free from any bias as we can make it. The importance of this cannot be exaggerated. Bias can occur without the researcher being aware of it.

Let us use an example of sampling which is customarily performed in manufacturing industry. A company manufacturing light bulbs needs to know how reliable its manufacturing process is. To do this, batches of light bulbs are selected and tested. The company has set a minimum standard of quality and reliability. If the selected sample does not meet this, it is assumed that this is true of the rest and the whole output of that production line may be rejected and the machinery stopped for investigation. It is obviously crucially important that the information provided by the selected sample represent reality. If, after taking a representative sample of them, we find, let us say, that 97% reach the required level or standard, we need to know with what confidence we can say anything about the standard of the entire output of light bulbs.

There are two main areas that we need to look at when considering the reliability of data like this. The first is the reliability of the sample itself. Was it truly reliable and free from bias? There are many ways in which bias can be there without our being aware of it. In a factory making light bulbs it would be necessary to take our samples at different times and on different days, especially if the machinery is operated by several different teams or shifts of people. People operating machinery can behave differently at different times of the day and week. If power failure or mechanical breakdown often interrupted the manufacturing process, this would also have to be taken into account. These and other factors might mean that the quality of output was uneven.

The second factor is the size of the sample. The larger it is, the greater the degree of confidence that we would have that our sample represented the true situation. I will look in detail at this point later.

It is worth noting that sampling is used in most mass production processes in order to monitor performance. In the same way we can sample people and when doing so we need to ensure that the sample is representative. Sampling is the process of selecting people (or things) to represent those who are not selected. Or put another way, it is the process of creating a small and manageable version of the universe under study so that the data we collect are of manageable proportions, but which nonetheless tell us something reliably about the whole. To do this we need to devise a means whereby every unit (person, light bulb or whatever) in the universe has an equal chance of being selected. This is the vital central principle of sampling. In order to carry out the discipline of sampling, and *discipline* is an appropriate word to use, we need to devise a sampling method that ensures that we can draw a reliably random sample. For this we need a *sampling frame.*

The Sampling Frame

The definition of the universe can often point us very quickly to a readily available and suitable sampling frame. An electoral register on which all eligible voters are listed with their names and home addresses, is an obviously valuable sampling frame which can be used when one wants a sample of electors. All those who are electors are listed there. The register is what qualifies and defines them as potential voters.

In each case we need to find the relationship between the population or universe we want to study and the sampling frame. Does the sampling frame adequately cover the population we are interested in? Is anyone we wish to include left out? Street maps may be viewed as adequate sampling frames, especially when they show dwellings. But there are three major weaknesses. First of all, maps are very soon out-of- date and omit new developments. Secondly they sometimes omit illegal, unplanned, 'squatter', 'informal' or temporary housing areas. The third weakness is that although they may show dwelling units, they usually give no indication of housing or population density.

Let us illustrate the latter problem. We might seek to use a street map of a city which showed dwelling units on it. We might systematically select a pure random sample of these units. But while it might be a random sample of homes and therefore useful if you were sampling households, it would be a biased way of sampling individuals. One might, for example, select ten people from one group of 100 dwellings with over 500 adults living in them. We might then select the same number of people from 100 dwellings in another part of the same city with only 150 adult residents. The two areas have widely different densities of people per dwelling.

Another kind of sampling frame often used in survey research involving sampling is provided by a population census. Geographical definitions of ways in which the population was counted are produced. A census, once it has been analysed and the reports issued, will provide the researcher with detailed data, broken down by enumeration area. There is usually a simple-to-understand hierarchy of analysis. Population data for the country as a whole is given, then a breakdown by region, then by sub-region or area, right down to enumeration areas of no more than a few hundred people each. The precise geographical definition of each of these population units is given. Data on both population and household numbers make census results of enormous value for the conduct of quantitative research among general populations.

Sometimes no ideal sampling frame is readily available. In many parts of the world there are no electoral registers. Up-to-date maps showing streets, houses may not exist. There may be no reliable or recent census data. You may have to create an adequate sampling frame yourself. This may seem daunting. It need not be!

Let us imagine that you have to take a representative sample of the population of an unmapped village or group of villages. You do not have a map, so why not draw one! It need not be a piece of professional cartography. A rough sketch map that does not need to be drawn to scale can meet your needs. On it you should note where the houses are, where they are clustered and where they are scattered. You will need to draw the boundaries of the area you want to study. Where does the village or group of villages end? You may need to ask a local and reliable informant. If you have data from a census, the enumerator or enumerators of the area will have already gone through the same process when marking out the area for the purpose of counting its population. But even if you do not have all the detail needed, the geography will often make choices quite easy. Rivers, lakes, ranges of hills and unpopulated land often make natural boundaries.

There are many other examples that could be given of sampling frames that can be used to make representative samples of the universe we have as the subject for study. Let us consider some examples.

We have written mostly about making samples of the general population. For this we require a sampling frame that covers the general population, which is why we were looking at censuses, enumeration areas and maps of streets and villages with all the dwelling units taken note of. But very often in research we want to study sub-groups.

Here are some examples and some suggested sampling frames:

Universe or Population sub-group	Possible Sampling Frame
Nursing mothers	Mothers visiting mother and baby clinic
Doctors	List published by professional body
School teachers	Ditto
Children attending school	Attendance/Registration lists
Farmers	Local Ministry of Agriculture lists
Subscribers to a TV satellite channel	List of subscribers

Exercise

There are some problems with some of these sampling frames. Do they include everyone you wish to study? The mother and baby clinics will not be visited by all nursing mothers. How could you ensure that all mothers are covered by your survey? How would you cover all children of school age and not merely those attending school? Are there some farmers not known to the agricultural officials and therefore not on any list? Will you always be able to obtain the lists you require? For example, if you want to survey subscribers to satellite TV will the company allow you access to their list?

How would you overcome these or other problems?

Consider some other examples. What sampling frames would you suggest for the following population groups? Might they exist or would you have to create something?

If so, how would you go about it?

Homeless people in a city
Unemployed people
College graduates
Regular listeners to a certain radio station
Regular viewers of a certain TV programme
Regular readers of a newspaper.

Sometimes a ready-made sampling frame in the form of a list will not exist and you will need to create one. In the case of the homeless you may be able to gain access to the people you wish to reach through an agency that serves them. But you might also need to add those who do not come into contact with that agency. One way might be to observe how many people are 'sleeping rough' – that is, those who sleep on the streets or in railway stations or other places. Note where they are to be found, make an estimate of how many there are and devise a way of taking a random sample of them.

Random or Probability Samples

These are theoretically the most accurate forms of sampling. Taking a random sample means that every individual in the area of your survey or within the universe for study – teachers, children of school age, nursing mothers or whatever – has an equal or known chance of being selected. If you were taking a nationally representative sample of adults, aged 15 and over, in your country you might set about making a list of the entire adult population, select names entirely at random, find these people and interview them. This would be a true random sample survey. In practice this is never done, at least not in an entire nation! It would be extremely time-consuming, expensive and needlessly complicated.

Pure random samples are however possible and often used with smaller groups, especially those for whom we can obtain or create universal or comprehensive lists. For example, the British Post Office frequently surveys its customers to assess their views of the quality of its services. A sample of customers using one or other of its services can easily be selected at random. A questionnaire is sent to those selected.

If you were seeking to do a survey of recent graduates from a college, you might obtain a list of names and addresses from the college. Suppose that a sample of 400 were required. A list of all recent graduates would be needed – the sampling frame. There are a number of ways you could make a random selection. One is to use a method similar to that used by lotteries. This might involve writing everyone's name on a slip of paper and mixing these very well in a drum. You would then select, without looking, 400 slips of paper to be your sample. Everyone in the drum has an equal chance of selection. We would obtain a pure random sample.

Having to write out everybody's name is a little tedious. An easier alternative is to use random numbers. These are easily generated on many computer programmes. I have used a computer to produce 396 random numbers between 1 and 1,000 in the appendices of this book. You can use these numbers in any order. Each number between 1 and 1,000 had an equal chance of being chosen each time that my computer made its selection. Another way is to throw dice. I also give a description of how to use dice to create random numbers in the appendices.

However, considerations of time and expense make the task of conducting a pure random sample rather rare when covering a general population. A pure random sample opinion survey of 1,000 Zambian adults is theoretically possible. Everyone is supposed to be registered with the National Registration Board and a random sample of 1,000 could be made. But having made the selection, finding everyone would be a time-consuming task, let alone the problem that the records of people's addresses are probably out-of-date. Supposing they could all be found, one would still find oneself making several very long journeys just to interview scattered individuals.

There is another problem. By the nature of random samples, anything is possible! You might actually select a sample that was unrepresentative. For example, when selecting recent college graduates, you might discover that most of those selected had been science graduates whereas science graduates were in a minority. Your method of selection had been correct. There was no bias in your method. And yet you have a sample that is biased. It can happen.

Stratified Random Samples

There are various ways in which we can improve the chances of a random sample being representative whilst not losing its randomness. These have the added advantage of saving time and expense. When there are well-defined categories within the population that you would like to be fairly represented within your sample, you can construct the sample accordingly while retaining the principles of randomness. You can decide on a pre-determined number to be selected within defined groups or strata within the population or universe under study.

Much sampling of general populations uses this method. What happens is that we usually divide the country into sampling areas and draw up sampling plans in accordance with what is known about the population in each part of the country. Existing administrative boundaries are useful for this purpose. Usually we will use the population size in each area to determine the number of people to be selected in each. Thus, for example, if we were carrying out a sample survey of adult Tanzanians (aged 15 and over) our 'universe' would consist of about 15 million people. We may decide that a sample of 3,000 will be taken to represent the whole country's adult population. We would need to determine from the last census what the distribution of our universe was between the different districts.

A sample of 3,000 in a universe of 15 million means a sampling fraction or ratio of one in five thousand. One in five thousand adult Tanzanians would be selected to represent the population as a whole. In a district of 500,000 people, 100 would be selected to be interviewed. In a district of 100,000, 20 would be selected, and so on. In practice we often over-sample in sparsely populated areas and make adjustments to the data in the analysis stage in a process called 'weighting'. A simpler alternative and one that avoids the need to apply weights is to divide the country into a number of areas each with a similar number of people. You would then take an equal sample in each.

Sampling of a country is often stratified by types of area, rather than just the formal administrative regions or districts. If we were, for example, creating a sampling frame for India, we might decide at first choose to divide it up into its component states and territories. These vary in size from Uttar Pradesh with 139 million people down to the territory of Lakshadweep with only 52 thousand.[10] You could stratify the states and territories by size. There are 15 states each with populations greater than 10 million people. In each of these states, areas could be listed by their population density. For example, cities of more than 1,000,000 could be one category. Cities and towns of between 100,000 and 1,000,000 could be another. Towns of between 10,000 and 100,000 could be another. The last category could be towns or villages of less than 10,000 people. Cities, towns and villages or areas could then be selected in each of these categories to be representative. One might choose a selection in each category for subsequent sampling. This is in reality a form of stratified sampling sometimes called cluster or multi-stage sampling. It is used when it is impractical for researchers to go all over a country to carry out research. A selection of villages, towns and cities may be chosen to represent others.

If we return to our Tanzanian example earlier, the point can be illustrated further. Our proposed sampling fraction was one person in five thousand. In an area of five thousand adults, this fraction would suggest that we would be selecting and interviewing just one person. But that would be time consuming and probably pointless. What we generally do is to group similar areas together in our sampling frame and select one of these to represent the others. Thus in an area of similar sized settlements one would group many together to add up to a larger number. Then one or two places may be selected to represent all. So if together the population of a number of similar areas adds up to 150,000, one would select one or two sampling points and select 30 respondents there to represent all the adults in the cluster.

Of course there are dangers in this approach. One must be especially careful if the population is made up of many distinct ethnic or linguistic minorities. In audience research, such differences can of course be major factors in media behaviour. If such differences exist, the stratification may need to take them into account. Deliberate stratification according to ethnicity or religion or similar category can ensure that people from all significant groups are included. This is one way in which careful stratification of samples can improve on pure random sampling. The latter can exclude or under-represent important minorities.

Stratified sampling, which may or may not be clustered, is thus especially appropriate when the population being studied is very varied or heterogeneous. Unstratified samples may be more suitable when the population is homogeneous – that is, it doesn't vary a great deal socially, racially, ethnically or in other major ways. A random sample may not always be relied upon to reflect all the major demographic differences in the population. A stratified sample may be a better method to use to ensure full coverage. We gave the case of India to illustrate a stratified sample that would ensure representative sampling of different sizes of communities from the very large to the very small. India would first be stratified by community size. Stratified sampling by ethnicity may also be necessary if we are to ensure that all the different ethnic communities are covered in a sample, simply because ethnic groups tend to live together. We find in many countries that there is a clustering by race, religion, nationality, economic status and even by occupation.

Random Sampling Within a Survey

A common method of sampling in a sample survey of the population is to use a *random walk*. In a given geographical area the person selecting the sample for interview may start at one house and select a respondent. It is very important to devise a method for selection of the starting point. Nothing must be left to interviewer choice in random sampling.

After the first home visited, the interviewer may be instructed to select the next house after a given interval, then to turn left at the next junction and select another house at a further given interval, and so on. An alternative scheme can be devised. What matters is that you have a process that chooses the sampled household and removes the bias that would come in if you allowed your interviewer to make the choice.

But who is to be interviewed at each house? Researchers need to be careful not to interview only the first person met. You don't want a survey solely made up of people who answer the door or greet any stranger who arrives! What we need to do is to randomise the selection of people at the household level.

At each house the person contacted by the interviewer can be asked how many people aged 15 years and over live in the dwelling which has been selected. One of these people is then selected by random for interview. If the person is not present an appointment should be made and the interviewer will return later to complete the interview with the selected person. This process is known as *call-back*. It should be agreed before-hand how many call-backs will be attempted on any survey. It cannot be indefinite of course. It is normal to say that there will be one or two call-backs during a survey when the selected person cannot be found. If after two or three calls, or whatever number you have decided on, the person is still not there to be interviewed, a substitution is made at another house, using the same sampling procedures as before. It is very important to get this process right and to avoid the risk of interviewers biasing the sample by being able to choose themselves whom they should interview. But it is also very important to make every effort to contact the selected individual. This applies not only to face-to-face sampling but also to telephone and other forms of random sampling of individuals. Otherwise we would be taking a sample only of people who are more easily contacted.

If all your interviews take place during working hours, you will find that many people will be out on the first and subsequent calls. It is a good idea to vary the times that you call at people's homes in order to maximise the chances of being able to interview people with the entire range of working and life patterns. And be flexible when you seek to find the missing person.

One way of selecting the respondent in each household is to use what is known as a Kish Grid. When houses or dwellings are selected, each one is assigned a number. When the interviewer meets a member of the household he or she is then asked to list all the eligible people (i.e. all those who have the demographic characteristics you are seeking – in this case all those aged 15 and over). All of one sex are listed first, then of the other, from the oldest down to the youngest. Using the Kish Grid reproduced here, the interviewer reads along the row corresponding to the household's assigned number until they reach the column giving the total number of eligible people in that household. The number at that point indicates the person by number who should be selected for interview.

Address Serial no	Number of persons listed in household						
	1	2	3	4	5	6	7+
1	1	2	1	4	3	5	7
2	1	1	2	1	4	6	1
3	1	2	3	2	5	1	2
4	1	1	1	3	1	2	3
5	1	2	2	4	2	3	4
6	1	1	3	1	3	4	5
7	1	2	1	2	4	5	6
8	1	1	2	3	5	6	7
9	1	2	3	4	1	1	6

Thus if we are at address number 7 and there are five eligible people in that dwelling, we interview the person who is number 4 on the list of all the adults in the household. There is a problem with what I have just described. It is basically a probability system of choosing households or homes, not individuals. Until the moment that we begin the selection of the individual in each household chosen, we have used a system in which every household has a more or less equal chance of being chosen. Once we use the Kish Grid the same cannot be said for individuals. According to this system, if for example, one house visited has one adult and another has six, we still interview only one person in each. You can see therefore that people living in homes with several adults have a lower chance of selection than those in homes with few or only one.

In probability sampling we have to endeavour, as far as we are able, to remove all sources of bias. The Kish Grid works well if we want a sample of one person per household. It is acceptable as a way of providing a reliable sample of individuals if household sizes do not vary greatly. But if there is a lot of variation in household size we may need a way around this problem that ensures that this bias is removed. One was devised several years ago by some British market researchers. What they came up with was a system whereby the interviewer would select respondents at fixed intervals. It depended to some extent on the existence of an electoral register. These do not exist everywhere. So I am devising a revised version of what Blyth and Marchant wrote about in 1973.[11]

At the first house selected, all adults should be listed. Then one is chosen by some pre-arranged random method. Also prearranged will be a sampling interval for individuals. It should approximate to the mean number of adults per household, a figure obtainable from the most recent census. Let us suppose that it is three.

At each house sampled a list of adults is made. It should be written in some prearranged order, alphabetical or in the order of birthdays or some simple system. The person chosen should in each case be the third person, not third in the home, but third on the running list since the previous interview. Let me illustrate. The names here are all fictitious and I have listed them alphabetically within each house.

	List of adults	Sampled individual
House 1	John Smith	
	Mary Smith	✔
House 2	Aisha Ahmed	
	Anwar Ahmed	
	Suluma Ahmed	✔
	Yusuf Ahmed	
House 3	Navjot Singh	
House 4	Sam Brown	✔
	William Brown	
House 5	Ali Saleh	
House 6	Adam Maganga	✔
	Sarah Mwanza	
	Tommy Mwanza	
	Obed Phiri	✔
	Peter Zulu	
House 7	Veejay Patel	
	Yolanda Patel	✔

Note that sometimes more than one person is interviewed per household (House 6) and sometimes nobody is interviewed (Houses 3 and 5). This system, if used with a random method of household selection will ensure a random sample of individuals also and one in which there should be little bias.

Quota Samples

Commercial market research companies often use quota samples. These are not random samples but are used when interviewers are instructed to look for fixed numbers of respondents of different categories or types. The categories are calculated in quotas that are typically of sex, age, housing type, social class, occupation or ethnicity. The interviewer is given a set of quota controls. One interviewer may be asked to select ten married women between the ages of 25 and 34 who live in a rural area. Another may be given a quota of five unmarried women of the same age group, in another area, and so on.

The selection criteria will be dictated by the purpose of the survey. If it seeks to represent the general adult population, the quotas will be based on the distribution of categories such as age, sex, social class, geographic area etc. that can be obtained from census or similar sources. If our survey is of a particular group, let us say of mothers of pre-school children, we may then draw up quotas to ensure a good representation of women in this category from all social groups. We would want to ensure that we did not select too many of the more well off, or too many who were living in towns. Quotas could be drawn up to ensure balanced representation in our sample.

Quota samples have a number of advantages that make them attractive to the researcher, including the media or audience researcher. They take less time than random samples. Interviewers conducting surveys using quota samples generally complete many more interviews in a day than when using any kind of random sample method requiring them to seek specific individuals according to the sampling plan. Because of the low cost and higher speed, quota samples are used in many commercial market research surveys. Interviewers are typically seen in a shopping street or mall in cities all over the world, holding a clipboard. He or she (more often female than male) will have been given a quota of interviewees to interview that day. Typically sex, age and possibly social class will define the quotas. The sex of the respondent usually offers no problems in the selection process, but age is a different matter! It is impossible to tell how old a person is before approaching him or her to request an interview. But the interviewer looking for a 35 to 44 year old man is unlikely to approach a man in his seventies or a youth in his teens. The interviewer can establish the age, social status and other demographic criteria of the respondent from the first few questions in the questionnaire. If the person does not meet the criteria of the quota or meets a quota item already filled, the interview can be politely concluded and the interviewer can continue to seek out the category required. It is often useful to link together some quota controls. If, for example, quotas cover sex and working status, link the two together in order to avoid finding yourself selecting too many unemployed men.

Quota sampling is subject to many biases. For example, quotas may all be filled in easily accessible areas while remoter areas are left out. Any system of sampling which leaves out certain areas or categories will distort the results if those excluded are different in significant ways from those included. If people living in remoter areas have different political opinions (as may well be possible) from those in more accessible areas, quotas which leave them out are likely to produce misleading results in an opinion poll.

The greatest weakness of quota samples is interviewer bias. With random methods the interviewer is given a strict scheme of selection and does not have any choice of his or her own about whom to interview. But the interviewer using a quota sample can choose the respondent, provided he or she meets the given criteria. The interviewer in the street or shopping mall can decide not to stop someone who appears to be unfriendly or the other one who seems to be too busy. Another bias is produced by the place in which the selection is made. We might think that a street is a good place to find a good cross-section of the population. But there are many people who spend little time in a street. There is the obvious case of the housebound and infirm. There are also people who spend a lot of time travelling by car or working in the fields. Quota samples conducted in the street are therefore likely to have a bias towards those who spend more time than others at the shops, those who appear to interviewers to be friendly and approachable and perhaps those who seem to have the time to stop and answer questions.

There are various ways to reduce these biases. One can vary the place where the interviewees are sought and the place of interviewee selection. Some people can be selected at homes or places of work. One can also introduce randomness into the way the quotas are filled. For example, one can start a survey using random methods where there is no choice left to the interviewer. The quotas come in when the interviewer checks what quotas have been filled and what categories are still to be found.

When conducting mass media audience surveys in Zambia in 1970-72 I used a hybrid sampling method with elements of randomisation, stratification, cluster and quota methods. First I stratified the country by geographical area – rural and urban districts. All districts were visited and quotas for age and sex were drawn up for each geographical category, urban and rural within each district. Using the 1969 national census I listed the number of men and women in each age group that I wanted to be interviewed in each district, in both urban and rural areas. In each district all towns were included. In Zambia there are relatively few towns and it was not necessary to make a selection. When it came to the rural areas, a selection had to be made. Within each rural district, census enumeration areas were chosen at random and interviews were clustered in each. Urban districts were stratified according to types of housing or settlement – high-density 'legal' or 'legitimate' housing, low density housing, and squatter or shanty areas. Using a random process of selection, houses were visited and quotas were used to select members of each household for interview. The resulting sample matched the census data by age and sex, on which the quotas were based. When the sample was complete we were able to check whether it matched the language or ethnic composition of the country and found that it did so within a small margin. We achieved a representative sample fairly simply and effectively by reducing, as far as possible, interviewer bias.[12]

Telephone Samples

As we shall discover in more detail later in section 3.8, the telephone has become an important tool in all forms of market research, including audience and readership research. Randomness of the sample is achieved by the use of what is known as

Random Digit Dialling or RDD. This is a system that selects any domestic subscriber's phone number at random and dials it automatically. Telephone companies usually provide, for a fee, a database of numbers for this purpose. The sampling frame can be all domestic telephone subscribers in an entire country, or all those living in certain geographical areas. If particular kinds of people are being sought, this part of the selection can take place when the phone call is answered. Sometimes a specialised database of telephone numbers of the kinds of people who are being sought may be available.

There are two biases inherent in this method. One is that telephone penetration can be quite low. This makes telephone sampling unsuitable in many countries. The other bias lies in with whom contact is made. It is obviously important not always to select whoever answers the phone. One of the methods described already of selecting individuals in each household needs to be used, and every effort should be made to contact that person, with repeated calls if necessary.

Snowball Samples

This is a technique of obtaining a sample of people who are difficult to find or in situations where it is not possible to do random samples in the normal way. It is not a method that is often used in quantitative work because the resulting sample may not be representative. I am describing it in this section on sampling, but it is more often used in obtaining respondents in qualitative research, described later.

Snowball sampling derives its name from the way a ball of snow becomes bigger and bigger as you continue to roll it. In snowball sampling you ask people with whom you make contact to suggest others they may know in the same category. If you are looking for people who are professionals in a particular field, snowball sampling may be an appropriate way to find them. However, snowball sampling is not random sampling and is subject to unknown but probably considerable levels of bias. It should be used only when other forms of sampling are impossible.

Sampling and Statistical Theory:

How large should a sample be? This is a question often asked. It is generally true that the larger the sample, the more accurate the data ought to be. However, if the sampling method is faulty increasing the sample size will not improve it.

In this section my intention is to provide an easy guide to some of the statistical basics which lie at the heart of sampling. They are relevant and useable only in the context of probability sampling. I will be introducing some statistical concepts. Some of these use Greek symbols. At this point many readers may be put off, finding these very off-putting. I know because I do! You should soon discover that statistical analyses are not as daunting as they look.

The principal underlying sampling theory is the *normal distribution*. This depends on probabilities. Let us suppose an imaginary situation where we are trying to discover something about a population. We are trying to find the value of x. It could be anything

– the percentage of individuals in households with a colour TV set, the number of people who have been to secondary school etc. The true result is at the centre of the horizontal axis of the following graph. If we take several samples of the same universe the results we obtain will fall within the following normal distributions. The mean of all results $\bar{x}$ should lie at the centre.

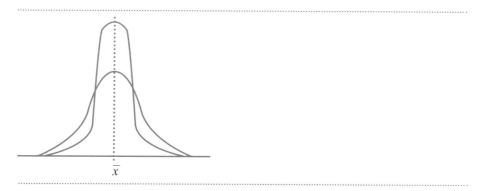

The sample that best represented reality would be one that gave us the result in the middle. But we can never be certain if we have achieved that result. Most of the samples we take will be on either side of this line. We never know for certain how far away from the true figure we are. What we can do, however, is to work out what the shape of the normal distribution for each sample probably is. In other words, we can say, with a reasonable degree of certainty, the likely distance, plus or minus, within which our results lie. That is what statistical probability theories let us do. That is why as researchers we really need to understand these things.

To calculate the range of reliability we need to work out the shape of the normal distribution for a variable. To do this we need to know two things, the arithmetic mean $\bar{x}$ and its standard deviation σ. This Greek symbol σ (Sigma) is used to refer to the amount by which the value of x is likely to vary. When the arithmetic mean $\bar{x}$ is low and the standard deviation σ is high, the value of x varies a great deal. This is when we get a flatter shape to the normal distribution shown in the graph. When the value of $\bar{x}$ is high, i.e. when many of the results we get for value x are the same or nearly so and therefore the standard deviation σ is low we get a taller narrower distribution and less variation in x. I will now show how we can calculate these.

When we carry out a survey to find the percentage of houses with colour TV sets we do not get the true figure but an estimate. Another survey would in all probability provide us with a different figure. If we continued to do survey after survey we would end up with a frequency distribution of these estimates for the percentage ownership of colour TVs. It would be in the shape of the normal distribution as in the graph. The most common results would be at the middle, but some surveys would give results at either side. Some would, by the laws of chance, give us low estimates at the left hand side of the graph. Others would, by the same laws, give us high estimates on the right. The area under each of the curves on the graph represents the range of results for x achieved. It can be shown mathematically that 95% of the estimates will lie within 2 standard deviations of the average, both above it and below.

33

$$2\sigma \quad \sigma \quad x \quad \sigma \quad 2\sigma$$

The areas at the two sides beyond the 2σ symbols (two standard deviations) constitute 5% of the area (2.5% on each side). 95% is between these two outer lines. We can therefore be 95% confident that the true answer lies within two standard deviations (2σ) of the average. And this is the usual degree of confidence that we give in survey research. To illustrate I will use the example of a survey measuring the percentage of individuals who live in homes with a colour TV set.

Our survey of 1,000 adults has produced an estimate of 30% for individuals with a colour TV at home. I will now show how near to the true figure this estimate is likely to be. And I will do so within a 95% confidence limit, the one most often used when we report the results of survey research.. What we have to do is to discover the size of the standard deviation, also known as the standard error.

The standard error is established mathematically by a simple formula:

$$\sqrt{\frac{x\,(100-x)}{n}}$$

x is the result – in this case 30% – while n is the sample size.

$$= \sqrt{\frac{30 \times 70}{1000}}$$

$$= \sqrt{\frac{2100}{1000}}$$

$$= \sqrt{2.1}$$

$$= 1.4$$

The standard error 1.4% is the value of σ. As you can see from the previous graph, there are 2σs on either side of the mean $\bar{x}$. 95% covers the area two standard deviations from the mean.

Our estimate of 30% therefore has a margin of +/- (plus or minus) 2 standard errors.

30% +/- 2 x 1.4 = 30% +/- 2.8

Therefore, the true figure for individuals living in homes with colour TV sets almost certainly lies between 27.2% and 32.8%. This may be sufficiently accurate for your purpose. What do we do if we want a margin of error smaller than this? As we noted earlier, to increase the reliability of a sample to make it twice as accurate, you have to quadruple the size. We would need a sample of 4,000 to have results twice as accurate as those given by a sample of 1,000 would. We therefore repeat the calculation:

$$= \sqrt{\frac{x\,(100 - x)}{n}}$$

$$= \sqrt{\frac{30 \times 70}{n}}$$

$$= \sqrt{\frac{2100}{4000}}$$

$$= \sqrt{0.5}$$

$$= 0.7$$

Using two of these values for σ we get a +/- range of 1.4, twice as accurate as before, with a probable range between 28.6% and 31.4%.

In quantitative research we have to remember though that the more people sampled the more the survey will cost and the longer it will take to complete and analyse. Somehow we have to find a compromise between the need for accuracy and the resources and time we have. A table giving the margins of error for findings from different sized samples is given in the appendices.

The other thing we often need to do is compare two results from different surveys with different sample or sub-sample size. You might find that between successive audience surveys of the same population the audience for a certain radio station has fallen from 43% weekly to 37%. Does this represent a real or only an apparent fall? In other words, how likely is it that this result represents a real change in the behaviour of the general population and is not the result of sampling error?

We need to know the sample sizes. If for both surveys it was the same, and 2,000 people were interviewed, statistical tests show that the fall in audience is probably (95% certain) real and not the result of sampling error. If one of the samples had been only 1,000 and we had the same result, we would not be able to say that the surveys had shown a real fall in audience. (For a table and further explanation see the appendices.)

Do remember though that these calculations and other statistical tests of significance or reliability work properly only with random samples. Mere size of sample is of no importance in establishing its reliability if the sample has been chosen by other means. For example, a radio station might give out questionnaires to people at a public event. It would be justified in feeling pleased if there were a good response. But it would not be justified in supposing that 2,000 replies, let us say, were any more reliable an indication of listener opinion than 1,000. This might seem surprising but it is true. The respondents are self-selected; they decide to participate and reply; they are not a random or representative cross-section of the listenership. They are likely to be different from the remainder of listeners in significant ways and increasing the number who respond will not make the replies any more reliable.

There are comprehensive and detailed books on sampling and statistical theory, which those involved in fieldwork of this sort, should study. Some suggested titles are given in the bibliography.

Exercise

The 5 rival radio stations in a certain city have each used different methods to find out what their listeners think of their programmes. Consider each of the methods they use and comment on each. What are the strengths and weaknesses (if any) with each approach? Is any radio station likely to know more about its listeners than any of the others? How would you suggest they might find out what their listeners think of their programmes? Give reasons for your answers.

1 *Radio One invites listeners over the air to write in with their answers to questions about what they like and dislike and their suggestions for what they would like to hear.*

2 *Radio Two sends a reporter out with a microphone to stop people in the street and ask them to express their likes and dislikes.*

3 *Radio Three meets listeners at its exhibition stand at the annual national fair in the capital city and gives out questionnaires for them to fill in and return.*

4 *Radio Four invites people over the air to write in and request a questionnaire that they then send out and the listener is invited to return.*

5 *Radio Five employs a trained team of interviewers who go from door to door in certain areas and ask questions of the people who answer the door.*

3.2   The Questionnaire: The Art of Asking Questions

The basic instrument of the sample survey is the questionnaire. We can obtain a representative and reliable sample. But if the questionnaire is not well constructed the results of our research can be spoiled.

Designing a Questionnaire

There is a saying in English "If you ask a silly question, you get a silly answer". Asking questions is one of the crucial basics skills of all opinion and market research, including audience and media research. Questionnaire design is a skill that is not quickly learned. But there is a logic to it that can ensure that the information being sought is provided unambiguously and in a way that can be codified and analysed.

The problem is simply put but only with some difficulty is it solved! Human behaviour is wonderfully varied and complex. No two people are exactly the same, even in their television and radio consumption behaviour! Opinions about anything are also very variable; no two persons think the same. We are all individuals and I think it is a good discipline for all market, opinion and audience researchers to remember this.

The reason I say this is because the process of research seeks to summarise and generalise about the immensely varied opinions, attitudes and behaviour of individual human beings. Audience research seeks to aggregate the enormously varied behaviour of thousands, even of millions of people and group them into different categories. The questions are designed to put people into categories that make analysis possible. In research we simplify and therefore, to some extent, distort reality in order to understand it, make sense of it and perhaps sometimes predict it. You could, if you had enough time, describe in detail every individual's listening, viewing and reading behaviour. It would take you an immense amount of time and you would not be helping anyone understand how people, taken as a whole, behave. Instead we summarise an immense quantity of different individual behaviour and produce aggregate data that provide us with generalisations. The questionnaire is the main instrument that makes this possible. We put the same questions to all the sampled individuals. Their combined responses give us a picture of people as a whole.

Questions need to be precise and help the respondent provide an accurate answer. Vagueness has to be avoided. This is why many of the questions we habitually ask in every day conversations will not do in a questionnaire. For example you might ask a friend 'What radio stations do you listen to?' Your friend may mention one station or several. Your friend might assume you mean, 'what do you listen to most? or perhaps 'what station do you most like listening to?. The question could be taken to mean 'tell me all the radio stations you ever listen to?.

Would the answer have been very different if you has asked your friend 'What radio station do you listen to?' Would the fact that you have used the word 'station' in the singular mean that you were expecting the name of only one? Would everyone you asked this question assume it meant the same thing? These concerns about meaning do not matter much in normal conversation, but when we are carrying out research we want each respondent to understand each question in the same way and for each question to compel the respondent, as far as possible, to give a precise response.

Asking questions about choice of radio or television station, or newspaper or magazine is a familiar requirement in media research. There are various ways in which it can be done. One approach is to ask about habitual behaviour. We may to ask people to say what they *usually* do. This is not an easy thing to establish or record using a simple question. People do not always recognise habitual behaviour in themselves. Or they can sometimes not report habitual behaviour at all accurately. They may say (and believe also!) that they habitually do one thing but in fact do another more often or more regularly! Moreover, asking about habitual behaviour may mean that we forget about occasional behaviour.

Another approach is to ask about actual behaviour. Questions can be asked about media behaviour on the previous day. This is a common technique in continuous media research when a survey is repeated on a regular basis. A picture of the behaviour of the population as a whole is painstakingly built up by taking a series of 'snapshots' of, for example, radio listening behaviour, by asking a large number of people what they listened to on the previous day.

How we ask questions, the manner we use, our facial expression, even our body language can affect the way people answer. Also the order in which the questions are put and the language used in the questions can have a major and unsought influence. You can ask about the same subject in a different way and get a different answer from the same person. This was illustrated in the British TV comedy series, *Yes, Prime Minister*. Here is an extract in which Sir Humphrey, a senior civil servant seeks to show another how an opinion poll can give exactly opposite results on the same issue, in this case the re-introduction to Britain of compulsory military or national service for young people. Compulsory national service ended in Britain in the 1950s:

Sir Humphrey:	*Mr. Woolley, are you worried about the rise in crime among teenagers?'*
Woolley:	*'Yes'.*
Sir Humphrey:	*'Do you think there is a lack of discipline and vigorous training in our comprehensive schools?'*
Woolley:	*'Yes'.*
Sir Humphrey:	*'Do you think young people welcome some structure and leadership in their lives?'*
Woolley:	*'Yes'.*
Sir Humphrey:	*'Do they respond to a challenge?'*
Woolley:	*'Yes'.*
Sir Humphrey:	*'Might you be in favour of reintroducing National Service?'*
Woolley:	*'Yes'.*

Sir Humphrey Appleby then poses the questions in a rather different way. See what happens!

Sir Humphrey:	'Mr. Woolley, are you worried about the danger of war?'
Woolley:	'Yes'.
Sir Humphrey:	'Are you unhappy about the growth of armaments?'
Woolley:	'Yes'.
Sir Humphrey:	'Do you think there's a danger in giving young people guns and teaching them how to kill?'
Woolley:	'Yes'.
Sir Humphrey:	'Do you think it wrong to force people to take up arms against their will?'
Woolley:	'Yes'.
Sir Humphrey:	'Would you oppose the reintroduction of National Service?'
Woolley:	'Yes'. [13]

Note the use of emotionally charged language. Note also how questions follow each other in an inexorable direction, leading the respondent, almost whatever his or her views, towards one opinion and then towards the exact opposite! No reputable researchers would ask such leading questions, nor would they 'funnel' questions in this way, leading the respondent, virtually without an alternative, towards a particular answer.

This is, of course, an extreme example to illustrate the point, but I hope it shows how sentence structures, the choice of certain emotive phrases and words can affect response. Tone of voice and 'body language' – the physical manner of the questioner – not reproduced on the printed page, are also major factors. There are many examples one could give from market and opinion research experience where results are biased by the way questions are asked.

The following questions were used in a survey in Delhi, India's capital city, designed to find out viewers' reactions to newly introduced cable television (CTV). Doordarshan is the national Indian state TV channel.

1. *Some of the CTV feature films contain sex/violence which affect the minds of children. What is your opinion about this aspect of CTV?*

2. *Do you think that exposure to such a large number of films (through CTV) with excessive sex/violence will affect the moral/ethical values in our society?*

   1. Yes   2. No   3. Don't Know/Can't Say

3. *It is generally believed that indiscreet showing of foreign films on CTV without removing objectionable scenes/dialogues (unlike Doordarshan which shows only classical/award winning foreign films and even removes some objectionable scenes) is a direct invasion on our culture. What is your opinion about this?[14]*

What is wrong with these questions? Many of us may agree that films containing sex or violence should not be shown on television. Others, while not necessarily approving of some things that are shown, believe that there should be no censorship and that viewers should be able to choose what to watch. But the purpose here, presumably, is to discover if viewers watch such films and what their opinions of such films are. The respondent should not be told what to think! The first two questions are very difficult to ask in a neutral way, but the effort must be made if the results are to reflect true opinions and not be what the respondent feels he or she is expected to say.

The third question is very biased. A better way would be to offer a range of opinions and ask the respondent with which he or she agreed.

The point to make here is that there is a reliable way to measure opinions. That is to use a question that offers the respondent a variety of different opinions with which to agree or disagree. This is a more reliable way of finding people's opinions without the questions influencing them unduly. Try these examples of a better way of measuring opinions about films on television. You could read out the following opinions and record whether a respondent agrees or disagrees with each of them.

Films often contain scenes which I find offensive

Films containing scenes involving sexual behaviour should be edited before showing on TV.

Films containing scenes of violent behaviour should be edited before showing on TV.

Films showing sexual behaviour or violence should be shown without censorship but with due warning of what to expect. The viewer can decide whether to watch or not.

Foreign films provide entertainment and variety and I welcome the freedom to choose myself what to view.

In each case the person questioned should be asked to choose his or her reply from the following categories:-

Agree Strongly
Agree Somewhat
No Opinion Either Way
Disagree Somewhat
Disagree Strongly

It is very important that thorough attention is given to the design of the questionnaire – its layout, the order and the wording of the questions. It is often the stage in research which is most neglected. Sometimes the faults in a questionnaire are very obvious and would be noticed easily if the researcher had simply tried it out on someone! New questionnaires should be pilot tested before use in the field.[15]

What goes into the questionnaire is determined by the purpose of the research. The designer of the questionnaire needs to keep a balance between the number of questions that could be asked and how many can be safely included. If the questions are too few to cover the requirements of the research, the project will fail. But it will also fail if the questionnaire is so long and complicated it wearies either the interviewer, or interviewee or both. There can be a tendency to 'play safe' and include everything that might be needed. The real skill is to reduce the number of questions down to those that are essential to meet the research objectives. Generally speaking, the accuracy of replies declines as questionnaires get longer. Opinions and practices vary in the research community. In my view and from my experience I would try to avoid a questionnaire that takes more than 45 minutes to administer, and one should plan for this to be a maximum, rather than an average.

Questions To Ask Before Designing Questions

There are four important questions for the designer of any questionnaire:-

Q1. Will all respondents understand the question in the same way and give the meaning intended?

Q2. Will the respondents know the answer?
Can you reasonably expect them to know?

Q3. Will the respondent, even if he or she knows the answer, tell the truth?

Q4. Will the question, as put, provide the information that you seek?

Only if the answer to each of these questions is 'yes' should the particular question be used. If you are not sure, pilot testing should provide the answer.

We have already considered Q1 – how the question is understood when using the example of how we might ask a friend to say what radio station he or she listened to. Vague, imprecise questions that can be understood in a number of different ways should be replaced by precise and unambiguous ones. "What radio station do you listen to most frequently" is more precise and is likely to provide a more consistent response. By consistency, I mean that everyone can be expected to understand the meaning of the question in the same way.

Q2 may be less easy to resolve. We often ask people detailed questions about their listening to the radio or watching the television yesterday. We may also ask them what newspapers or magazine they have read that day or the previous one. Can we expect them to remember two days ago? Perhaps we can, but what about three or more days before the interview? Respondents may be unable to answer a question about household income. We often need information on levels of income in order to categorise respondents according to their level of wealth. The wage earner can be expected to know, but if the wage earner is the husband and we are interviewing the wife, she may not know what their household income is.

There is no easy solution to this problem. Experience within different circumstances and cultures will point to the best solution. Sometimes a general ranking of the household's level of wealth can be obtained by asking questions instead about household ownership of various items – bicycle, radio set, electric or gas cooker, refrigerator, colour or monochrome television, motor car and so on. The more of these items owned the greater the effective wealth of the household. There is usually less of a problem about asking questions about what people own than what they earn.

The issue of not knowing some things overlaps into Q3. The respondent may know the answer to the question about income but not be prepared to tell you! He or she may not tell you the truth, fearing, despite assurances of confidentiality that the information may be passed to the income tax authorities. The respondent may give an answer that is less than the truth.

One solution to this is not to ask for a precise figure but to show a range of income levels on a card or read them out and ask the respondent to select the category into which he or she fits. I recently received a postal questionnaire that asked the question in this way and offered the following range of annual incomes. All I had to do was to select the category into which I fitted.

Less than £10,000
Between £10,000 and £20.000
Between £20,001 and £30,000
Between £30,001 and £40,000
Between £40,001 and £50,000
More than £50,000

Q4 is one that you need to ask about all questions used. Will the question, as put, provide the information intended? Let me illustrate this by returning to the question of income because it contains many other problems and illustrates the wider issue of designing questions that need to cover all kinds of people in very different situations. Remember that the same question needs to be addressed to both the very rich and the very poor and all levels in between. You might think the question "what is your current income?" would be acceptable, provide that we can overcome the problems already addressed. But what will the respondent suppose 'income' to mean? Is it household income? Do we mean cash only? In many societies, cash is not the best indicator of real income, especially, for example, among peasant farmers.

The problem is that unless you make it quite clear what you mean, the definition of income will be provided by the respondent and there will be uncontrolled variation in how people answer. A way around this problem can be to ask those in paid employment about cash income and then to ask all respondents about their other means of income in cash or kind. The question or questions used will need to reflect the local situation. This is a good example of the importance of pilot testing and of thinking carefully about the meaning and purpose of each question and of relating the questionnaire to the cultural circumstances in which you are operating.

Not All Questions are Answerable!

You should avoid asking questions cannot be easily answered. It is surprising how often this happens, even in areas where there is a lot of experience in survey research. Most common of all is the question which requires a respondent to remember something in too much detail. In Europe it is common practice in audience research to ask detailed questions in surveys about what respondents listened to yesterday. Respondents are taken through the day in clearly defined time 'slots' sometimes each as short as five minutes. But one has to doubt whether anyone can remember what they did on the previous day with this degree of accuracy. Fifteen or thirty minute time periods are in more common use.

Questions asking people in great detail about something in the past may be a waste of effort. How far back is it reasonable to expect people to remember things with a fair degree of accuracy? And does this vary according to culture and tradition? Generally, accuracy declines with the length of the period of recall. People remember what they did on the previous day better than what they did on the day before that, and so on.

This is an important issue for questionnaire design in radio and television research because recall or memory questions are often used and probably more than in other forms of opinion and market research. But we must not expect too much of our respondents' memory.

The degree of detail required may determine the length of the recall period. As has been noted, it is a common practice in Europe to build up a picture of daily radio listening by asking respondents in a face-to-face interview what they listened to on the previous day. With the assistance of the interviewer, most people are usually able to build up quite a detailed account of what they heard on the radio the previous day. It greatly helps if the interviewee has a detached list of times of programmes and programme sequences on the different networks on the previous day. But to ask the interviewee to remember the same degree of detail for the day before yesterday would increase the difficulty. Both the difficulty and inaccuracy increases the further you try to get the respondent to remember.

In audience research we often need to measure media behaviour on different days of the week. We need, in effect, a lot of different 'yesterdays'. This is a problem in radio audience research and it can be dealt with in one of two ways. One way is to carry out interviews with a sample of the population every day. But this is an expensive option.

43

An alternative is to give out self-completion diaries to a representative sample of the target population. These are, in reality, self-completion questionnaires, with the respondent being asked to note what times he or she listens to the radio over the next few days, to what network, and so on. I will describe the methods in more detail later.

Types of Question

There are many things that the designer of a questionnaire needs to know. Some are the well-known rules or guidelines that I have outlined. Others will be learned through experience; what works in one culture or society may not work in another. A questionnaire is itself a cultural product; it is very important to make sure it is appropriate to the social and cultural context in which it is used and does not import inappropriate assumptions, values or opinions from another.

Questions can be put into nine broad categories:

A. Open-Ended or Verbal Questions

The expected response ranges from a single word or phrase to an extended comment. Let us use an example that relates to what you are doing right now. Someone could ask you "What are your opinions of this book so far?" If the question were an open ended one, your reply would have to be written down by the interviewer. This poses problems. You might speak very fast and the interviewer would have to try write down whatever you said, or else try to summarise it as best he or she could.

Open-ended questions can elicit a wide range of responses and can reflect a true diversity of opinion and behaviour. But a major disadvantage, among many, is that they can be extremely difficult to analyse and report. When you have collected all the answers – and there could be a very wide range of them – they have to be categorised in order to produce some kind of summary of responses.

Another problem is that there is a high risk of interviewer bias. The interviewer may not have either the time or the space to record all that the respondent says and so has to try to summarise the reply. Interpretation is involved and this may differ between interviewers, leading inevitably to bias and distortion in what is recorded and reported.

Open-ended questions are often used in a pilot test to provide the list of likely responses to be used in the final questionnaire. However, there is another important use of the open-ended question. It is often important and valuable to give people the chance to express themselves freely on one of the topics being researched. Respondents may well have something to say which is not covered by the structured part of the questionnaire. An open-ended question may be a valuable 'safety-valve' for the expression of strong opinions. This technique can be used at the end of a questionnaire and interviewees often welcome the chance to express views freely.

In face-to-face interviews, open-ended questions can help to sustain interest. A long and fully structured questionnaire may become rather tedious to both interviewer and respondent. An open-ended question can help to focus attention at the beginning of a new set of questions about a new topic. Open-ended questions are also very often used in self-completion questionnaires when the respondent is free to write down views and opinions. In this case there is, of course, no interviewer bias.

B. List Questions

With this kind of question, a list of prepared optional answers is offered, any of which may be chosen. Sometimes only one answer can be chosen, at other times the respondent may select more than one answer.

List questions are often used to measure opinions. A pilot survey carried out beforehand with open-ended questions can collect a range of opinion about something. The most common responses, simplified and summarised, can be listed on the final questionnaire. The respondent may be asked which opinion is closest to his or her own, the alternative of 'other response' also being offered and recorded where appropriate.

Use of list questions in place of open-ended questions removes interviewer bias. It also has the advantage of uniformity of meaning, making comparisons possible.

How long should a list of options be in such a question? There is no fixed maximum, but remember that the longer the list, the greater the difficulty you will have in interpreting the data! A smaller number of possible answers may distort reality more but makes interpretation easier. As noted earlier, we attempt in research to generalise and summarise the infinite variety of human behaviour and opinion in order to understand it better, quantify it and be able to explain and predict it more accurately. But all forms of quantitative research by questionnaire attract the legitimate criticism that they distort reality. They do, but only to make sense of it! This is the paradox of all quantitative research.

List questions can be used in several ways and for several kinds of information. Here, for example, is a list question from a media research questionnaire used in Namibia.

What is your main source of news. That is, where do you receive information about what is happening in the world, in your country and in your area?

[Interviewer instruction:] Record ONE answer

Television	*Radio*
Newspaper	*Magazine*
Family	*Friends*
Colleagues	*Other (State)* _____ [16]

In the 'Other' category, the precise answer stated should be recorded. If the respondent can choose more than one answer this should be clearly indicated in the interviewer's instructions.

List questions may be used to record household equipment – electric cooker, refrigerator, water closet, electric light etc. In this case obviously multiple answers may be given and recorded.

There is a tendency for items at the beginning or end of lists to be selected. This *list order bias* effect can be neutralised by changing the order in which the list is read out, usually by rotating it, choosing a different starting point with each successive interview.

C. Category Questions

These are a variation on the list questions. Categories are provided in order to group a range of responses. For example, when we ask a person the educational level that they have achieved, there might be a wide range of responses. What we can do is to create a list in which educational levels are grouped into categories. The question asked is usually something like "What was the level you reached in education?" The interviewer would have a list summarising the different levels from no education up to a university degree or post-graduate qualification. The response is marked accordingly. A category question was illustrated earlier as a way of collecting information about income.

D. Ranking Questions

These provide another way of measuring views and opinions. The respondent is asked to put possible answers in rank order of importance. Respondents might be asked to rank in order of desirability a list of choices for new radio services or programmes. Some detail might have to be given to help people make informed choices.

You might ask people to say what were, for them, the most important types of programme on radio or television. Number one could be given to the most important category, number two to the next, and so on. In the analysis it is simply necessary to add the scores and the overall response with the lowest score is the most favoured. One could, of course use the numbers around the other way, giving the highest number to the most important down to the lowest number to the least important. From this one obtains a rank order of responses which may reflect no single individual's view but is an average of all of them.

A famous example of a ranking question is one that has nothing to do with audience research. It is in the annual Eurovision Song Contest held on television throughout Europe each year. Each participating country votes for the songs of the others. Each country (the decision is made by a panel of judges usually with local viewer participation) chooses the top ten songs and assigns them each a score from twelve down to one. The top song is given the score of twelve, the second is given the score of ten, the third is given the score eight and then the rest in descending order down to one point. The winner is the song from the country with the most points.

You might well use a similar scheme to test the popularity of presenters or to rank entertainment programmes. The same method could also be used for more serious purposes. Let us suppose that you wanted to know how farmers wanted to get information about new seeds or fertilisers. You might ask a question something like this:

The following are possible ways in which information about new seeds or fertilisers could be announced or made available to farmers. Please rank them in order of preference for you. Give your first choice the number 1, the next choice the number 2 and so on down to the number 8 for the information source which is the least important to you.

Announcements on the radio
Announcements in a farming magazine
Information to come from agricultural extension workers in this area
Information to be sent to you in the mail
Information from the suppliers
Other — Please state

Analysis would give you a series of scores for the different ways of obtaining agricultural information. The one with the lowest score would be the most popular means or the one with the highest overall priority.

A modification of the ranking question is one in which the respondent is given a set of scores or numbers to assign to a list of possibilities. In the above example, every item is given a score. Instead, the respondent may be given a fixed number of points or numbers to distribute. He or she can then give no points at all to those things of no interest or importance and give more points to those things that are really wanted. For example we might give the respondent 36 points to distribute among all the possibilities. He or she might distribute these evenly among three or four favourite projects and give no points at all to the others.

E. Scale Questions

Respondents may be read a statement "The television network should always play a feature film after the evening news" or "Most locally made television programmes are of poor quality", and then be asked for an opinion ranging from strongly disagree to strongly agree.

A coding frame is provided thus:-

Strongly disagree	*0*
Disagree somewhat	*1*
Neither agree nor disagree	*2*
Agree somewhat	*3*
Strongly agree	*4*

I suggested this scheme as a better way of assessing opinions about foreign films on television in India in the example cited earlier. The order can equally well be reversed. Each point is assigned a number 0 to 4. The overall score will be a measure of opinion. This can, for ease of comprehension, be converted into a percentage. The sum of scores for each category of answer is divided by the number of responses (omitting non-responses). The resultant number multiplied by twenty-five gives a score out of one hundred. In the above case the score would indicate the level of agreement and would enable comparisons to be made with similar questions or with the same question over time.

Some experts think that one should try to remove the middle position 'neither agree nor disagree' in order to obtain a clearer idea of opinion. I will again use an example from Namibia to illustrate. Here the question is designed to discover what viewers and listeners think about the national broadcaster, the NBC.

In our work as market researchers, people have told us about various opinions they have concerning radio, television and the Namibian Broadcasting Corporation. Would you please tell me how much you personally agree or disagree with each of these statements by giving me one of the answers from this card? Would you say you agree strongly, tend to agree, tend to disagree or disagree strongly that the NBC. . . . . ?

[Interviewer instruction:]
Read out each statement in turn and record ONE answer for each.[17]

Statements	Agree strongly	Tend to agree	Tend to disagree	Disagree strongly
a. understands the needs of the people				
b. is wasting money				
c. is educating the needs of Namibia				
d. is government controlled				
e. is promoting English as the country's language				
f. is helping you with your education				
g. is important for the country				
h. has programmes of a very high quality				
i. is politically neutral				
j. represents the people of Namibia				
k. is a parastatal				
l. is controlled by an independent board				

Note there is no middle position – 'Neither agree nor disagree'. The respondent is urged to choose one side or the other. The question uses the word 'tend' to encourage respondents to indicate which side of the argument they tend towards even if they do not hold strong views.

Exercise

There are many points to note from this Namibian audience research question. What is the first thing you notice about the statements on which opinion is sought? What kinds of opinion are being offered here for the respondents' comments? Can you think of reasons why this range of opinion statements should be used? How would you go about creating a similar list of opinion statements about some organisation or service that you were seeking to research?

Comment

These statements are all things that people have said at one time or another about the NBC. But the main point to note is that the list includes statements which are critical of the NBC ('is wasting money') and those which are favourable ('understands the needs of the people'). It also contains statements which for some would be critical and for others not so ('is government controlled' or 'is promoting English as the country's language').

Opinion statements can be a good way of helping respondents to feel more relaxed about expressing opinions. I once helped to run an audience survey in Vietnam, where people are unaccustomed to expressing criticisms either of the government or of its institutions and services. We wanted to find out what people really thought about the national broadcaster, the Voice of Vietnam. We found that by offering them a list of opinion statements they felt more relaxed about agreeing or disagreeing with statements that reflected a range of opinions from critical to approving.

In the above examples a four or five point scale has been used. There is no rule against a greater or a smaller size of scale. In my experience, four or five give the most easily analysed results.

In the Namibian case, the results, once added up and a mean score calculated, would tell the NBC on which side of the line – agreeing or disagreeing – the listeners tended to fall, and by what margin. Sometimes it will be necessary to analyse results further. For example, a mean score right in the middle of the two extremes might mean that there were no strong opinions either way. But it might also mean that strongly opposing views were evenly balanced. These are rather different and you may want to know in which groups of the population the opposing and strongly held opinions were expressed. Analysis of the data should provide an answer.

F. Quantity Questions

The response is a number, exact or approximate, in answer to a question asking for information that can be supplied in numerical form. How many people live in your household? How many radio sets in working order are there at home? How many television sets do you have? The actual number can be recorded.

G. Grid Questions

In these a table or grid is used to record answers to more than one question at the same time. These require practice but in the end they help both interviewer and the person who does the analysis!

For example, you might need to know what audio-visual equipment is available for use in the home and what is out of action needing repair. A typical grid question might be as follows:

Which of the following items does your household have? How many are in working order and how many in need of repair?

49

	Number in household	Number in working order	Number in need of repair
Car radio			
Portable radio set			
Other radio			
Television (black & white)			
Television (colour)			
Satellite dish			
Video recorder			
Audio cassette recorder			

H. Two Choice Questions

These are sometimes called *binary* or *dichotomous* questions. Some examples can illustrate the type.

Did you listen to the radio yesterday?

Is your TV a colour or black and white only set?

When you want to hear some music, given the choice of listening to the radio or your own tapes or records, which would you usually choose?

These questions, often of the Yes/No type, are easy to handle and analyse by computer, or manually. They make routing within a questionnaire relatively simple. Someone who answers 'Yes' to the question 'Did you listen to the radio yesterday?' can then be asked further questions about radio schedules, networks, programmes and so on, while the one who answers 'No' is taken on to a later section of the questionnaire. The two-choice question makes it very easy to group respondents into sub-groups for subsequent analysis.

However, the two-choice question should not be over-used. You might want to divide your respondents into heavy and light users of the radio. It could be tempting to use one question to determine this. Perhaps you might ask whether on the previous day the respondent listened for more or less than one hour, using this as the criterion for light or heavy listening. But this could be very misleading. A better way would be to look at listening behaviour over a longer period. If you do use two-choice questions to categorise or group respondents make sure you use a question which defines them fairly and accurately.

I. Probing Questions

These may not be written into the questionnaire. But they can be standardised in order to avoid interviewer bias. For example, a standard probing question would be 'Anything else' or 'Can you explain a little bit more?'

There may be other kinds of questions that might be devised but the above list covers all kinds that are normally used in quantitative market research.

Making Questions Work

The quality of the answers you get depends greatly on the way the questions are worded in the questionnaire. It is easy to forget the need to be precise and to avoid language that means different things to different people. Consider the following question and the range of responses offered:

'How much time do you spend watching television?' (Tick box)

A great deal ☐
A moderate amount ☐
Not a lot ☐
No time at all ☐

The only precise answer would be the last one! The others would have no definite meaning. All you would be measuring would be subjective opinions of the amount of time spent watching. For one person, an hour a day would be 'a great deal' while for another it would be 'not a lot'! If questions are imprecise, no amount of clever statistical analysis afterwards will give the results any greater precision.

There is another kind of problem. Can you see any difficulty with the following two questions?

Does your radio have the facility to receive FM? Yes/No

What kind of radio do you have? (Tick box)
Portable ☐
Car radio ☐
Tuner in a stereo system (with record or c.d. player) ☐

How would you deal with the problem(s) you have noticed? (There are at least two!). The key thing to check is this. Do the questions work equally well for the person with ten radio sets and the person with only one? Are there clear instructions for the interviewer?

The first question would be more precise if it were: 'Do you have any radio with FM or VHF?' (The only problem then is that many people are not familiar with technical terms. It may be better to ask to see the person's sets to verify if they do indeed have the facility to receive FM broadcasts.)

The second question about the kind or kinds of radio sets at the respondent's home provides no data on the numbers of sets. If you need to know, you will have to add a question in which you ask how many of each category the person possesses.

There is another problem which is trickier but which is essential to tackle. What do we mean by 'you'? Usually we need to find out about access at the respondent's homes.

The person interviewed may not be the head of the household or the owner of any of the equipment asked about. He or she may not personally own media equipment of any kind. In many cases, because of random selection within a household, we will be interviewing a child, another relative of the head of the household or other person normally living there. We should beware of asking questions implying ownership of radios, televisions and other household equipment in large, extended households where such things may be shared. Guard against imposing views of family structure or of the respective roles of men and women from your own background. Be ready to notice when your questionnaire, perhaps drawn up against a different background of assumptions and attitudes, does not really fit the situation. Be prepared to change it!

Sometimes questions may presume certain views. Consider the following question:

'Does your local radio station provide an adequate service?'

The presumption here is that the respondent has an idea of what an adequate local radio service would be. This question might work quite well but may need to be followed by more questions for clarity.

There is another point to look out for or be aware of. Opinion tends to lead towards leaving things as they are, generally people tend to prefer 'Yes' to 'No' and they tend to approve positive statements more than negative ones. These tendencies are related. Let us use some hypothetical examples. Consider these questions:

Do you think that the proportion of films shown on TV from other countries should be reduced?

Do you think our TV should increase the proportion of our own country's films shown?

These are different questions of course, but each is the reverse side of the other. If you increase the proportion of indigenous material you reduce the proportion of non-indigenous or foreign material. If respondents were logical and consistent the support for the first proposition should be the same as for the second. In reality it might not be. There is a tendency in many cultures to approve of positive steps (increase, improve, enhance) and disapprove of negative ones (restrict, prohibit, prevent).

I noted above that respondents often do not understand technical terms. Avoid specialist language and try to find the words that people are more likely to be familiar with. All fields of human activity develop their own specialist language. It should be avoided in questionnaires. Broadcasters speak of *genres* of programme. It is best in questions about *genres* to use words like *types* or *kinds* of programmes. If you want to know about the *technical quality of radio reception*, avoid these words and ask how well the radio can be heard. Radio is subject to *interference* but you may find that few people use this word. 'Can you always hear the programmes clearly?' or 'Do you sometimes find difficulty in hearing programmes?' are better ways to obtain information about reception quality.

The Order of Questions

The structure and order of questions is important. Funnelling is helpful here, but not in the way that Sir Humphrey did it in the passage from the TV comedy *Yes, Prime Minister!* Good funnelling is when the questionnaire moves from the general to the more particular in a way that will not bias the response. For example, if you asked the question 'Have you read the Daily Mail in the past seven days?' as your opening question, you might get a startled response. One should start with a general question and then focus on the particular. It might run something like this:

I want to ask some questions about newspapers and magazines.
Do you ever get to read any? (If yes) What do you read most?
Have you ever read the Daily Mail? When did you last read the Daily Mail?

Funnelling like this is appropriate. The danger is when it comes to opinion questions; funnelling can then tend to bias response.

It is important to avoid undue influence or contamination between one question and another. In the example quoted earlier from the TV comedy show, Sir Humphrey's questions were asked in such a way as to lead almost inevitably towards a particular set of replies. What he did was not only to use biased language but also to use the juxtaposition of questions to assist the process of obtaining the response he wanted. He does this to prove a point about how opinion research can make anyone say almost anything! There is some truth in his charge and that is why we need to be aware of the danger and take all steps to remove it. The example I used was taken from a TV comedy, but there are some examples from real life.

In 1939 when the Second World War began in Europe, the United States was not at first involved. There was a poll containing these two related questions:

1. *Do you think that the United States should permit American citizens to engage in the German army?*

2. *Do you think that the United States should permit American citizens to join the British army?*

The questions were asked in a different order in order to see if this affected the response. It did to a significant degree:

		Order 1-2	Order 2-1
	Yes	22%	31%
Question 1	No	74%	61%
	No opinion	4%	8%
	Yes	40%	45%
Question 2	No	54%	46%
	No opinion	6%	9%

53

18

Public opinion in the United States was generally against involvement in another European war, but there was more support for the British and Allied cause than for Germany. When the question order was reversed and serving in the British forces was suggested first, there was a greater degree of support for the idea of US citizens serving in a foreign army. And note that this applied to both questions.

How can this be avoided, and which is the truth? The answer is that probably the only way to avoid this contamination across questions in this particular case would have been to separate the two questions and put them in different parts of the questionnaire. As to which is the truth, the answer is that both sets of responses are equally valid but that in both cases respondents' views as expressed have been affected. If uncontaminated responses are essential then the questions have to be separated.

Checking or Testing the Reliability of Questions

Reliability is a measure of the extent to which a questionnaire produces similar results on different occasions. A tractor that sometimes pulls a heavy load but at other times cannot even be started, is unreliable. A question that produces one answer on one occasion but a different answer (from the same person) on another may be unreliable. But how can we ever tell?

There are various ways of testing reliability. One is to test a question on the same person on different occasions. But a better method may be to try questions out on a number of people chosen in a similar manner. A crucial question is, would different interviewers asking the same question of two random samples of people get similar results? Note the use of random samples here. We can assume, with a reasonable degree of safety, that two random samples of the same universe will possess the same characteristics. We can also assume that if two interviewers produce different results from two such separate samples of the same universe using the same questionnaire, then the differences arise from differences between the two interviewers or from a fault in the questionnaire that somehow gives different results in different circumstances. This is an essential point. Unless we can be absolutely sure that the questionnaire will produce the same results when applied to samples of the same population we cannot use the questionnaire to make comparisons between populations. We would say the questionnaire was unreliable. There are various ways of measuring reliability; some of them are rather complex. Usually it is through experience that we establish which questions can be relied on to give consistent results, and of course the reliability of questions can be tested for most purposes on a pilot survey.

Social and Cultural Acceptability and Self Portrayal

There is always a danger that respondents will answer questions in ways that fit in with socially acceptable norms rather than with what is true. The respondent may say he/she smokes less, drinks less, listens to more 'good' programmes, reads more educational material and so on, than is actually the case. There is no easy way around this problem. Obviously the interviewer must ensure that all questions are asked in a wholly neutral manner and that no hint of approval or disapproval is suggested by his or her manner or expression. Sometimes it is possible to use different questions about the same or similar topics in different parts of the questionnaire and these can act as a cross-check.

Validity

Validity is defined as that quality in a questionnaire that ensures that what is measured or described reflects reality. Consistency of results is not enough. A questionnaire can produce consistent results, ie. be *reliable*, but still be invalid; the results may not accurately reflect reality but instead consistently get it wrong! How can we tell?

It can be quite difficult to find out. A good example of a validity problem is experienced in radio audience research. Let us suppose that we are using a face-to-face questionnaire in which the interviewer asks a large number of respondents, randomly selected from the population, about what they listened to yesterday. The process of selection and interviewing carries on over several weeks, using the same questionnaire. From the results you would expect to be able to calculate various things about radio listening such as, for example, the average daily audience as a percentage of the population, and the average number of hours listened to per person per day. If instead you use a self-completion listening diary to another random sample of the population, we would also be able to calculate the daily audience and the average number of hours of listening. But the two sets of data will unfortunately be different; the self-completion diary method is likely to produce higher figures. Which is valid? Do diaries encourage people to overstate their listening? Do people listen more because they are filling in a listening diary? Do people who listen very little to any radio simply not bother to send in their diaries, with the result that those who do are taken erroneously as fully representative? Does an aided recall, face-to-face interview produce an underestimate? No one is certain; it is probable that both happen. But which is the valid measure? It is doubtful if audience researchers can ever satisfactorily answer this question, but it may not matter too much, provided that we consistently use the same method of measurement. There may be some distortions in each but these will be consistent over time; each means of measurement will therefore be able to tell us what we need to know.[19]

3.3   Pilot Testing

We generally need to test a questionnaire to see if it is going to work in the way intended. In effect what we do is to run a mini-survey. Let us suppose we are carrying out a survey to measure the impact of a radio and TV campaign on infant nutrition. Perhaps there has also been a campaign using posters and advertisements in the press. We have decided that the best method to use is a random sample survey of women with children. A questionnaire has been designed and produced. The questions cover all the areas for investigation by the research project. What is to stop us from just going ahead?

You may well obtain acceptable results along the lines of what was needed and expected. But there is a risk, especially with attitude and opinion questions, that some questions will not work in the way intended. Some sections of the questionnaire may be found to be unnecessarily complex. You may have made some assumptions about attitudes that are not justified. There is no point wasting resources on questions that do not work; it wastes the time and effort of everyone. Pilot testing helps you to avoid making mistakes and can save time and effort in the long run.

To do a pilot survey it is not necessary to go to the trouble of selecting a fully random sample. But it is important to select people who will represent a wide range of possible respondents. Will the questionnaire work equally well with old and young, rich and poor, educated and illiterate, people of different ethnic backgrounds or religious affiliations and people of different occupations and life styles? Here is the chance to find out. We can test the questionnaire on as wide a range of interviewees as possible. Pilot testing is also an excellent opportunity for giving interviewers experience of the questionnaire. Mistakes and misunderstandings can be corrected. It is at this early stage that the experience and skill of the interviewers can be used to improve the questionnaire. Their comments on the way that the questionnaire works in the field should always be given proper consideration.

The pilot survey is not only a way of trying out questions and training interviewers. We can also use the exercise to see if the results provide what is needed. Sometimes even well designed questions don't provide useful information. They may just lead to the research equivalent of a dead end! Leave out redundant questions like these and save everyone's time. Remember also the use of open-ended questions to provide a range of possible answers for list or category questions.

3.4 The Interview

How the interview is conducted plays a large part in the success or failure of research. Training and supervision of interviewers and quality control of interviews are key elements in the success of quantitative research.

The Role of the Interviewer

The manner, the tone of voice, the 'body language' of the interviewer and the relationship between interviewer and interviewee are all important. They can influence the answers given. Not only can the person being interviewed be influenced. The interviewer can interpret answers in a way determined by expectations and prior attitudes. Consider this true story from a research methods training course. Participants from various African countries were being taught the need to avoid leading respondents towards certain answers.

They were divided into three groups for a pilot study in a rural village. A key question they were to administer asked farmers to give reasons why they did not expand their agricultural activity.

Each group of interviewers was given, separately, identical instructions. Interviewers were told not to suggest answers and not to supply examples. However, before they started, the instructor casually mentioned three likely reasons. These were mentioned separately to each group and a different reason was given to each!

To the first group the instructor suggested that the likely reasons that the farmers would give was the shortage of land, labour and equipment.

To the second group, the instructor suggested that they would hear their respondent farmers say it was a lack of money, seed and fertiliser.

To the third group of interviewers he suggested that they would find their respondent farmers saying that it was the lack of roads and the distance of markets.

The interviewers selected, at random, a number of farmers. The most frequently stated set of constraints in the responses were identical with that mentioned casually by the instructor to each of the three groups! The interviewers, who had been given to expect that the problem was the shortage of land and labour, recorded this as the most common reason given by the farmers. Those who had been told to expect the lack of money, seed and fertiliser recorded this as the most common reason, and those who had expected transport difficulties recorded that this was the main constraint.

The 'casual' remarks of the instructor had influenced the results. It may have been that despite the firm instructions, interviewers confronted by the difficulty of asking an awkward question of a stranger, actually helped the person to answer or interpreted responses in the expected way.[20]

Even when the interviewer scrupulously follows the rules and says nothing apart from reading the questionnaire verbatim, there is still a tendency for the interviewer's expectations to have an influence on the way responses are interpreted and recorded. There are two ways of minimising this bias. The wording of questions need to be as neutral as possible to avoid giving the respondent the impression that certain answers are expected. Secondly, interviewers need to be thoroughly trained to maintain a self-critical awareness of the twin dangers of influencing interviewees, and of a subjective interpretation of responses.

The manner and tone of voice, even the 'body language' or posture of the interviewer can be a big influence. Let us imagine you are asking questions about plans to change a TV service, or it might be a proposal to open a commercial popular music radio station, or it could be a question about the current government in power. In each case you may have very strong views yourself. It may be hard to ask questions in a tone of voice and manner that does not communicate these views to the respondent. But it must be done, otherwise your results may be distorted and give a false reflection of reality.

There are other ways in which interviewer bias can intrude. For example, the interviewer may think it is pointless to ask all questions of everyone. One might think it is not necessary to ask questions about TV viewing of very poor people, or assume by a person's demeanour or appearance that he or she was illiterate and skip over the readership questions with a lack of attention. But appearances can be very deceptive and assumptions are often wrong. Many poor people do actually watch a lot of TV.

Some people may appear to be uneducated but may in fact be otherwise. The golden rule in research is 'Don't ever make any assumptions about anybody, anywhere'! Sooner or later your assumptions will be wrong! The danger is that you may not notice and record a lot of false information.

Politeness and courtesy are very important. The interviewee is giving his or her time to provide information. It may be ultimately of benefit to him or her or even to the community, but at this stage this may not be at all clear or certain. The interviewer needs to treat the person interviewed with care and respect. One problem that can interfere with this is social class or caste. In many cultures it is difficult to avoid the bias which can be brought in to the situation by differences in social status between interviewer and interviewee. It is often the case that the interviewer comes from a higher social class than the person being interviewed. The reverse can also happen. Both can affect the reliability of the answers given.

Class difference can produce a range of feelings among interviewees ranging from resentment to deference, with varying degrees of unease and even embarrassment. There are various ways of dealing with this problem. One is to recruit interviewers from all social backgrounds and use them where appropriate. But this is not always a practical solution. There are no rules about this; each circumstance requires different sets of solutions. Research fieldwork supervisors need to be alert to the problem and choose and train their field workers to be sensitive to it. Often one finds that the best team of interviewers are made up of people who seem relatively classless to most people being interviewed. But whatever one writes here will not be of much help in a general sense. Conditions and circumstances vary enormously between cultures and experience is the best guide.

Different ethnic and religious backgrounds can also play an important part in affecting response. In many societies it is not possible for a man to interview a woman at all, or at least the woman's husband or other close relative may have to be present. Such considerations of social propriety can also affect the response. A woman may say rather different things in response to a strange man, especially if a close male relative is present than she might say to a woman with no one else present. This even applies in what we might think is the relatively 'safe' area of broadcasting. In 1985, in a survey conducted for the BBC in Pakistan, the research agency carrying out the interviewing found that among Afghans living in refugee camps, some men said they did not like their wives to listen to the radio when they were not present. Women did in fact sometimes listen to the radio, whether or not their husbands knew or approved. It was therefore important to be sure to interview women not in the presence of their husbands. For this it was essential to use women interviewers when interviewing women respondents.

There are some useful rules for administering questionnaires that all good interviewers should follow.

Introduce yourself in a friendly way and explain in simple terms what the research is for.

Always say how long the interview is likely to last.

Explain that the information given is confidential and anonymous. (There may be occasions when anonymity and confidentiality may be waived but this can be done only with the prior permission of the interviewee).

Check back at the end of the interview with the respondent and ask if there are any points of uncertainty or if he or she has any questions.

Don't waste the interviewee's time or in any other way abuse the privilege he or she has granted you by agreeing to be interviewed.

Ghana Broadcasting Corporation's audience research department reported some interesting problems when their interviewers go out into the field to select random interviewees. Evidently 'gifts' are required for some of them. For example, some old women demand tobacco before being interviewed! Often it is essential (and at least courteous) to secure the help of a village chief, which may require the provision of 'the usual customary drink.'[21]

Checking Interviewers

During normal survey conditions, one should look out for major differences between the results obtained by different interviewers. If it is obvious that these differences arise from the fact that they have been interviewing people in different locations with people from different lifestyles and backgrounds, then all may be well. But if they are mostly interviewing people drawn at random from the same universe, their results should be broadly similar. If they are not it can be an indication that one or more of the interviewers are biasing the responses. Remember that while the questionnaire is constant, the interviewers and enumerators are not. To what extent do one interviewer's responses differ from another's because of their different ways of administering the questionnaire? Our aim should be to reduce such interviewer bias to an absolute minimum.

This is why the training of interviewers is so important. They work on their own almost all the time. In most quantitative fieldwork it is usual to have a team of interviewers under the management of a supervisor who not only directs the fieldwork but is also responsible for quality checks. Sometimes he or she will attend interviews but obviously this can happen at only a small proportion of them. The supervisor will also be involved in some back-checking, which I will explain shortly. But most interviews are neither supervised nor back-checked. A great deal of trust is put in interviewers and it is vital that they are highly motivated, well-disciplined and responsible individuals. The job of interviewing involves skills that need to be learned. One of the most important skills to develop is that of consistency. Interviewers need to do everything in the same way with each respondent so that the differences between them are entirely due to genuine differences and not something produced by the differences in the way questions have been put or in the manner of putting them. This is how we will produce results that reflect the respondents' realities in a consistent and reliable way.

But how can we tell if interviewers are inconsistent? If we are involved in a very large-scale survey in which each interviewer may be responsible for very many interviews, inconsistencies and differences between results can be spotted at an early stage. It may be noted that an interviewer has a significantly larger number of responses of a particular kind while in other respects the people interviewed were similar. One would need to investigate. In most cases, inconsistency and unreliability can be detected very quickly by appropriate methods of quality control. These take place while the survey is going on if we want to avoid additional problems later. Adequate quality control prevents a survey having to be repeated later when it becomes clear at the data processing stage that the results are not reliable. It should be noted that it is important that each questionnaire form has to record the identity of the interviewer.

Interviews can be supervised of course, but it is impossible for supervisors to be present at every interview. The supervisor should be present for some interviews and will be able to notice errors, inconsistencies, inappropriate behaviour etc. It is also common practice for a proportion of interviews to be 'back-checked'. The supervisor who checks that the answers given were accurately recorded revisits a proportion of interviewees. The services of an interviewer who was found to be unreliable may be dispensed with, unless, the fault can be corrected through further instruction or training. Persistently faulty interviewing should always lead to the dismissal of the interviewer concerned.

3.5 Checking and Editing of Questionnaires

The supervisor who goes out into the field with the team of interviewers should continually check through all questionnaires as they are completed. He or she needs to look out for inconsistencies, omitted questions and other errors. Sometimes it may be necessary to go back to the interviewee to put things right. Certain checks can be, and often are, built into the questionnaire so that most inconsistencies can be spotted at the time by the interviewer and corrected by checking with the person being interviewed. But if this fails the supervisor should be able to spot the error and, if needed, go back to the respondent and check for a correction.

Checking and editing also involves making sure that the questionnaire is ready for data entry - the point when the results are entered into a computer file for analysis. The supervisor can also use the checking process to determine whether the interviews are going well, that the interviewers are administering the questionnaires correctly and that all the answers are being recorded correctly. Questionnaires usually contain routing instructions. The supervisor can easily see if these are being followed correctly.[22]

Back Checking

As I noted earlier, it is good research practice to specify a certain percentage of interviews that will be back-checked. It may be decided that 5% of all interviewees will be recontacted by the supervisor to check on the reliability and accuracy of the data recorded by the interviewer. The drawbacks here are first, the time factor and second, interviewee fatigue. The person interviewed in the first place may not take too kindly to being bothered again, especially with questions he or she has only recently answered! However, the co-operation of interviewees can usually be ensured by a simple explanation of why it is necessary. It is usually not necessary to check the whole questionnaire but the supervisor will usually check a few key or difficult questions to ensure that interviews have proceeded properly. The main purpose is a check on interviewer reliability and consistency. Much survey research around the world is conducted by commercial survey research agencies and you will find in their specifications for survey research that they always build back checking into their research proposals.

3.6   Some Common Problems Encountered in Field Research and Some Solutions

At the end of any research project in the field it is very important to find out about the experiences of the field researchers. The interviewers and their supervisors will have a good deal of important information about the project itself, problems with fieldwork, sampling difficulties, and the like. They will be able to provide information that will help in the analysis and interpretation of the results. 'Debriefing' the field force will also provide valuable information to assist in the better design of future projects.

Few things ever operate perfectly. This is very true of field research when so much can be unpredictable. The weather, political upheavals and crises, civil disturbances and unrest and other events, usually unforeseen, can interrupt or influence the research in unpredictable ways. Those in charge of the research have to decide what influence or effect any events may have had on the results. When reporting any research project one needs to relate results to prevailing circumstances.

In a recent radio audience survey in the capital city of a less developed country, the following problems were reported. They are problems encountered in many countries, both industrialised and less developed, but tend to be encountered more often in the latter.

It was sometimes impossible to use a Kish Grid because the household member first contacted was suspicious that it had to do with security or taxation. Some interviewers reported that it was often difficult to find men over 24 years of age at home. Two or three visits at arranged times had to be made. Then the person selected would often not turn up because of a general distrust of strangers in a city beset by both terrorism and an arbitrary police force.

When researching in areas of higher income, it was often a household employee who opened the door. Sometimes, despite a careful explanation of the purpose of the research, the employee or servant would be reluctant or even refuse to call someone else to be interviewed. Sometimes the interview would be conducted through the intercom without the front door even being opened!

61

Contacting and interviewing people at lower socio-economic levels of this city was relatively easy. However, there was another problem familiar to anyone who has commissioned research in less developed areas. Other people in the household tried to influence the answers of the persons selected, even answering for the respondent at times. One interviewer reported that this was a persistent problem, even when she made it clear that personal answers were sought. In about half the cases she reported that interviews had to be abandoned. The problem was said to be most acute with women aged 40 and over with low levels of education. When interviewing such women, other members of the household, very often the husband, would seek to intervene and 'assist'.

Some interviewers reported that questions about one of the radio stations seemed to create in some respondents certain expectations that they would receive some present if they said they listened. Evidently the radio station in question had recently engaged in some promotional activity, rewarding people identified as listeners. Consequently there was probably some over-claiming of listening to that station.

Educational levels were sometimes difficult to establish reliably. Young respondents, both male and female, sometimes claimed university education when they were obviously not telling the truth. Interviewers established whether the claim was accurate by adding a question asking the name of the university.

I like solutions invented on the spot by interviewers to overcome problems. Asking a supplementary question to ascertain the reliability of a reply is acceptable provided that the interviewer does not make the respondent feel inadequate or foolish. This obviously requires experience, tact and sensitivity. The interviewer needs to consult the supervisor about any such problem and to agree on a solution. This should be recorded in the field notes.

Addresses of some respondents were difficult to establish in some shanty areas. Dwellings were not numbered and were not in named streets. This made it difficult or impossible to trace the person interviewed for back checking. How can we answer the problem of identifying dwellings in shanty areas? The same problem is encountered in many rural areas of the world. The solution is to ask at the dwelling how it could be found again. Usually people locally have a way of identifying dwellings, very often by the name of the owner or head of household.

Once again there are no absolute rules. The skill of good field research, is to find appropriate and effective answers to problems as they come up. Then, having found a solution, one should keep a record of it. Supervisors, and very often interviewers too, need to keep a fieldwork diary to record anything out of the ordinary, problems encountered and how they were dealt with, and so on. Interviewers and supervisors develop skills and knowledge from their experience. These can be an immensely valuable resource.

There may be various ways of mitigating or removing some problems. These will depend largely on local circumstances. Here are some suggestions. Suspicions of the reasons for research are enormously difficult to overcome. Sometimes it may be necessary to give a careful account of the purpose of the research and to make a very big effort to build confidence. It may be necessary to do this at each selected household.

This can, of course, be very time-consuming. There are sometimes short cuts that can help. People may be very suspicious of the police, government officials and the like, but there may be a local person who is trusted by everyone. It may be a priest, an elder of a village or a respected local figure. If the purpose of the research is carefully explained to that person, his or her word of reassurance may help remove suspicion. This is more difficult to achieve in cities where there is less social cohesion, more anonymity and less prominent or widely accepted opinion leadership.

The presence of other people at the face-to-face interview is more problematic. In western societies where individualism is seen as of some importance, most opinion and market research interviews are conducted away from the presence of other people. It is simply not possible to ensure this in most parts of the world. Does it matter? The text book response is to assert that it does matter because people will not always give their own personal views or be completely frank and honest when neighbours and relatives are listening. But if we accept that it is usually impossible to interview people as isolated individuals because they do not live in that way, then to attempt to insist on one-to-one interviews may be unrealistic and pointless.

If the reality is that people's individual behaviour is always influenced by others then we should not seek to create a false and unfamiliar situation in an interview. On the other hand, when one is investigating the views and behaviour of women in societies where they take a subservient role it is important to ensure that interviews take place without the presence of a man.

One has to make a sensible and practical judgement. It is important to explain patiently and carefully that the interview is not a test. There are no correct or incorrect answers. It should also be made clear that it doesn't matter in the least if the person being interviewed does not have an answer to a question.

Radio and television producers, journalists and media managers inhabit a world of separate and rival programmes, networks and identities. The audience may not share those perceptions. While media people might think that a station identity or programme and name are of great significance, the audience are very often inconveniently oblivious to these things. In research we sometimes find that people have only a vague idea of what programmes and networks they listen to or watch. They are sometimes just as vague about what papers or magazines they read. Or they may simply get it all wrong! Just as the brand name of 'Hoover' may be applied to all vacuum cleaners or 'Thermos' to all vacuum flasks, so also can viewers, listeners and readers confuse radio, television and newspaper titles and apply these to other channels and sources. I remember in a survey in Ghana one respondent saying that he listened to the BBC from many countries – from America, South Africa, Germany and Britain. It took some time for us to realise that he was using the term 'BBC' to apply to any international radio broadcasting.

Such kinds of errors may be rare, but their existence points to the need for care and alertness. In radio and television audience measurement, when using the diary or interview method, we may need to use 'prompts' – that is titles or phrases likely to help respondents recall and identify correctly what they watch or listen to. In both diaries and face to face interviews it is sometimes necessary to give not only the 'official' name of a radio or television station but also other names by which it may be popularly known.

The same thing applies to magazine and newspaper titles. Very often these are not clearly distinguished from each other. There may be several magazines with titles like 'Farming Monthly', 'Farming Today', 'Modern Farming', or 'The Farmer'. It is not surprising that some respondents may make mistakes in reporting accurately what they read. It is much the same with the names of individual radio and television programmes. It is often a painful thing for producers to realise but the audiences for many quite popular shows often have only a limited knowledge of the actual titles!

3.7 Translation of Questionnaires into Different Languages

In most countries of the world, on any survey with national or major regional coverage at least, you will normally need to administer any questionnaire in more than one language. For example, in a recent national media survey in Zambia, the questionnaire was produced and printed in English. But at least seven other Zambian languages were used in the field.

Sometimes this is done by translating and printing questionnaires in each of the major languages that will be used. For example, in Morocco it is usual to print all questionnaires in both Arabic and French. In Cameroon and Canada English and French are usually both used. In India, a common practice is to print questionnaires in three languages – English, Hindi and the main other language of the area being surveyed. A national survey in India will usually use several versions of the same questionnaire, but since this is an immensely complex operation, national surveys in India are not very common. A good deal of market and media research in India is state-based, relying on state-wide surveys which may be later brought together into compilations of data for the whole country. For an example of this, see Section 12.3.

If we remember how crucially important the wording of questions can be, having the questionnaire carefully translated into every language that is going to be needed would seem to be the correct way to proceed. But it does increase costs considerably, as also does the need to pilot test each language version of the questionnaire.

In my experience the challenge of language is best dealt with in two ways. In many cases it is simply not possible to provide printed translations in all the languages needed. Moreover it is even less likely that there will either time or resources to pilot test questionnaires in every language. The solution, a compromise between research perfection and the realities of limited time and resources, is to ensure that there are agreed, printed and tested versions of the questionnaire in at least the major languages. The interviewers in the survey team will usually speak these major languages between them. The ability to speak fluently more than one language is a major asset in any interviewer! Sometimes it may not be necessary to print the questionnaires in different languages. The interviewers may be provided with translations in various languages on separate sheets of paper to use as necessary.

For the lesser languages (lesser in terms of the numbers who speak them), interviewers can be taken on especially for the purpose in the respective areas where these languages are used. These interviewers will need to be thoroughly trained in the purpose of the research and the meaning and intention of all the questions. You have to make every effort to ensure that the words used in verbal translation of what is written on the questionnaire are appropriate. Back-checking interviewers who speak a language not known to the supervisor poses a major problem. Solutions have to be found which are appropriate to the local conditions.

An established way of checking translations is to back-translate. Let us suppose that we are running a media survey in Peru. For any national survey, the questionnaire will normally be prepared and tested in Spanish. But we will also need a version in the main indigenous language Quechua. After translation we would give the questionnaire to another Quechua speaker who has not seen the Spanish original nor been involved in any way with the research. This person would be asked to translate into Spanish. This *back translation* can then be compared with the original and any discrepancies investigated and corrected where necessary.

The same or similar method can also be used in the field by tape-recording interviews and getting these back-translated into the original. However, this practice is cumbersome and expensive and should be avoided if possible.

No solution to the challenge of multilingualism is perfect. But the issue arises in most countries and the professional researcher needs to be aware that different languages may carry with them different meanings and emphases. All these are related to the all-important question of culture and the need to make all research sensitive to the differences between people and the need to adopt appropriate procedures in our research. This is easier when you are dealing with a piece of research focused on a community or area rather than something on a larger regional or national scale.

3.8 Audience and Media Measurement Research Methods in Use Today

Radio and television audience research and readership research are required by broadcasters, publishers and advertisers on a fairly constant or continuous basis. In radio and television, programmes and schedules often change. There are seasonal

65

variations caused by changes in weather and in the human behaviour associated with it. Many radio and television stations therefore need regular or continuous research. Similarly, advertisers have campaigns that last for a certain period of time. Newspaper and magazine publishers have special promotions and special editions. They launch sales campaigns from time to time. They may see sales rise or fall. They will also however want to know what readership reaction there has been.

Whereas a sample survey may tell you everything you need to know about listening, viewing and readership, it remains true only for the period when the research was done. Generalisations from a single survey about TV and radio consumption habits and behaviour, or about readership or awareness of advertising campaigns may be reliable for a while. Much depends on how fast the media market is changing. But broadcasters and publishers need up-to-date information and usually expect it more frequently than annually.

Advertisers also need to have data which are up-to-date on which to base decisions on their future campaigns and on the allocation and placing of their commercial 'spots' on television or radio or their other media buying policies. Various methods are in current use in media research. I will deal first with the methods mostly used in radio and television audience research, although some of these are also used for readership research.

Self-Completion Diaries

A sample is selected to represent the population as a whole, over a certain given age. Those selected are invited to keep a diary of listening or viewing on a weekly basis. A precoded diary is provided listing stations and times of day. Examples of diaries (TV and Radio) are given in the Appendices.

Each diarist is provided with instructions. Sometimes the diary is handed over personally by a research field worker who can explain what needs to be done. Most diaries are kept for seven days but can be for longer or shorter periods. Diary keepers are often recruited by mail or telephone, a less expensive option than through personal contact by a fieldworker, but the latter is probably the required method in most less developed countries.

There are many recognised weaknesses of the diary method. People can forget to record all their listening or viewing or they may complete the task at the end of the week just before it is to be sent by post to the audience research headquarters or research agency. By this time the respondent may not have an accurate recall. Respondents can make mistakes in time, programme, channel or some other aspect of their listening or viewing activity.

There are not only errors of omission. The respondent may record what he or she intended to do, not what actually happened. The respondent may fill in what usually happens rather than what did actually happen. Diary keepers also can try to please or impress by their listening or viewing behaviour as recorded, a conditioning element that is less common in other research methods.

Another major problem is one that is unique to the diary. People who listen to little radio or watch little TV may be reluctant to keep a diary about something they do not often do. And yet, if our diary method is to be representative of the whole population, the diary keeping sample needs to be representative of people with all existing levels of radio and TV consumption. This includes those who listen or watch very little, and those who may watch or listen to nothing during the period they are asked to record.

What about the person who never listens to radio or watches television? These will be encountered when first contacts are made with prospective diary keepers. The field worker placing the diaries keeps a record. To find 1,000 television diary keepers it may be that one encounters 100 for whom keeping a diary would be a pointless exercise because they never watch television. In each of these cases we could 'return' the diary immediately and enter the data as a nil viewing response. Or we can, when projecting the results to the adult population as a whole, make the necessary allowance for the fact that for every 1,000 viewers who see any TV there are 100 more (in this hypothetical case) who watch none. Thus if 20% of the diary keepers had seen a particular programme we could not say 20% of the population had seen it. We know that those who never watch need to be accounted for. In this case we could say that for every 200 people who watched it, 900 did not. (800 + 100). The audience in the population as a whole (1000 +100 = 1100) would be calculated as follows:

200 ÷1100 x 100 = 18.2%

This is an obvious and easy adjustment to make. Other distortions occur with diaries and are more difficult to cope with. How do we overcome the problem of illiteracy?

We do not wish to exclude illiterate people from our research. We cannot assume they are non-listeners or non-viewers. If the percentage of illiterates in the population is small (less than 5%) it may not matter much to exclude them. But if the proportion is larger we must either avoid the diary method or find a way around the problem. In the Zimbabwe All Media and Products Survey, ZAMPS, the diary method is used to record detailed information about radio and television use. Many Zimbabweans, especially of the older generation and living in rural areas, are illiterate. ZAMPS includes illiterate people in the sample. When fieldworkers find that a selected individual is either unable to read or write or who would have some difficulty in filling in a diary, they ask for a neighbour, a friend or another member of the household to complete the diary for them. This is an imaginative and appropriate response to the problem. If this solution is not possible, and it may not be in all cultures or circumstances, the diary method should not be used where there is widespread illiteracy. It is important that illiterate people should not be excluded from research, especially as the media behaviour of illiterates may be significantly different from that of the literate. More-over, a good deal of broadcasting activity is specifically targeted at the less well educated and those with no education at all. Radio can be a powerful and effective way of reaching the disadvantaged and it is important for this reason that research is designed to include them.

Another recurrent problem with diaries is that it is often difficult to recruit a representative number of people from lower socio-economic groups or classes. And those who are recruited are less likely than others to complete the diary and send it in. This introduces serious distortions in the results for which allowance should be made. This can be done at the analysis stage. For example, if 35% of the population are in lower socio-economic class but only 25% of the diarists and only 15% of the responses sent in come from people in this group, one would 'weight' or increase the value of the results of these 15% to be 35% of the sample and thus to reflect the appropriate proportion in the population as a whole. At the same time and by the same process the responses from over-represented socio-economic groups would be weighted down to appropriate proportions. However, one should still make every effort to find sufficient respondents from all socio-economic groups and ensure, as far as it is possible, that their diaries are returned.

There are various ways of encouraging maximum response. One way is to offer rewards for the return of completed diaries. These do not have to be substantial or expensive. Or a small number of larger prizes could be offered in a draw in which all respondents participate. Only a few will be rewarded but the rest may feel sufficiently encouraged to return their diaries diligently with the hope of being lucky.

Some research companies find that it is a sufficient inducement to tell respondents that by taking part in the diary research, they become part of the ratings of television or radio programmes. Respondents like to feel important and why not! The only slight problem with this is that some respondents might feel induced to report listening or viewing in a not entirely honest way, or even to increase or change their viewing or listening behaviour because they know it is being measured.

While there are all these disadvantages or weaknesses of the diary method, many of which can be overcome, there are also many advantages. The diary method has the great advantage of being cheap! The recruitment of the diarists usually requires interviewers to go out into the field to select the respondents. But no long questionnaires have to be administered. The diarists do most of the work! In some cases the chosen respondent may be asked to complete only one week's diary and another selection of respondents is then made for subsequent weeks. In other cases the same respondent can be asked to complete subsequent week's diaries and this also helps to keep costs down.

The diary method can be made to work in most circumstances. It has the enormous advantage of making it possible to plot listener and viewer behaviour from day to day. This is virtually impossible with single face-to-face interviews, the method I will describe later. Another great advantage over face-to-face interviews is that people who are difficult to contact in normal face-to-face interviews may agree to fill in a diary. People who spend a lot of time away from home or who work long hours are hard to contact for a personal or telephone interview. But they may agree to complete a diary.

As noted earlier the diary method is likely consistently to record higher levels of listening than the face-to-face aided recall method. However, allowance can be made for this and it has been established that, provided allowance is made for under-represented groups and for non-listeners or non-viewers, it can give a fairly accurate picture of media behaviour.

How do we deal with a person who may listen to the radio or watch television on only a couple of occasions in the week? His or her viewing or listening behaviour is of equal interest if one is seeking to build up a truly representative and reliable picture of the behaviour of everyone. Response, even from low users of radio or television, can be improved by the way the diary system is administered. The fieldworker should emphasise, when explaining to the respondent, the fact that the diary of an occasional listener or viewer is of equal interest and importance. Of course, all postage costs for sending in the diary must be paid by the organisers of the research.

Television and Radio Audience Meters

We can use electronic technology to record very accurately just what the radio or TV is tuned to and exactly when it is switched on or off. A meter can be attached to the set and can be so designed as to keep an accurate record of what happens to the TV or radio over a period of time.

The use of meters is not new. Radio began what many have called the electronic age. It was appropriate that, at a very early stage, someone should have suggested an electronic means of measuring the audience. Only a year after the first radio audience survey using face-to-face interviews in March 1928 in the United States, the invention of a meter device was announced. But commercial use of meters for audience measurement did not happen until 1935. This was before the invention of successful magnetic tape recording apparatus. The information that needed to be recorded – date, time and radio channel or network – had to be marked onto a moving paper tape. There were many problems, not least of which were power failures, blown fuses and disconnections, not uncommon occurrences in these early days. The patent for these Audimeters was acquired by the market research company AC Nielsen, still a big name in market and media research today. The system was gradually improved and developed until in 1942 there were 1,300 meters in 1,100 homes in the United States. The system went into decline when in the 1950s car radios and portable radios came into common use and listening on these sets increased to the point when meter data became unreliable. At that time, Audimeters had to run on mains electricity and could not therefore be used on sets outside the home.

These early meters were very limited in what they could do and the data they recorded. They provided information about stations tuned to and the time and days. But they provided no information about who was listening.

> '...the record shows the audience flow only in terms of homes. Nothing is revealed concerning the people who listened. For example, the recorder may show tuning to three consecutive programs in a given home. But there may have been no actual flow of audience; for the first may have been listened to by a child, the second by a man and the third by a woman.'[23]

69

Now meters for radio have been made possible again. But they use a totally different technology from their forebears and, if the remaining technical and other difficulties can be solved, they will collect data about networks and times of listening. It is proposed that the listener carry the new meter, either as a wristwatch or a small pager-sized device that 'hears' what the listener hears and records this in a digital form. At the end of a given period, the data collected by the instrument can be downloaded via a telephone with a modem to the research agency. The data can then be analysed and reported. The technology of these remarkable instruments is immensely complex and beyond the scope of this book. It is, as you would expect, very expensive and it is not yet certain whether there will be sufficient resources within the radio industry, even in the wealthiest markets, to pay for this high technology solution.[24]

Today meters are used for television audience measurement in most countries in Europe and in Japan, Australia, New Zealand, the United States, Canada and an increasing number of countries in the developing world. Meters on TV sets in selected homes are used to provide data on viewing patterns and behaviour.

The first television meters recorded only the date, time and the network to which the set was tuned. They did not record whether anyone was actually watching what was on the television, nor did they record how many people were in the room watching the set, nor anything about those people. They were in fact very similar in their limitations to the early meters measuring radio use in the United States, whose shortcomings are noted above.

This situation was changed when 'peoplemeters' were introduced. These also record date, time and network tuned to. But they also require people to press a button on the meter to record their presence in the TV room. A different button or number can be assigned to different members of the household. There are even buttons or numbers to record the presence of visitors to the household who may be watching. In this way, theoretically at least, the peoplemeter can record not only the time of viewing and the programmes and channels being viewed, but also who was watching and their demographic characteristics – age, sex, occupation etc. There has been, and still is, some scepticism about whether the meter records real viewing behaviour. The respondents have to remember to record their presence in the room and their departure from it. And being present in a room with a television set switched on is no guarantee that the programmes are actually being paid attention to or watched!

One may ask at this point how all this relates to what has been said about the principles of sampling and representativeness. Obviously a meter is not like a questionnaire. But the selection of households for the placement of meters follows the principle of sampling outlined earlier. The aim is to find a sample of television households that will accurately represent the population of television households in the country or region being researched as a whole. What usually happens in Europe is that a research agency first needs to do an *establishment survey* to determine the nature and composition of television households and of households with no television. Data are collected on the size of households, number of television sets, income, class, age and sex distribution and, where relevant, ethnic and other demographic data. Data are also collected on the proportion of the population who have access to cable or satellite services. A model of the television owning population is built up. From this model, a sample is constructed in which all the significant population groups are represented and in the correct proportions, from single person households to large family households, from poor households perhaps with only one monochrome set, to wealthy households with many sets and all of them colour. The agency then selects households that socially, geographically, ethnically, and in such matters as household size, number of sets, wealth, age and sexual composition, represent the population as a whole.

In fact the model is never perfect. It cannot be, for the peoplemeter cannot yet, for obvious practical reasons, be used in institutions like hospitals, schools, hostels and prisons where a large number of people may be watching. Peoplemeters cannot be used in hotels, public bars, community centres or cafes where, in some countries, a lot of television viewing takes place. Peoplemeters exclusively record viewing in households. In countries where a lot of viewing takes place outside the home, they do not record the whole situation very well. Moreover, the factors that led to the demise of the radiometer have begun to raise questions about the efficacy of television meters. I sat next to a man on a commuter train recently watching television on a 10 cm screen portable set. Television is now potentially as portable as radio has been for the past forty years.

Presently meters in use are connected to the telephone system. At fixed times, usually at night, the research agency's computer automatically 'calls' by telephone each household. (The ringing tone is suppressed so as not to wake anyone in the household!) This method means that meters are difficult to use in households where there is no telephone. Various solutions can be employed, ranging from the use of cellular phones to the collection of data on computer diskettes from the households.

For obvious reasons, portable sets taken outside the home, in cars, in caravans, even on trains, cannot be metered. If out-of-home television viewing is as significant as out-of-home radio listening, a new kind of meter system needs to be developed. At present the meter system ignores or excludes all viewing outside the home as well as all viewing in large groups and in hotels, shops etc. It could be that the new radio meters being developed will provide a solution. These meters can record any radio listening, wherever it takes place. They could also similarly measure and record all television viewing by picking up and recording the sound of the television set. They would exclude any television viewing where the sound was not being used, but this is not a major problem. This development, if adopted, would mean a shift away from the household as the unit of measurement to the individual. This makes it, potentially, the most accurate means of measuring the actual viewing or listening of individuals.

Meters are mostly used in western industrialised countries and Japan. However they are not unknown in less developed countries. TV meters for audience measurement are used in China, India, the Philippines, South Africa and various Latin American countries. It should be noted however that in most of these less developed countries, television meters tend to be used only for measuring audiences in the urban areas.[25]

Personal Interviews

There are two basic methods. Either the interview takes place face-to-face or it is conducted over the telephone. There are many variations in approach with each.

A. Telephone Interviews

The use of the telephone in audience research is found mainly in the richer countries. Telephone interviewing is widely used where there is a high level of ownership of telephones. In some places it is now virtually essential to use telephones; security systems on apartment buildings and other restrictions on access to people's front doors make personal calls hazardous or impossible.

Both the advantages and disadvantages of interviewing by telephone are obvious. On the plus side, telephone interviewing takes less time than conventional face-to-face interviewing. Interviewers stay in one place and are provided with special equipment both for making the telephone calls and for recording the respondents' answers. Computer software packages are now available for telephone interviewing which facilitate the immediate input of data so that results are available immediately the sample has been completed. The interviewer does not then need to fill in separate forms; the answers can be entered directly, the interviewer being supplied with a keyboard and screen on which the questions appear. No time is taken nor is money spent in travelling or looking for the next respondent. Normally many more interviews can be conducted in the same time. Back-checking is done by the supervisor calling a certain proportion of all respondents.

As I explained briefly earlier, randomness of a telephone sample can be achieved through Random Digit Dialling or RDD, a system that selects subscribers' phone numbers at random and dials them for you automatically. The person who answers the phone, who could be a child or a visitor, may not be the one who is interviewed. The same random selection procedures described earlier may be used to select a household member. When the selection has taken place, explain the purpose of the phone call, assure confidentiality and say how long the interview will last. Telephone interviews need to be very much shorter than face-to-face interviews. Even half an hour could be regarded as too long on the telephone. Refusal at this stage should be avoided if possible.

Telephone interviews have some major disadvantages. Even in the wealthy United States, about 5% of television households have no telephone. In most countries, the proportion having no telephone is of course higher. The method is unsuitable for surveys of the general population in countries where telephone penetration is very low. However, surveys using the telephone can be appropriate where particular groups of people are the target for research. Telephone interviewing could be an appropriate way of assessing the use of satellite television in many African and Asian countries. People who have satellite dishes tend also to have home telephones.

72

Another disadvantage of telephone interviewing is that it is not a very suitable means of obtaining a lot of detailed information. Respondents sometimes resent and reject an unexpected phone call from a complete stranger, especially if it turns out to be a long one. What is more, if one just happens to be enjoying ones favourite radio or television programmes, one may especially resent being interrupted to answer questions about it!

Ironically, it was this factor which was, for some users of research, the most attractive feature of the method. Telephone interviewing could be used to determine what people were actually listening to or viewing at the moment the telephone rang. It was as near as you could get to an exact measure of real behaviour.

Various techniques have been used in the United States making use of this fact. One method is known as 'telephone coincidental'. A very short questionnaire is used:

"What were you listening to on the radio when the telephone rang?"
(If the respondent named a radio programme or presenter rather than a radio station a second question was then asked:-)

"What station was that broadcast over?"
(If however the respondent named a station in response to the first question, this second question was asked instead:-)

"What was that station broadcasting?"
(A further question was then put:-)

'Please tell me how many men, women and children, including yourself, were listening when the telephone rang.' [26]

The well-known American audience research pioneer CE Hooper used this method from 1934. It is fairly easy to find fault with the questions! As worded here they seem to assume not only that the person who answers the phone has a radio but that he or she was listening. These two facts could bias replies.

A similar technique was also used later for television:

"Do you have a television set?"
"Were you or anyone in your home watching TV just now?"
"What programme or channel?"
"How many men, women or children under eighteen were viewing?"
"Who selected the programme?" [27]

Telephone interviews are nowadays used in Europe for some audience research but not so much for coincidental measurement as for the method in far more common use, known as 'telephone recall'.

73

This involves a conventional interview using a questionnaire which asks respondents to recall either what they listened to yesterday, or for the 24 hours preceding the call. Many variations can be used, but typically telephone recall interviews ask about:

The time the radio (or any household radio) was in use the previous day.
What was heard during those hours.
The station or stations listened to.

There is a lot more that could be written about the use of the telephone in media research. Its use is growing in market research in the industrialised countries. It provides results rapidly and relatively cheaply. However, it remains very difficult to obtain an unbiased sample. There can be a high refusal rate – usually very much higher than for face-to-face contacts. This is the weakest point of telephone interviewing.

The method may be appropriate in large countries where distances to travel are very large. Telephone interviewing is very suitable in countries where it is difficult or impossible to gain access to people via their front doors. For example, it is nowadays extremely time consuming and, in some places, positively dangerous to attempt door-to-door surveys in the United States. Obviously telephone penetration has to be very high for it to be a useful method for general population surveys.

In most developed countries, telephone penetration is now over 90% of households. But telephone surveys can be used in countries where telephone penetration is low if one seeks to reach a sample of people in the highest income brackets. Moreover, telephone interviewing can be used to supplement face-to-face interviewing in those areas and with those people where front-door access is difficult or impossible. For example, in the more prosperous areas of some cities in some poorer countries, security is such that access to interviewers arriving on foot is virtually impossible. Telephone surveys may have to be used to gain access to people in this class.

Even where telephone penetration is very low it may still be possible to use telephone interviewing for all kinds of respondents. For example, there are often telephones in villages or in poorer areas of cities and towns. These phones may be in cafes or hotels, community centres or the houses of local officials. It may well be possible to devise ways of using these phones and calling selected people to the phone for interview. A procedure for selection would be needed to remove or reduce bias. I am not aware that this method has been used, except in Russia where many apartment blocks have pay phones on each floor, shared by all occupants. Some research agencies have devised a way of using these phones to make reliable representative samples and do telephone interviews. The same methods could be used elsewhere. The advantage of speed, cheapness and the fact that literacy is not required, make the telephone method very attractive where resources are limited. Using telephones for research in poorer countries is a challenge for ingenuity! But the major weakness of bias arising from high refusal rates remains a matter of concern.

B. Face-to-Face Interviews

The sample to be contacted and interviewed is chosen by one of the methods outlined in Section 3.1 on sampling. Many audience research departments of non-commercial public service broadcasting have traditionally used face-to-face interviews in which people are asked about listening yesterday. (It has also been used for television research, although meters have largely taken over in industrialised countries.[28])

Face-to-face interviews are probably the most practical method for use in most of the less developed countries. The method is not the least expensive but it is usually the only feasible method in areas of high illiteracy and low telephone penetration. Meters have to be excluded from consideration in many countries because of the high costs involved.

The BBC's *Daily Survey* of radio listening (and for some years, of television viewing also) began as the *Continuous Survey* in 1939. At one time 2,500 people were selected each day of the year and interviewed face-to-face in their homes about what they had listened to on the radio and watched on television the previous day.[29]

In the United States the advertisers clamoured for day-by-day and hour-by-hour ratings. They wanted to know how many people were listening to commercial announcements between programmes. But in Britain and almost all other European countries there was a monopoly of broadcasting allocated by the state, either to a state-run broadcasting service or to one run on the public's behalf by a public body like the BBC. There was no radio advertising in most European countries. In Britain the BBC existed to provide broadcasting as a public service. No one demanded to know how many middle class housewives were listening at precisely 2.10 p.m. on a Wednesday! But advertisers and programme sponsors involved in commercial broadcasting, both then and now, do want to know just that kind of detailed information.

However, public service broadcasters did want to know quite a lot about the public's behaviour. Programme planners – the people who decided to place a light entertainment programme after the evening news, or light music in the early evening or more serious talks and features in the early afternoon – wanted to know in quite a lot of detail about public listening habits. BBC planners had, over the early years between 1922 and 1938, gradually devised a daily pattern of programmes. Did it suit the listeners? Were any groups seriously disadvantaged? Early research had shown senior management at the BBC just how out of touch they were with the daily habits and lifestyle of the British public. The results of an early survey were something of an eye-opener to the middle and upper class hierarchy at the BBC who had believed that nobody ate their evening meal before 8 pm. They 'were staggered to learn that most people had finished their evening meal by 7.00 pm.'[30] This had major implications for programme scheduling; managers realised that they had, in this respect, been getting things wrong for some fifteen years! Would they find that in other respects they were badly informed about audience behaviour and tastes?

Interestingly the stimulus to providing more systematic and reliable data on listening in Britain was the Second World War. There was a major disruption of social and economic life. As Silvey put it, 'programme planners found themselves very much at sea'. It was decided that a fully representative sample survey should be conducted to find out facts about the population in respect of its use of the radio. After this initial survey took place in October 1939 it was decided that similar research would be needed on a continuous basis and the *Continuous Survey*, later to be known as the *Daily Survey*, was born. Its objective was to estimate the actual audience for each programme. It began in December 1939 and continued until August 1992 when it was replaced by a self-completion diary system. Between 1949 and 1981, it was also the vehicle by which television viewing was measured. This is now done by a peoplemeter system in co-operation with commercial television. It was the emergence of commercial radio that eventually led to the *Daily Survey's* demise. Commercial broadcasters' requirements could not be fully met by aided recall of listening yesterday employed by a continuous survey of this kind. This is mostly because a questionnaire which records only the previous day's listening or viewing does not provide figures for weekly reach or weekly share and cannot be used to plot changes in individuals' listening or viewing behaviour over several days. These can all be provided by the diary and meter methods. The diary method is the one now used by both BBC and commercial radio for radio audience measurement, while the meter system is in use in most developed countries for television audience measurement.

The *Daily Survey* was based on the assumption that people could give an accurate account of their listening or viewing behaviour on the previous day, especially if the interviewer reminded them of what the programmes had been and at what times. The questions were limited to a single day, the previous day. A day has, for most people, a natural beginning and end. People can be taken through the day from when they woke up to when they went to bed and to sleep.

A major task, as with all interviews, is to try to ensure honest and accurate answers. A lot of attention was given to training interviewers. She (most interviewers on surveys of this kind in Britain are women) would need to be in full control of the conversation. Everything said to the interviewee, from the introduction and explanation at the beginning to the thanks at the end, was prescribed and was the same for all interviewees. Silvey's account sets the scene and approach very well.

"I am working for the BBC, finding out what people listened to yesterday. Will you tell me what you listened to yesterday, please?"

The interviewer followed this question immediately with another:

"For instance, did you happen to switch on when you got up yesterday morning?"

This was followed by another question if the respondent was unsure:

"Well what time was that, do you remember?"

Having found out what time it was, the interviewer would consult the details with which she was supplied and follow with:

"That was when ... (programme title) ... was on. Did you hear that?"

It should be noted here that at this time the only broadcaster in Britain was the BBC. The interview would then continue quite rapidly with the respondent being taken through the day.[31]

Silvey had some important observations to make about the process, which are worth noting. They are still valid today.

> *"This rapid approach was calculated to convey the impression to the informant that the interviewer was businesslike and that the interview would not take long and also to encourage him to regard the encounter as a friendly challenge to him to see if he could remember something as recent as yesterday's listening. If he took it in this spirit, the focus of his attention might be diverted away from a possible preoccupation with the impression his replies were making on the interviewer. He would have told her all she wanted to know almost before he had realised he had done so."*

It should be pointed out here that later on, the interviewers stopped the habit of identifying themselves as being from the BBC. Silvey claims it made no difference, but in this respect he was certainly mistaken. It is bad practice for interviewers to identify themselves in this way. Independence is vitally important.[32]

To start with, the sample for the *Continuous Survey* was 800. That was the number selected and interviewed everyday. Originally it excluded children under 16 but later included children down to the age of 4, who would be interviewed with the assistance of a parent. Originally the sample was selected in the street. Interviewers were instructed to select by quota a given number of people of each sex in four age groups. No one was omitted if it turned out that they had not listened at all on the previous day. The idea was to get the whole picture, and non-listeners are part of it.

The survey throughout its 53-year history has usually included extra questions at the end designed to answer contemporary issues for the broadcasters and planners. For example, at the beginning of the Second World War, there was much controversy about how bad news of the progress of the war was being reported and about the continuation of light and humorous entertainment. In 1940 the news was regularly about disaster for the Allied powers as one country after another fell to the Axis powers and British forces had to retreat. Some said that in view of the situation it was inappropriate to have light entertainment programmes. The question was asked:

"When the news is grave do you think the BBC should cut down on variety programmes?" [33]

A clear majority (over 60%) said "No" and only 20% said "Yes". Moreover further analysis showed that most of those who had said 'Yes' did not listen to entertainment or variety programmes.

Another recurring issue was 'vulgar' jokes in comedy sketches on variety programmes. Many letters were received complaining of poor taste, a theme that has continued in listener mail to this day. Questions on the *Daily Survey* have been used to find out what the listening public as a whole thought. As has often been the case, the letter writers have been shown to be unrepresentative of the general opinion. As a general rule it seems safe to assume that those who write do not represent those who do not!

3.9   Research among specific target groups

Often one may not want to obtain data from the general population. For example, specific media may be aimed at certain groups. Farmers, school teachers or pupils, people in the medical profession, rural development workers, children, members of ethnic, linguistic or religious minorities, people with disabilities and many other groups form targets for special programmes or broadcast services. They can be researched in such a way as to provide data just about them. For example, one could organise a survey among children to find out specifically about their reading, listening and viewing habits and preferences. If they are included in a general population survey, there may be enough children in the sample to provide the data that you need. But there may not be enough, and in any case the normal coverage by survey may not include people younger than teenagers. Also, you may have some special questions just for children. In these cases a specially designed survey among children may be called for.

The general survey may provide information on other subgroups, like professionals, farmers, members of ethnic or linguistic minorities, housewives and students. But very often the subgroup in which there is interest will not be represented sufficiently in a general survey. For example, many public service broadcasters in Europe seek to provide services for members of ethnic and linguistic minorities. These will be selected in the normal way during surveys of the general population. They will be found among households with TV meters and they will be among those who are asked to complete diaries. But normally their numbers in such samples will more or less reflect their proportions in the population as a whole, and there may be too few for separate analysis. For example, an ethnic minority accounting for 5% of the population will normally form only 5% of any representative sample. If that sample is, let us say, 1,000 or 2,000, the sub-sample of those from the ethnic minority would be only 50 or 100 respectively. These numbers would be a little too small to do any very detailed further analysis. When you want to understand the media habits of minorities, especially designed surveys of these minorities may need to be carried out.

3.10 Survey Research for Small Stations

Can small radio stations with limited funds do their own surveys? I believe that they can, provided that they follow certain basic guidelines and rules. But remember that poor research can be worse than no research at all! It can give spurious validity to data that can be quite wrong.

The main disadvantage of a station doing its own survey research is that there is a loss of independence; when an outside body does the research the results may have greater credibility. The experience of Australia seems to have a wider relevance. Although there is a regular system of radio audience measurement through a commercial company, McNair Anderson, this is mainly confined to the large cities. Australia is a vast country and there are many local and regional stations not covered by this research 'omnibus'.[34] But many of these stations are non-commercial and cannot afford to commission research in their area from a research agency. Some of these small stations do their own surveys and the national broadcaster, the ABC, has provided them with guidelines on how to go about it, mainly advising the use of telephone surveys.[35]

3.11 Other Methods of Audience Measurement Research

New methods can be devised to meet the special needs and circumstances of less developed areas. A good example of an innovative approach to audience measurement was demonstrated a few years ago in India.

At that time a high priority had been put on getting television to the villages. But existing research did not cover the villages adequately. Another important factor to consider was that while most television viewing in the towns was household based, viewing in the villages was mostly to community sets. A different approach to research was needed in order to obtain data from these viewing groups. The diaries used at that time to measure TV viewing would not be suitable because of the high proportion of illiterates. What is more, diaries are used to record the behaviour of individuals living in households and in India at that time much viewing behaviour in villages was communal rather than based on individual or family choice. And of course the new meter systems now in use in India and elsewhere cannot be used in such a situation. Meters are capable of recording the presence in the room where the TV is placed of up to about ten people, but they are not designed to measure communal or group viewing.

Doordarshan's need was not only to find out who and how many were viewing programmes in the villages, but also to find whether programmes were relevant to and enjoyed by rural viewers. What did they think of the programmes? Were they understandable, useful or interesting? What Doordarshan did was to appoint literate people in some of the villages to be a point of contact for the purpose of the research. Each of them was provided with self-completion questionnaires. These asked for information about the numbers of people viewing the television, their ages, sex and similar information. Also asked for was feedback and response of the audience.

Problems were encountered in the long time it took between initiating each wave of research and Doordarshan receiving the results. The research department decided for this and other reasons to concentrate on speeding up reaction in order to provide continuous feedback to producers from their village audiences. Doordarshan refined the questionnaires and set in place a routine and continuous system built around television viewing clubs that sought to ensure the maximum involvement of rural viewers. The contact person in each club or viewing group provided information on a pre-coded questionnaire about the composition and size of the audience watching the community set. The research was continuous and therefore provided data on viewing behaviour over time. It also provided qualitative information on viewing behaviour, reaction, comprehension and interest.

Wherever a community set had been placed, there was one person given responsibility for looking after it, the set custodian. In most cases it was the custodian who filled in the questionnaire and posted it in a reply-paid envelope to the respective Doordarshan audience research centre. In addition to the official community sets there were also many rural voluntary 'teleclubs'. In these an educated person was invited to perform a similar task.

This interesting example of a method designed for the special circumstances of India is no longer in use. It was appropriate when so much rural viewing was communal. This appears not to be the case any longer. There are now a large number of rural households with television in India. According to the current head of audience research at Doordarshan, one in six rural households now has a set. There is still a good deal of community viewing and there is also much viewing of television at neighbours and friends' homes. In India today, as in many other countries with substantial rural populations, this TV audience is not regularly measured, nor is much notice taken of the views and responses of rural viewers. For the most part, continuous audience research, in India as elsewhere, tends to be financed and directed by the commercial advertisers and broadcasters. In India they are interested mostly in the top 20% of the population living in the major cities.[36]

This is a matter for concern to all who are interested in understanding the full picture of media use in a country like India. Whereas only a few years ago audience research activity attempted to cover all viewing activity, both urban and rural, today television audience research is confined mainly to the cities. With the rapid development of cable and satellite television in India, funded mainly if not entirely by commercial advertising, the concentration of research in the cities has increased. The rural audiences and their needs and interests are in danger of being forgotten.

Part of the reason is that it costs a great deal more to cover rural as well as urban areas in a vast country like India. Commercial advertising is mainly targeted at urban audiences and consequently there is little interest in providing the extra funds required for the coverage of rural areas where most Indians live. Advertisers are not really interested in knowing about the poor living in the villages. But these people matter to any public service television station, like the Indian national broadcaster Doordarshan. They are also important for anyone who wants to see the full picture.

Television audience measurement in India is carried out in two different ways. Diaries are used and have been for many years. But now the television meter has come to India, but at the time this manual was written, all of these are in urban households. If you ever see audience data on television viewing in India, based on data from the meter system, treat the results with a great degree of caution, if not outright scepticism. The meters are placed only in urban households; it is as if the rural television viewer does not exist![37] Then what often happens is that data from urban television meter systems are extrapolated or projected to cover the entire populations. But as you will discover, rural people's television consumption patterns tend to be quite different.[38]

Exercise

(Allow some days for this as a project).

Investigate how radio and television audiences are measured where you live. Is there a joint industry committee? How are the data collected? What methods are used? How often are measurements taken or is the process continuous? Who pays for the audience measurements and how are the data used? Note the differences, if any, between the use made of the data by different media. To do this you may have to enquire at a local television station or at an advertising agency. What channels are covered by the measurement system or systems used? Are new satellite and cable television channels included? Are all radio networks covered? If not, which are left out and why? What area or areas of the country are covered? What are left out and why?

Find examples of the use of audience measurement in the public domain. Do audience figures for different TV or radio programmes or services appear in the press? Is the apparent 'success' or 'failure' of different services and channels commented on? Do audience figures or ratings play any part in the way in which publicly funded radio and TV services are described and commented on? To what extent is public discourse about the electronic media informed by data from research?

Comment

Some of you will find that it is relatively easy to find this information. There may be a joint industry committee in which all TV channels, or all radio networks, both public and private co-operate with the advertising agencies and ensure that there is only one set of audience statistics about TV viewing or radio listening. This is the case in, for example, Germany, the United Kingdom, South Africa, Canada, Italy, Austria and many developed countries.

But some of you will find this task not so easy. In many countries you may find that there are two or more rival audience research methods and sets of data, supported and paid for by different broadcasters and advertisers. This is the case in India, Russia, Bulgaria, France, the United States and many Latin American countries. In the least developed countries you may find it very difficult to find any regular research. What is done is usually not regular but ad hoc. This is the case in too many countries to list here, but includes most African and Asian countries.

Audience Opinion and Reaction

The measurement surveys described above can also be used to provide some reaction to programmes, but these will usually be limited. Surveys may not be suitable for obtaining detailed opinions. Often the best way to assess audience reaction and opinion is to design specific research vehicles for the purpose.

4.1 Panels

Panels were one of the earliest methods of regular research into audience opinion. Listeners, viewers or readers are selected and invited to help by being members of a panel. Members are asked to give regular feedback on selected programmes, networks, periodicals or services. The panel never meets; the word is used to refer to a group of people who may have little else in common other than they are chosen to carry out a specific function or several tasks over a given period of time.

One of the main advantages of panels is that they enable behaviour and opinion to be measured or assessed for various programmes over time among the same people. This is not normally possible with face to face interviews.

One of the first uses of the panel approach in audience research was in the BBC when listeners to 'variety' (light entertainment) programmes were sought to give regular feedback on this kind of radio programme. The means of recruitment was to invite listeners to volunteer. A series of appeals was made via the press and on radio programmes. The announcements or appeals explained that volunteers would be asked to complete some relatively straightforward tasks that would not take a lot of time. It was explained that completing these tasks would help the BBC to give a better service to listeners.

The response astonished and rather overwhelmed the BBC. 47,000 listeners sent letters offering themselves as volunteer panel members. It was decided to enrol only 2,000. But how should they be selected?

Exercise

Consider three points. First of all, can you see any problems that arise from this method of recruiting panel members? If you ask for volunteers in this way, are the people who volunteer likely to be representative of the audience as a whole? What biases might there be as a result of recruiting in this way? Can these biases be eliminated or reduced?

Secondly, can you think of other ways of recruiting such panel members? How would you do it? What other problems might be faced by using this different approach. Remember that many approaches to research problems are imperfect. All have their advantages and disadvantages.

4

Third, faced with 47,000 eager and committed volunteers, what would you do? You can't use them all. Resources will not permit that. They have written because they want to help and probably feel positively towards the radio station. You need to recruit just 2,000 of them. How do you do it?

Nowadays, faced with such a number of volunteers we would try to select a panel that would match what we know about the demographics of those who listen to (in this case) light entertainment programmes. But at that time (1937), audience measurement had barely started and they had no data on which to base any selection. Instead they sought to match the panel with the general population whose demographics were known from census data.

Those who had volunteered were not an even cross-section of the population. Their demographic composition did not match that of the population as whole. There were more men than women. They were younger than the population as a whole and they had a slight middle class bias. The south-east, generally more prosperous and close to London, was over-represented.

The BBC attempted to reduce this bias, making the sample of 2,000 as representative as it could of the population as a whole. They were enrolled for a twelve-week period. Each week they received by post, a list of the forthcoming week's light entertainment programmes–usually about 35 of them. Panel members were asked to report which of them they listened to, and whether they had listened to all or part of each of the programmes.

The main purpose of this exercise, before the establishment of regular audience measurement, was to find out what was listened to, for how long and by what kinds of people. Later all this could be better supplied by a fully representative survey. As was soon discovered, the nature of volunteers makes them untypical of the audience as a whole. A volunteer panel like this was an unsatisfactory basis for 'inferring the absolute quantity of the general public's listening programme by programme'. However, this method can be a reasonably reliable guide to the relative popularity of different programmes.[39]

I have mentioned this early experiment to show that inexpensive and simple methods can be used for research when representative surveys are impractical or cannot be carried out very regularly. They can be used between surveys to plot the relative popularity of different programmes and the demographic nature of the different audiences for them. If selected to be representative of the whole population, panels can also be used for quantitative measurement. They are more usually used nowadays for the assessment of opinions and reactions in audience research. To obtain the most representative results it is best to select a panel according to criteria set by the nature of what is being sought, and to be fully in control of the selection.

It is best to illustrate how panels may be selected by an example. Let us suppose we need a panel to provide us with regular feedback and reaction to a network that specialises in cultural and arts programmes. We want to obtain a representative panel of the audience. But what constitutes the audience? Someone who normally listens or watches the channel in question everyday is obviously a member of the audience in which we are interested. But what of the person who watches or listens very occasionally? He or she is also a part of the audience.

It is not a good idea to encourage panel members to do any duty listening, viewing or, because we can use this method for reactions to printed media, reading. We want them to behave normally and we should ask them to report on or react to the programmes they encounter as a result of their normal viewing or listening behaviour, or the articles and content that they would normally read. You may find that a panel member has nothing to report in the period of his or her membership of the panel. That has to be accepted as a reflection of the reality we are attempting to measure and understand. However, we may decide to eliminate the occasional audience, concentrating instead on those with a greater degree of commitment and interest.

Practically speaking, your panel may have to consist of those who listen or view programmes or read papers or magazines on a fairly regular basis. Instead of recruiting people as volunteers, a procedure which requires them to volunteer or 'self-select', it is possible to find a more representative sample and avoid the bias of self-selection, through face to face interviews. During the course of quantitative research a respondent who, from his or her answers, fits the description required for the panel being recruited can be invited to become a member.

One disadvantage of this approach is that it can take a long time to find a panel for minority programmes, magazines, papers or services. Another is that having selected a panel you may find that their viewing, listening or reading habits provide insufficient data for analysis. For example, you may select 1,000 people to be panel members and send them all the weekly or fortnightly questionnaires asking for reactions to programmes or articles listed. But response to any one of these may be only ten or twenty people – too few cases for analysis.

You can, of course, guard against this by greatly increasing the size of the panel so as to ensure that even for minority programmes you would probably get a sufficient response. But this can be very expensive in postage and labour. Maintaining panels involves continual work, updating addresses, sending out reminders and generally keeping records in good order. The larger the panel the more work there is to do.

For more than forty years, listener reactions to programmes on the BBC were collected via a volunteer general listening panel. 3,000 panel members aged 12 and over were recruited by broadcast appeals for volunteers on the three, later four, national radio networks. A panel made up from listeners who responded was then selected to be representative of each network's audience in terms of age, social class, sex and geographical region. The panel members, who served for two years, each received a weekly booklet with questions about programmes in the radio network they listened to most. The system succeeded in supplying regular reactions to programmes. But how representative were these? Were volunteers different in some way from those who didn't volunteer?

Inevitably, what was really a self-selected sample was different in being more articulate and biased towards the middle class, despite all attempts to correct this. Listeners to the more serious kinds of programmes dominated the panel. The system was replaced in 1984 by panels based on a controlled recruitment method. The *Daily Survey* provided an excellent source for this. Light listeners – those who listened to less than 10 hours of radio in a week – were excluded. It meant excluding one in three of all listeners to the BBC but it was the only practical way to proceed. Infrequent listeners would hardly maintain interest in the task if they found themselves regularly returning blank questionnaires. Excluding them undoubtedly reduces the representative nature of the panel, but it was noted that the infrequent listeners accounted for only 10% of listening to the networks in question.

The new panel was selected to represent the radio audience, structured by class, sex, age, social class and geographical distribution. It was grouped into nine categories according to the listening habits of the individuals. The groups represented listeners to any of the then four national BBC networks or combinations of networks. However, there was a problem about the arts and culture network, Radio 3. In the sample recruited for the panel, few had listened to any Radio 3 programmes in the previous week and many were only infrequent users. With Radio 3 and other networks like it, it is necessary to over-recruit in order to secure enough data for analysis. And so it was that the Radio 3 panel was boosted by appeals in the traditional manner for volunteers whose replies were used only for the analysis of response to Radio 3 programmes.[40]

Panels can be used effectively even when many listeners are illiterate. If what is needed is informed, considered feedback from literate listeners and viewers, panels can be very useful provided that it is remembered that they do not represent the opinions of illiterates. It is a good idea to give a modest incentive to members of a listening or viewing panel. Members of the Ghana Broadcasting Corporation's listening panels in Ghana used to have a free subscription to the now defunct Radio and TV Times. They now get a free TV licence and, if they have rediffusion radio (an early form of cable or wired radio still in use), they pay no hire fee. This is an acceptable policy in a broadcasting monopoly, but when there is competition it would be methodologically safer to use incentives unrelated to the broadcast services in any way.

You might wish to have another kind of panel, one which is not representative of listeners as a whole, but only of those you particularly wish to reach. For example, you might have a radio programme or a series of programmes for mothers with children. You might also have a magazine or newspaper for the same target group and perhaps television programmes as well. Others not in your primary target group might also be in the audience. Almost all kinds of radio and television programme and many kinds of printed materials are regularly consumed by people for whom they may not be primarily intended. You may well decide that in your research you wish just to concentrate on your primary target audience. That may well be an appropriate and efficient approach.

In this case you would need to devise an alternative way of recruitment. Do you have or can you devise a suitable sampling frame from which to recruit?

Exercise

You need to devise a method for providing regular feedback for radio and television programmes, as well as other communications and messages, about child health. Your target group is mothers with young children. How do you go about recruiting a panel among them who can be relied upon to give you regular and useful feedback on what they receive?

4.2 Postal Self-Completion Questionnaires

Postal research is sometimes regarded with some disfavour, both because it is difficult to make a random postal sample of the general population and because response rates can be very low. Both problems can be overcome to a large extent when the population to be surveyed by post is defined by some category that by its very nature provides you with a readily accessible and up-to-date postal address list. If we want to survey doctors, members of an association, subscribers to a magazine, or any other group of people for whom addresses are known and accessible, postal survey research can be a very appropriate and cost-effective method of research. If the number is not too great, a postal survey of all people on the list may be feasible. For example, if you want to know the opinions of members of a group numbering only a few hundred up to two or three thousand, it could be appropriate to send questionnaires to all on the list. This would be, in reality, not a sample but a census. But if numbers are greater, as they usually are, a random sample should be used. Random numbers (there is a table in the appendices or you can easily generate one) can be used to select those to whom you will send a questionnaire.

Postal research now seems to be in favour again in the market research business. Much impetus has been given to the use of postal research by the growth of *direct marketing* – an approach to selling goods and services that depends on databases and mail addresses, mostly people's home addresses. It has also been boosted by the growth of focus on customer care and what has become known as *relationship marketing*. This is a way of encouraging or ensuring continued business by developing and retaining customer loyalty, by keeping in touch with customers, learning about their needs and interests and ensuring that the company develops goods and services in line with customer requirements and preferences. Research becomes a part of the marketing process, an essential part of the relationship that needs to be developed between provider and customer. One can think of parallel uses outside the strictly commercial field where the same process could be involved. For example, if a broadcasting station runs regular programmes for health workers, the relationship and contact between the station and the programme makers can be enhanced and strengthened through regular postal contact with health workers on a comprehensive address list. These contacts can involve the use of questionnaires encouraging feedback and response to programmes.

When sending out a questionnaire it is essential to provide a readily understandable explanation to the recipient. The person to whom the envelope is addressed needs to know what is being asked, by whom and for what purpose. The importance of the covering letter cannot be over-emphasised. It has to 'sell' the purpose of the exercise to the recipient. He or she is being asked to do something. There is some persuading and convincing to be done!

There are always some people who will fill in questionnaires, even without being asked or having anything much explained to them! But you don't just want replies from them. You would have a sample then consisting of some rather odd people! You want to persuade as many as possible of those who receive the envelope to respond, including some that might be very reluctant to do so.

Questionnaires can be sent by post to listeners, viewers or readers with explanations and instructions on what to do. Postal questionnaires have many advantages. They avoid the need for expensive fieldwork involving sample selection. The only costs are those of postage, printing, data input and analysis. Postal questionnaires are very widely used. You may have received a postal questionnaire at some time. Perhaps you have seen one when staying at an hotel or found one in a magazine, asking you, respectively some questions about your opinion of the hotel's service or the magazine's contents.

There are many drawbacks and pitfalls. Not the least of these is, of course, the fact that they are restricted to literates. They must be well presented and constructed, with the minimum of ambiguity. There is no one present to answer questions or explain anything about the questions! They must leave nothing to chance.

Reply postage has to be paid and if you know the name and address of the person who has received the questionnaire (in the case of the hotel or magazine questionnaire they usually don't!) it helps to send reminders.

Although mail surveys are cheap, they are not as widespread as they might be. One problem is that the response rate can be very low. A 40% response to a postal survey would be well above average. But if you had a 60% refusal rate on a face-to-face survey you would be doing very badly indeed.

It can require a lot of skill and determination to obtain a high response rate to postal research. The highest rates are experienced by organisations that send postal question-naires to their members. 75% can be expected, sometimes higher. If you send to people who are not formal members of any group and therefore have no shared commitment to a common purpose the response will be lower. Response rates are usually higher when you pay for the return postage. Other ways of encouraging a higher response include the offer of incentives. These can include the promise that a specified gift will be sent to all respondents. This can be expensive. An alternative can be to put all responses into a draw for an attractive prize or prizes. Reminder letters can also boost response.

Experience is the best guide. You will learn by experience what response to expect.

This will be an important factor in how you design the project. If you expect a 60% response and you decide you need, say, over 1,000 responses for effective analysis, you will need to send out 1,700 questionnaires.

In many countries, the national postal administrations operate a reply-paid system whereby special envelopes, post cards or fold-up forms can be used. These have to be printed according to a format laid down by the postal administration concerned. A licence normally has to be applied for. These specially printed envelopes, cards or forms are sent out with the questionnaire. They can be incorporated into the questionnaire so that when folded the questionnaire makes a postal item. The recipient posts the item in the normal way but does not have to buy a stamp. You, the organiser of the research and licence holder, then pay the post office for all items received. The charge is usually a little higher than the normal internal postage rate, but the advantage is that you pay only for what you receive. The other way of paying for return postage is to send everyone a stamped addressed envelope. This can be very expensive both in the time it takes to individually stick thousands of stamps on envelopes and in the fact that you will inevitably be spending money on stamps which are not used for the purpose of returning the questionnaires.

Some say that mail surveys are slow and that they should not be used when survey data are required urgently. I do not share this view entirely. If the project is well planned, it is possible to complete all stages within four weeks. It is hard work but possible. The main problem is one of representativeness. How do you avoid obtaining replies only from particular kinds of people who may not be like the rest who do not send in the questionnaires so readily? And what do you do if you do not have a comprehensive and up-to-date address list of the kinds of people you wish to reach?

One way of obtaining listeners names and address to which to send postal questionnaires might be to use the listeners', viewers' or readers' letters you have recently received. Recency is important because addresses can soon become out-of-date. But to use the addresses from letters means that you are, in a way, using a self-selected sample. The important point to remember is that people who write letters to radio or television stations, or newspapers and magazines are not typical of the audience or readership as a whole. They are unusual; most consumers of the media never write! Those who do may be habitual letter writers and have characteristics that make them different from the rest of the media public. There is no easy solution to this problem unless you can obtain a representative address list of listeners, viewers, readers or whoever your target groups is, to use as a sampling frame.

With magazines and newspapers a simple and practical solution can to be to insert a questionnaire into every edition on a certain date. But this method produces a very low response rate. Figures below 5% are quite normal. Do not expect therefore to obtain very reliable data through this method.

If people who write letters are untypical and unrepresentative can they ever be used for postal questionnaire research? With caution and within limitations they can. Postal research may often be the only method open to you. Sometimes the information one needs may not require a strictly representative sample to be used. An example from BBC World Service experience can illustrate. Senior managers had decided to switch a new transmitter covering Area A in order to cover Area B. Both areas had other transmitters giving some service. But Area B was an area that was believed to be badly served. But one senior manager was unhappy. He worried about listeners in Area A. The decision was postponed for just over a month to give time for research. If it could be shown that Area A would be seriously adversely affected the decision might be reconsidered.

There was no time for an on-the-ground face-to-face survey in Area A. Telephone penetration was low. Listenership to the service affected was probably loyal and keen but relatively small and scattered. The only way to discover how much reliance was placed on the transmitter in question was to send a simple questionnaire to recent correspondents in Area A asking them which of the radio frequencies available they used to listen. The results from the returned postcard questionnaires showed a very high level of reliance on the service provided by the transmitter in question rather than to the other signals available. The decision was rescinded and alternative arrangements were made to serve Area B. The exact numbers and percentages did not matter. All that was needed was an answer to the question 'if we move the transmitter from Area A will a lot of existing listeners be affected?' The answer was 'yes'.

4.3   On-air Questionnaires for Radio Stations

On-air questionnaires are usually employed only for radio audience research and usually only by small radio stations with few resources. As the name suggests, this method involves asking listeners to write in with their answers to some questions. Announcements can be made within or between programmes. Only four or five questions or fewer may be asked. Things need to be kept very simple. Prizes can be offered from a draw as an incentive, but you may find that listeners will respond without any offer of prizes.

On-air questionnaires can be used quite effectively, especially when other methods are not possible. The main weakness is that you obtain an entirely self-selected sample which cannot be said to be representative of the audience as a whole. People who write in response to an on-air appeal are likely to be different in some important respects to those who do not respond.

There are at least two ways in which I believe the use of questions on the air can be effective and appropriate. Experience in the BBC World Service's audience research department shows that self-selected respondents' replies on technical and reception matters are fairly reliable. Research has shown that the responses of those who reply to on-air questions do not give information very different from that given by a representative sample. Or to put it the other way around, those who respond seem to be reasonably representative of all listeners if we just take what they say about matters of radio reception.

In 1990 the BBC World Service asked on-air questions about the radio frequency being used by the listener at that moment. More than 100,000 answers were received from all parts of the world. The analysis of the replies to what we called the 'Can You Hear Me' project provided a very valuable comparative global picture of the way in which the BBC World Service's various frequencies from different transmitters were being used at that time. It enabled some major savings to be made on transmitter costs by switching off or reducing the service hours of those transmissions that were being used little or not at all.

Another way in which the method can be used is when areas are closed to field research for political or other reasons. International radio stations sometimes use this method to learn something about their listeners in such areas. One good example I have seen was carried out by the Christian radio station FEBC based in the Philippines whose Burmese broadcasters obtained useful and encouraging feedback from and information about their listeners in Burma, a country that has for a long time been virtually entirely closed to outside researchers. Listeners were asked to write in with a few simple answers to questions about themselves. The station was able, for the first time, to gain an idea of who some of their listeners were, where they lived and the issues that interested and concerned them.[42]

There may be other uses for on-air questions. For example, you might appeal for certain kinds or categories of listeners to write in with information about their response or reaction to broadcasts intended for them. Teachers could be asked to write in and describe how they use educational programmes with their pupils. A model set of on-air questions might go like this:

If you have listened to these programmes, please write to us with answers to these questions:

What is your name and address and the name of the school?

How often to you use these programmes? Is it every time or occasionally?

How many pupils usually are in the class when you listen?

Please give us your views about the usefulness of the programmes. Do they meet your needs? If they do not please suggest ways in which they could be made more useful to you and your pupils.

You might think of other questions you might wish to ask, but do not have too many. Try to avoid more than five.

When you ask questions on the air do remember that listeners may have difficulty taking down all the information they need. Warn them before you make the announcement that they will need a pencil and paper. After giving out the details it is a good idea to say that the questions will be repeated. You should at this point tell them when this will be.

4.4   Appreciation Indices

Producers, programme makers and planners need to know not only who listens or watches and how many, but also what they think of the programme. And they may need to obtain information or feedback in a more systematic way in which response can be compared over a period of time. We have seen various ways in which opinions can be measured. Appreciation Indices or AIs are a commonly used method in some countries. They have strengths and weaknesses.

Audience size is a useful guide to overall performance of a particular network or programme on that network. But it will never give you the whole story. We need also to take account of audience appreciation as a measure of a programme's achievement. People may listen or view a programme merely because it was on at a time when they usually listen or view. We may want to know what they really think of it.

A programme may attract a low audience but be appreciated very much by those who did watch or listen. This might well be thought to be a satisfactory and worthwhile achievement, especially within public service rather than commercial broadcasting. Sometimes a programme with a small audience and a high AI may attract new listeners or viewers. The enthusiastic minority may talk about the programme and others may hear about it and try it out, like what they see or hear and become regular listeners or viewers. Sometimes high AIs can be predictors of audience growth for the programme in question.

This is how AIs are achieved. They are often used in the kinds of diaries described earlier. Listeners or viewers are asked for their reaction and response to named programmes. Often only a selection of programmes will be asked about; sometimes the viewer or listener is asked to give a view on all programmes encountered.

On the BBC *Daily Survey*, which was used to measure radio audiences, all respondents aged 12 and over were asked to complete a booklet called *What You Think of What You Watch*. In it were listed various TV programmes over the next five days. They were asked not to do any special viewing but to answer questions only about their normal viewing.

Most of the questionnaire concerned AIs. Each respondent was asked to rate each programme they watched on a six-point scale from 'extremely interesting and/or enjoyable' to 'not at all interesting and/or enjoyable'.

For every television programme the percentage of viewers who recorded each level of appreciation is calculated. The following could be the results from such an exercise:

Extremely interesting and/or enjoyable	6	5	4	3	2	1	Not at all interesting and/or enjoyable
	28%	29%	26%	8%	6%	3%	

The AI is the mean of all these calculated as a percentage. The score of 1 is eliminated. In effect we are giving the judgement 'Not at all interesting or enjoyable', the score of 0. We are left with 5 scores of appreciation of different levels. Assign scores to each from 5 to 1 and divide the sum by 5.[43] This is how it is done:

$$\frac{(28 \times 5) + (29 \times 4) + (26 \times 3) + (8 \times 2) + (6 \times 1)}{5} = 71$$

We divide by 5 in order to obtain a score related within the range to the scale 0 to 100. If everyone had given the top rating of 6 – 'Extremely interesting and/or enjoyable' – to which we assign the score of 5, the calculation would give us a score of 100.

$$\frac{100 \times 5}{5} = 100$$

If everyone, equally unlikely, had given a bottom rating of 1 – 'Not at all interesting and/or enjoyable' – to which we assign the score of 0, the result of our calculation would be a score of 0.

We say that the programme in the above example has an AI of 71, a typical result. These AIs are not absolute measures. Their value is in comparability between programmes of a similar type, or of the same programmes in a series. Experience shows what AIs a drama programme will normally achieve. One can then see if a particular programme achieves a higher or lower than normal AI.

For radio a similar method can be used. In Britain a five point scale ranging from 'Very well worth hearing' down to 'Not worth hearing' has been used. The number of points in the scale can be higher or lower but experience shows that 5 or 6 point scales work well.

Indices can also be provided on specific opinions about a programme. For example, a radio service may have featured an interview with a leading politician, perhaps the Prime Minister. A specific question or set of questions can be asked.

	Agree strongly	Agree somewhat	Neither agree or disagree	Disagree somewhat	Disagree strongly
X was a good interviewer					
X was too deferential – he did not ask really searching questions					
The Prime Minister dealt with questions well					
I learned a lot from this interview					
I found this interview interesting					

Individual scores and overall indices for each aspect can be given. The decision on how to report results may depend on how the results emerge. The issue with all research reporting is how to make complexity simple. Instead of a set of figures it may be sufficient to report in words what the average of opinions in each category was – most listeners found it interesting, most found x a good interviewer, although a substantial minority thought he was too deferential, etc.

4.5   Other Measures

Audience researchers often seek to devise new ways of measuring the way people view or listen to programmes, especially in response to the concerns of programme makers. In The Netherlands, the public broadcaster NOS has been using a novel way of looking beyond ratings, share and appreciation. Do these really tell us all we want to know? NOS researchers have come up with a way of measuring two other important factors about radio listening behaviour, *attention* and *group or individual listening.*

On their regular diary measurement for radio, NOS asks respondents to say where they listen, whether in the car, at work, at home etc, and to grade their enjoyment of programmes on a scale from 1 to 10. They later select some of the diary participants to complete a further diary on which they are asked to record two other matters. Were they listening with attention or not? Were they listening alone or in company? Also, in addition to the usual list of stations an additional 'station' was added to the diary charts – the respondents' own record, cassette or CD player. The results are of great interest and importance.

Attention to programmes varied at different times of the day and at different parts of the week. It was highest in the early morning and late evening and lowest during the day in between 10.00 a.m. and 4.00 p.m. Listening alone or with others also varies in a similar way. There is a greater tendency to listen alone in the early morning and late evening. Older people also tend to listen more on their own.

There were also great differences between stations. For example, the popular music stations with the highest shares, Radio 3 and Sky Radio, have the lowest attention scores among the major stations. The news station, Radio 1, has a lower share but enjoys a high score for attention among its listeners. It is also more likely than other major stations to be listened to alone. Some minority interest stations with a low share have the highest scores both for appreciation and attention, and among the lowest for listening in the company of others. It seems very obvious that NOS have discovered two very important measures that must surely be a factor in the respective impact and importance of these stations. I am not aware if these measures have been tried elsewhere. It seems reasonable to suppose that similar findings would be made. It has important implications for the use of popular communications media as educational and developmental tools.[44]

93

Qualitative Research

We are now going to look at a rather different kind of research. Whereas in quantitative research we have been dealing mostly with numbers, in qualitative research we are trying to discover or understand human attributes, attitudes or behaviour in a more exploratory or interpretative way. Numbers cannot describe or explain everything. Human behaviour and everything else that can be said about people cannot be fully encapsulated in or understood from numbers and percentages. Although these are valuable and often necessary to give an overall picture of some aspects of human life, they can never provide the whole picture of it. As good researchers we need to embrace other methods in order to give this broader, more comprehensive view.

Qualitative research was first developed within the study and discipline of psychology and later in the more general field of social sciences. But in recent years it has found its fullest development in the field of commercial market research. The success of qualitative methods in market research has in turn influenced social scientists in the academic world to make a greater use of the method.[45] They have found in qualitative research a very useful way of understanding human behaviour. Focus groups are a good way of exploring how media messages are interpreted.[46] We know from many studies that people are influenced not just by media messages but, perhaps more, by the intervening influence of other people. Qualitative research can bring out these influences more clearly than is the case with quantitative methods. This is partly because quantitative research tends to focus on individual behaviour within a household or family, whereas qualitative research in focus groups puts the respondents into a social setting in which the personal influences that operate in social settings are reproduced and can be observed.

One method, qualitative or quantitative, is not superior to the other, although it is often true that researchers enjoy being involved more in one than the other. This sometimes leads to a rivalry between practitioners of the two broad research disciplines. But each group of methods is used for different purposes.

Qualitative research is often able to add depth, perspective, colour and understanding to the 'dry' data and figures from quantitative research. This is why we find that very often qualitative and quantitative research projects are done in conjunction with each other as part of the same project. The one set of methods can often complement the other. Results from quantitative research can often be understood better when combined with qualitative research. Conversely, the findings of qualitative research can be given a broader social perspective by quantitative research conducted at the same time. And, as I hope to demonstrate, the use of qualitative research is an excellent way to ensure before you set out on a quantitative project that you are making your research culturally appropriate and sensitive.

Qualitative research can also be used as a prelude to quantitative research by exploring those issues and motivations that are most relevant in the choices people make when using the media. Comments and opinions discovered through qualitative research can be tested in a systematic quantitative way to discover which of them receive general support and agreement and what the strength of that agreement may be.

There are three main qualitative research methods – *focus groups, in-depth interviews* and *participant observation*. Sometimes focus groups are referred to as *group discussions.*

The techniques of qualitative research are not very easy to describe. Whereas questionnaire design and sampling both have procedures to be followed that are relatively straightforward and can be itemised, the same is not so true for qualitative research. The main difference is implied in the word itself. *Qualitative* denotes interpretative and exploratory activities, rather than factually descriptive ones. In qualitative research we are not usually involved in precisely defined terms nor in accurate measures of human behaviour or attitudes.

In qualitative research we normally use only relatively small numbers of people. Structured questionnaires are not used and the results are not normally open to any kind of statistical analysis. Qualitative research usually cannot prove or disprove anything in the way that quantitative research may be able to. But used effectively and appropriately, qualitative research may be the only way we can really understand peoples' motivations, attitudes and behaviour. There are good disciplines and professional methods in qualitative research which, if followed, can ensure that qualitative research is both reliable and valid. How are qualitative data different and how do we handle them? What relevance do they have for audience and other media research?

5.1 Focus Groups, Sometimes Known as Group Discussions

The most common form of qualitative research is the focus group. People are selected and invited to meet together with a trained moderator to discuss some aspect of, in our case, media use. The same techniques are used in product and advertising research.

A focus group is a kind of group interview. But unlike the face-to-face interview, a focus group is not a structured dialogue between an interviewer and a respondent, with the latter's answers carefully recorded. What happens, and this is what gives focus groups their great strength for research, is interaction within the group. The interaction is always based on topics supplied by the researcher or *moderator* whose important role I will describe shortly. This interaction produces information and insights into the behaviour and attitudes of people that would not be likely to emerge from a straight one to one interview.

The first task in any research project is the definition of the problem or issue to be addressed – the intended focus of the discussion within the group. Unlike much quantitative research, which is often repeated in order to watch changes in behaviour over time, qualitative research is almost always carried out *ad hoc* – that is to say, each project is a separately constructed activity, starting more or less fresh each time.

Those who need the results and those carrying out the research need to agree the objectives and expected outcome. The members of the research team need to make sure that they obtain clear information about what is expected of them. Very often, those who are seeking answers through research have not worked out in any great detail what needs to be investigated. For example, radio producers involved in creating programmes for, let us say, the entertainment and enjoyment of youth, may have found out from audience measurement surveys that their programmes are not popular and do not attract large or appreciative audiences. They want to do something about this but do not understand what is wrong nor have much idea how to find out. Qualitative research, conducted among the target group, could give them pointers to what could be done. It could help them to see what potential listeners think of the programmes, how they compare them to what else is available to watch or listen to, and it could set all this in the context of the listeners' daily lives. But the commissioners of the research – in this case the producers of the unsuccessful programmes – may have little idea of how the research is to be done, nor even of what has to be investigated. The professional researcher will work with them to develop an understanding of the problem from the broadcasters' point of view, and then to turn this into a carefully constructed research plan.

A research proposal like this will be turned into a research brief, agreed by both commissioner and researcher, before the research can begin. The research brief will usually contain three crucial elements.

The *Background* to the research – in this case the problem about the poor performance of certain programmes. What is known about the programmes and their present audiences. The broader broadcasting context.

The *Objectives* of the research – in this case almost certainly to discover why the programmes are not popular and to give guidance on ways of improving or changing what is being produced.

Research Methods to be used to achieve these objectives.

Two things then need to be agreed. A *discussion guide* is drawn up. This translates the research objectives into subjects to be covered during focus groups (if that is the chosen method). The discussion guide, like the questionnaire used in quantitative research, needs to be written by those who are actually going to do the research. The usual practice is for the discussion guide to begin with general matters before gradually narrowing the discussion down to the particular. A discussion guide will always begin with subjects that help the participants to relax, gain confidence and develop relationships and understanding within the group. One would not start the discussion on these programmes with a question like "Why don't you like these programmes?"

The second thing to be decided is the kinds of people and how many of them are to be invited to take part. Normally, groups need to be matched quite deliberately and carefully. It is unusual for people of different sexes to be included in the same group.

It is also usually inappropriate for people of widely different ages, social classes, wealth or education to be included in the same group. Knowledge and experience of the subject being researched is also important. It is not a good idea to mix experience with inexperience, for the former will overwhelm the latter. What we usually look for is people who will relate well together by having some experiences and backgrounds in common. We might be investigating the way farmers in a particular area use the media. We would probably seek to select groups of farmers who have broadly similar backgrounds. We might want to select farmers of similar wealth or similar amounts of land, or be engaged in similar kinds of farming. The success of a group lies in the group dynamics that develop in the conversation led by the trained moderator. If the differences between the members of the group are too great, these differences are likely to make conversation difficult.

You can see already that in order to cover all possible combinations of demographic and other relevant characteristics, one might need many groups. If, for example, we divided people into the two sexes and, let us say, three age groups, we would have six groups:

	Age 15 to 24	Age 25 to 40	Age 41 and over
Male	I	I	I
Female	I	I	I

Then if we divided by class, education and wealth (usually these are to some extent inter-related) and made three categories of these, we would have 18 groups. Further three-way categorisation, by experience or knowledge of the matter being researched for example, would give us 54, and so on. What is more, usually we might want to have more than one group in each category.

In practice this degree of subdivision of groups is unnecessary. The subject matter and the resources available for the research determine the choice of groups and their categories. One very commonly used way of organising groups is to divide them by whether or not they use the product or service being researched. If, for example, you were investigating attitudes towards radio as a medium for learning about health, it could be a productive method to divide groups according to whether or not they used radio in this way.

Recruiting for focus groups is done in various ways. Young mothers might be sampled through their attendance at mother and baby clinics. Farmers could be recruited by visiting them at a selection of farms. Radio listeners and television viewers are often recruited through quantitative surveys. A question, usually asked at the end, asks the respondent if he or she would be prepared to take part in further research. They would be told what it would entail and where the focus group would be held. Not everyone on the survey would be asked; the interviewer would have a list of the qualifications required for taking part in the focus group. It could be that listeners to a particular radio station were being sought, or people of a certain age group, occupation or social class, or any combination of these or others. The name, address and telephone number (if they have one) is noted and the person is contacted later with directions about where to go and when.

The moderator plays a crucial role and it is worth spending a little time looking in some detail at the moderator's function. There are dangers inherent in group moderation. Remember that you want to bring out genuine and real relationships and attitudes that arise in the group. But the presence of the moderator, an outsider in effect, can, if you are not very careful, introduce a false element. The situation is somewhat unnatural. Participant observation, which will be described later, overcomes this to a great extent but takes very much more time. All qualitative research is to some extent an intrusion into normal social interactions. Experienced moderators learn how to reduce the influence they inevitably introduce.

The moderator is trained to lead the discussion, beginning with general matters before moving on to the particular. It is important to involve everyone present. The moderator has a discussion guide which may include a series of questions. This is not a rigid framework but is designed to keep the discussion going along the desired lines and is a reminder to the moderator of the purpose of the research. A good moderator plays a low-key role. He or she should not express opinions but seek to ensure that the attitudes and opinions of everyone present are heard. A good moderator certainly asks questions, but these should normally reduce in number and frequency as the discussion proceeds. A good moderator should not only avoid expressing opinions; he or she must avoid showing any negative reaction to anything anyone in the group says. Positive reactions are OK provided that they are to encourage further contributions and interchange. No opinions are 'right' or 'wrong' even if the moderator thinks so! People in groups often admit to practices that are unwise or foolish. The point is not to put them right but to allow these things to be expressed and discussed. It is, of course, alright for other members of the group to disapprove of or disagree with what others have said.

Moderators should look out for opportunities to promote further discussion on items that come up and which seem relevant to the topic. Sometimes what is said may not be the whole story; moreover what seems to be apparent may not be what is actually being said. The following questions are typical of the kinds of things a moderator might say in a focus group:

What do others think about that?

Tell us a bit more about that?

X, do you agree with what Y has just said? Have you had the same experience?

X said earlier how much she enjoys Radio One's morning show. Does anyone else feel the same?

What do others enjoy in the mornings on the radio?

The moderator will normally seek to get the group as a whole to express and discuss experiences and opinions. The plan should be to get each group member to participate and interact with each other rather than just with the moderator. The moderator is there to ensure that the discussion continues to be about the subject being researched, to ensure that all the areas for discussion have been covered, to stop any one person from dominating the event and to encourage the less vocal participants to have their views heard.

Sometimes the discussion will flag; the moderator's task is to get it going again along the right lines. The most successful groups are usually those that develop a natural dynamic of their own, when all the member participate and talk between themselves, interacting freely and without much prompting or guidance from the moderator. When groups work really well, ideas, opinions and attitudes emerge that would be far less likely to do so in formal interviews using a structured questionnaire. The moderator needs to be well prepared, having anticipated possible problems that might emerge. He or she should know the discussion guide very well and not need to refer to it often, if at all. The moderator needs also to listen very carefully at all times to the discussion as it proceeds and be ready to be very flexible, not always sticking rigidly to the plan implied or laid out by the discussion guide. The focus group must not degenerate into a sterile series of questions and answers between moderator and group members. The whole point is to get a free discussion going which develops its own momentum and dynamic. A good group is often one that could have gone on for much longer than the time allocated because everyone is enjoying the occasion and there is a creative and interesting interchange of ideas and experiences.

Focus groups are nearly always recorded, either on audiotape or increasingly these days on videotape. This frees the moderator from the need to take any notes and it provides an accurate and thorough record of what happened and what was said. Participants should always be told that they are to be recorded, but confidentiality must be assured. The moderator must tell everyone that the tapes will be used for no other purpose than the analysis and reporting of what was said. The identity of individuals in the group should not be recorded in any report and group members need also to be reassured on this point.[47]

The moderator's skill is to enable the group, brought together for a short time, to coalesce into a body of people that will trust each other, argue, agree or disagree, explore each other's backgrounds and contributions and illustrate, by what they say, some important aspects of the topic under review. You won't get to this point immediately. There are several stages to go through. First of all the moderator has to help the group to form, to relate to each other and to develop trust. Then the topic can gradually be introduced and discussed. When this has been fully aired, the group can be encouraged to become more creative. It is at this stage that some of the projective and other techniques described later can be introduced. At the end of the time, the moderator needs to attempt to bring things to a satisfactory conclusion, summing up what has been said and confirming if there is agreement or otherwise. Moderators should always give everyone a chance to say anything that they feel still needs to be said.

A good moderator can shift the discussion in any direction and this can lead to the discovery of information that can be wholly unpredicted and unexpected. Questionnaires, by their very nature, measure ranges of expected behaviour and attitude. But they cannot deal with the more subtle and hidden meanings in human response and behaviour, which can be very important in media research. Very often people don't know their own attitudes and motivations, or they know them only superficially. A person may express a mild opinion in favour of something in response to a question, while in conversation in a group he or she may make it clear that the views held are very strong ones.

Qualitative research is most commonly used in media research to: -

Discover behaviour and attitudes that can be tested quantitatively.

Define areas for systematic research on a larger scale.

Eliminate irrelevant areas from larger scale quantitative research that follows.

Illustrate or expand what has been discovered in a quantitative survey.

Provide insights into the way existing services and programmes are used.

Provide a richer range of responses to particular press, radio or television content than is provided by the questionnaire methods so far described.

Provide ideas for communicators and planners.

Group discussions usually involve between 6 and 10 people in each group. Too large a group can lead to some members losing interest or to the development of sub-groups within the group. 8 seems to be the ideal number in most current practice. The discussion usually takes between one and a half and three hours. The same group can be reconvened to carry on a discussion or, more often in audience research, to listen to or watch programmes. Reconvened groups can help you to gauge perceptions and attitudes and discover how these change over time. In media research reconvened groups can be very useful for considering new programmes or content and then later to plot attitudes and responses when these innovations are developed and introduced.

Sometimes group discussions can last longer than two or three hours if the subject matter really does require some in-depth discussion. The point to make about groups is that the 'rules' are only guidelines and can be modified according to requirements. There can be a lot of interaction within a relatively short space of time and a lot of data can be generated for analysis.

There are many techniques can be used in qualitative research to stimulate better response and many ways of leading discussions and conducting in-depth interviews.

Focus Groups and in-depth interviews often use creative techniques to reveal aspects of human behaviour and attitude that do not become so apparent through normal conversation. Many of these are described as *projective techniques*. Here are some examples of techniques quite commonly used:

Role Play

Respondents may be asked to act out their perceptions, becoming actors in a make-believe enactment of something related to the subject of the research. For example, you might ask respondents to act out the roles of radio or television producers. This might give you some revealing information about how their place and role is regarded. When a group is going well and the respondents have learned enough about each other to feel confidence and trust, role-play can work very well.

Photo Sorting

Respondents are given a pile of photographs and asked to select those that they might associate with the product or service being researched. This is sometimes used, for example, to understand a brand's image. You might ask people to find all the photographs that seemed to go along with a particular brand of soap as against those which seemed to go with another. You can do this with radio programmes or networks and can learn a lot about the perceived image and status of each of them.

Collages

Respondents can be asked to create collages – pictures made up of bits of coloured paper, cuttings from magazines and other visual material of different texture and appearance – in order to express or depict what they feel about a product or service. They might be asked to depict the ideal or something as it is now.

Personification

"If this radio station were a person what would he or she be like?" Respondents are asked to stretch their imaginative capacities. Often they enjoy this and come up with perceptive observations. Some focus group research using this technique was carried out for the BBC World Service in Egypt in 1986. Participants were asked this question about the BBC and other stations they listened to.

There were many similarities in the depictions. The BBC was seen as:

A serious, truthful person   *A classic man with a moustache*

A good spokesman   *Solid as Mokattam Mountain*

A strong personality   *A person with 'etiquette'*

Snobbish   *Stand-offish*

Like Margaret Thatcher, a woman of strong personality

Nearly all the personifications of the BBC were masculine. The BBC was seen as reliable and trustworthy, doing things 'properly' but rather stiff, formal and not very friendly.[48]

By contrast, Radio Monte Carlo, another international radio station popular in Egypt and elsewhere in the Middle East, had a quite different image:

A nice attractive lady with a lot of make-up

A young man, wearing an open shirt, a gold chain and driving a BMW.

Monte Carlo is a good person – a priest, a wise teacher – cheerful and entertaining

A cheerful, intelligent young girl, lively and entertaining

The association of priest and teacher with cheerfulness and entertainment is not one that is familiar to all cultures but it is not necessarily at odds with the other images. This list is a reminder that it is very important that qualitative data are interpreted objectively but by someone who has some knowledge of local cultural reference points and conventions.

Picture or Scene Completion

Respondents are given a picture to complete or provide a caption to. You might ask respondents to write in what they imagine a television viewer to be saying to a non-viewer after seeing a certain programme. You might ask respondents to imagine that the picture is of someone from a particular radio station and ask him or her to use coloured crayons to give an impression of the kinds of clothes they wear. I have seen these and other ideas for picture completion working very well. You might think that people would be embarrassed by being asked to behave a bit like a child, to draw or colour pictures when such a thing is something they may not be accustomed to doing. In my experience and that of many colleagues, it is something that, after a little diffidence, most people enjoy doing.

Word Association

Respondents are asked what words come to their minds when a product or service is mentioned. This can be tried out using the names of radio or TV stations, newspapers and magazines, presenters and personalities and so on.

Product and Service Mapping

There are various ways of mapping or positioning a product. One approach is to ask respondents "What kind of person uses this product?" The image of a product or service can be illustrated by discussion of this question. The lifestyle, class, social status, and many other attributes of the user of a radio, TV station, newspaper or magazine, as *perceived by others* can tell you a lot, not about the real customers but about how people perceive different media and their users. These perceptions influence people's choices. Consider how people might ask themselves, 'If I associate in my mind that radio station with that kind of person does that attract me to the station or repel me? Is that the kind of person I am or want to be?' Perhaps nobody ever asks that question in that clear, conscious, explicit way, but there seems little doubt that this is one consideration which influences the choice of radio station as it influences choice of many other products and services.

Sentence Completion

'The perfect radio station for me would be one which . . . . .'

'The kind of broadcaster I like to listen to is one who . . . . .'

'If you want to know what is really going on in this area you need to . . .'

The answers to these can be the starting point for a further exploration of these subjects. Like the other projective techniques they can be a very good way of unlocking ideas and opinions.

Obituaries

"Imagine this radio/TV/newspaper were to die and you had to write an obituary. What would you say about it?" "What were the strengths and weaknesses?" "What will you remember it for?" "What do you think that radio/TV/newspaper would like to be remembered for?" These and similar questions can bring out some of the main qualities as perceived by users.

103

This list of projective techniques is not exhaustive. New ideas can and do emerge and you may think of new ideas that could be tried out to reveal people's inner thoughts and views.

Examples of Focus Groups used in Audience Research

Qualitative research using focus groups is used quite extensively in audience research in the process of developing new programme ideas and services or of modifying or transforming an existing one. An example will help illustrate this.

In 1982 a new science series, *QED*, was launched on BBC television. The target was a mass audience not a well informed, technically educated one. It presented a series of programmes, each one of which was on a different scientific or technical subject. The aim was to do this in an appealing and easily understood way.

Research was needed to find out, among other things, how well the programmes were understood, how viewers had categorised the programmes and their satisfaction with, interest in and enjoyment of the programmes. If the researchers had provided the programme makers with figures or percentages showing that most had enjoyed and understood the programmes, no doubt the producers would have been pleased, but their understanding of audience response would have been little improved. Instead it was decided that in order to understand better the audience's values and attitudes, qualitative research would be used. Producers wanted detailed in-depth reactions from viewers. So it was decided to convene six groups each of eight viewers of *QED*. The groups were to discuss programmes about science in general and *QED* in particular. At each group a recent edition of the programme was played about halfway through the session.

The groups were kept fairly informal. They were conducted in the homes of the moderators. Respondents who were invited to take part were allowed, indeed encouraged, to talk freely and among themselves about the subject of TV programmes on science. None of those involved knew beforehand what the subject of discussion would be. Selection was straightforward; six groups of 8 each were recruited from the general public. Those recruited had to be people who had watched *QED* programmes. The usual method of doing this is to have what is known as a recruitment question on a survey questionnaire. In this case during the course of a regular face-to-face interview in which general questions about TV viewing were being asked, the respondent would be asked if he or she was a regular viewer of the *QED* series. If the answer was in the affirmative the respondent would then be asked if he or she were prepared to take part in further research at a future date. If the person is willing, name and address details are taken down and the person is recontacted later.

The discussions showed that the issues identified as important by the viewers were broadly similar to those of the producers. Viewers did categorise the programme in the area of 'science for the layman' intended by the programme makers. The research underlined the importance of presentation in helping the understanding of otherwise complex subjects. Respondents were quite enthusiastic about an informative series that was nonetheless entertaining and not heavy-handed or dull. Some criticisms emerged however, and they did so sufficiently across the groups to convince one that this was probably a reliable reflection of more widely held views. Most of the criticisms grew from the series' own success and popularity. Its viewers expected more than the programmes were able to provide. For example, there was some criticism of the structure, some viewers complaining about the lack of logical flow of subject matter.[49]

Although most selected group members could understand the programmes they did not always feel they had learned very much. They wanted simplicity, but this should not mean a lack of content. Interestingly, when viewers felt they were able to learn something, enjoyment was greatly increased.

What did the producers do with the research? They were pleased to discover that the audience welcomed and appreciated the programme idea, that the level of content was about right and that the variety in style in the programme was not an obstacle.

As a result of the criticisms however, certain changes were made. The narrative structure was improved. Producers tried to avoid inconclusive or muddling subjects and they tried to ensure that programmes contain more 'nuggets' of information. The series, which had little identity of its own for the viewers to remember, was, after the research, given a stronger identity with its own presenter, more use of programme logos and use of the title, *QED*.

Quite often, qualitative research through group discussions can show that audience and producer definitions of what a programme is about can differ considerably. This may not matter but it can be an eye-opener to a producer! This is actually one of the greatest strengths of qualitative research, appreciated and understood by creative people – writers, producers, performers and similar communicators – in ways that quantitative research rarely can be.

5.2 In-Depth Interviews

The second main form of qualitative research often used is the in-depth individual interview. The intention and broad purpose is broadly similar to other forms of qualitative research, which is to *reveal* or *understand* rather than to measure or describe. In-depth interviews are characterised by being open-ended, flexible, respondent-centred and designed to use respondent creativity and imagination. Like focus groups they also are used to attempt to go beyond those things which are on the surface.

Although in-depth interviews are often discussed and described alongside focus groups, they are quite different in many important respects. There is no social interaction. The emphasis is on the individual. This is the crucial point of choice between the two methods. When one wants to probe highly individual, personal reactions and behaviour, in-depth interviews are appropriate. There are a few other reasons why we might use the method, which I shall come to later.

105

In-depth interviews can provide quite detailed and rich data on individual behaviour and attitudes. In the field of media research they can be appropriate in a number of areas. In many cultures, radio listening has become very much an individual rather than a family-based or group activity. The new medium of the Internet is, by its very nature, almost entirely an activity for an individual operating alone. In a field where so little may be known about how people use this new medium, a series of in-depth interviews with users of the Internet might be a very good way of beginning a research project designed to show how the new medium is used.

Another major use of in-depth interviews is when you want individual creativity rather than group work. Some of the projective and imaginative techniques described earlier can work better when done with individuals working on their own.

There are a number of other reasons why we might want to use in-depth interviews rather than focus groups. For example, certain sensitive or controversial issues may be difficult for some people to discuss with others in a group. If you were investigating attitudes towards aspects of sexual behaviour or its depiction on television, group discussions might not be possible in view of the diffidence that many people might display when asked to discuss such matters in a group. This will vary greatly between cultures and sometimes within those cultures.

In-depth interviews may also be used when it is difficult to collect together participants for a focus group. The population might be very scattered. The people you are looking for may not be easy to find. It may take a lot of effort to find enough people to form a group, especially one that can come together on a specific date and time in a specific location. You might wish to explore rural schoolteachers' use of radio. By their nature, rural professionals are thinly scattered. It might take a long time and be very difficult to arrange a focus group of rural teachers, remembering that ideally focus group members should not know each other.

There are also some people who, because of the nature of their job will rarely or never be able to take part in group discussions. Senior civil servants, managing directors of large companies and other senior executives, politicians and other high status people may be of interest in media research. But their involvement in qualitative research may be possible only through in-depth interviews.

Questions used in in-depth interviews are not derived from a structured pre-arranged questionnaire. An interview guide will be prepared, but the interviewer always needs to be alert and flexible and to watch out for things that the respondent says which will need further elaboration and ad hoc questions. The following examples, all taken from transcripts of in-depth interviews that I have seen, give an idea of the kinds of questions that are asked. You can see that all of them could not have been thought of beforehand.

What did you feel like on that occasion?

Why did that make you feel that way?

Did you discuss your reactions with anybody else? How did they react?

Are there other occasions when similar things have happened?

What was your experience with this product/programme/service etc.?

Remember to probe anything that might lead you on to deeper understandings of how the media are used and thought of by the respondent. Watch for hidden assumptions and unspoken, underlying beliefs.

5.3   Participant Observation

Participant observation means what it appears to mean, which is always helpful! The researcher, to varying degrees, participates in an activity, a social group, lives with a family or families, joins a club or some other social formation in order to observe and understand it and the people involved. The focus group is an event of social interaction that we hope will replicate something of the cultural and social realities of the real world. But it is a somewhat unnatural event. Can we always be sure that people are like that in real life situations? There may be some aspects of life, especially in the family situation, which are not revealed in focus groups. Participant observation is a less unnatural procedure much used in ethnographic and anthropological research, far less so in commercial market research.

The main differences between focus groups and participant observation lie in the degree of control the researcher has and in the time it takes to do. In a focus group, although the moderator tries to avoid too much intervention, he or she is still in control. Participant observation by its very nature involves much less control. The researcher sees people on their home ground behaving as they do normally. For it to work it is essential not to even try to control events. The advantages are in being able to see real-life social interaction and behaviour. More openness and less control may enable you to see what might otherwise not be known.

In focus groups you rely almost entirely on people's verbal and body language. You may give participants tasks to perform but these are always to some extent artificial. You are left with the question: 'Is this how they would behave in real life?' Participant observation enables you to find out. You have the chance to observe a whole range of behaviour and social interaction. People communicate within a focus group because that is what they are asked to do and what is expected of them. In participant observation they do what they normally do in every day life.

Participant observation is not often used in commercial media or market research, largely because of the time and expense involved. However there is much of relevance and importance that could be gained through this method. Most media consumption in most societies takes place in the home. A BBC colleague running an audience research survey in Morocco was staying in a rural village home. He reported that a male member of the household came home while he was there, took a key out of his pocket, unlocked a cupboard and took out a radio set and went off to another room to listen. Later he returned the set to the cupboard, locked the door and left. Is this typical behaviour or something peculiar to this household? We do not know, but the episode reminded us that the mere existence of a radio set in a home does not guarantee that everyone has equal access to it. It might explain why many survey results from around the world show a higher reported level of access to radio by men than women, whereas the figures for each sex should be nearly the same, unless there are a significantly large number of male-only or female-only households. These are common in many developed societies, but the differences in access to radio and television by sex tend to be found mainly in less developed societies where single person or single sex households are much less common. The probability is that many women when asked the question "Do you have a radio or television where you live?" answer that they do not, even though there may be a set or sets, because they personally do not normally have access or control.

Participant observation can be a way of seeing and recording who turns the radio or television on, who chooses or switches the channels and at what time or times of the day different people in the household do this. If there are newspapers, magazines and other reading matter in the home, where are they, who picks them up, when and for how

107

long do they read? These and other observations collected in a number of homes give you an idea of the ways in which media are used in that society and these can give you a guide on how to structure and word any questionnaire you subsequently use in a survey.

Arthur Asa Berger in his excellent book for college students on media research suggests the use of participant observation for studying that very modern phenomenon, video game players who frequent amusement arcades. Here are users of a contemporary and new medium with their own sub-culture. Participant observation is very suitable, he suggests, in eliciting information that might be otherwise very difficult to obtain. Berger suggests that the participant observer note such things as the location of the arcade, where the players come from, their sex, age, apparent lifestyle, apparent class and status, ritualised behaviour, interaction with each other and conversations. He suggests that the researcher should also carry out some short interviews to supplement these observations to complete the picture.[50]

The practice of participant observation requires the researcher to have a good discipline of how he or she is going to record the observations. Practice is needed to avoid writing things down in full view of everyone being observed! People can become uneasy at this kind of behaviour. It is best to write notes at the end of the day or at periods when you are alone. Sometimes it is possible to use recording equipment, either audio or video, but you need to be aware that the presence of cameras and recorders can make people self-conscious and perform differently. Photos can assist memory and illustrate some aspects of life, but again great care needs to be taken not to either offend custom or affect actual behaviour.

There are a number of difficulties with participant observation, quite apart from the long time it takes to obtain data from many households or other situations. How, for example, do you know what behaviour is significant? How do you record what is going on without this affecting the behaviour you are there to record? Experience and sensitivity are required and like all qualitative methods, it is a learning process in which you can expect to improve techniques and discoveries over time.

5.4   Reliability and Validity in Qualitative Research

One might suppose that qualitative research, in the way I have described it here, is difficult to define in precise procedures, is therefore vague and must be either unreliable or not valid or both. It is true that there appears to be less precision in qualitative studies. But this should not imply a lack of objectivity or distance from truth. We are dealing here with a different way of investigating and describing reality.

There are ways of testing both the reliability and the validity of qualitative research. Remember that the reliability of a method (questionnaire, sample, focus group etc.) is the degree of consistency whereby the same results would be produced by different researchers using the same method. Does the method we employ give the same data when used by someone else? If so, the method can be said to be reliable. But remember also that something may be reliable but wrong. Validity is the degree to which what we find through research corresponds to reality. Does the method we employ get to the truth of the matter?

I do not have the space here to address the complex question of proving validity or reliability. However, there are relatively simple procedures that can maximise the confidence you have in qualitative procedures. The raw data – recordings, notes, transcripts and results of any written or visual tasks done from a series of focus groups – can be given to analysts separately to analyse and report. A new moderator's conduct of focus groups can be monitored by more experienced ones and any deviation from objectivity can be corrected through training.

We need to remember that one of the great strengths of qualitative research is that it helps us to discover or uncover aspects of behaviour that otherwise might not be apparent. But the method does not tell us how widespread some kind of behaviour or set of attitudes is. We don't get numbers from qualitative research. What qualitative research may do is help us create hypotheses that can be tested quantitatively.

The key to best practice in qualitative research is objectivity. The researcher needs to develop a critical discipline that will minimise subjective judgements and interpretations. To help this process it is a good practice to carry out regular exercises in what is referred to as 'inter-rater' reliability. The following exercise is derived from one suggested by Silverman in his excellent book on this subject.[51]

Exercise

After a qualitative research project has been carried out – focus group, in-depth interview or participant observation – obtain the data and carry out an analysis of it. Ask some colleagues to do the same independently of you and of each other.

When you have each finished bring your analyses together and study the similarities and differences between them. Consider the following:

What are the major similarities and differences in the ways you have categorised, classified and sorted data?

Discuss between yourselves which of your analyses require revision or abandonment, and give reasons.

Do the similarities in your analyses necessarily mean that you have found the best approach?

Do you perceive aspects of your colleagues' analyses that portray a lack of objectivity in them? Do some of them say the same about you? (This is an excellent way of discovering each other's biases which may not otherwise be apparent to any of you.)

What have you learned from this exercise and what will you change as a result?

Sometimes when doing qualitative research you will get a consistent story or set of data, yet it may prove invalid. Kirk and Miller in their book on reliability and validity in qualitative research describe research into the social and cultural place of coca in Peru. Coca, the source of the illegal drug cocaine, was potentially difficult to research, yet the writers obtained good responses and their results seemed to be consistent and reliable. They soon discovered they were wrong. Their respondents had not been telling the truth. Their suspicions were roused because the results were too perfect. So they introduced the topic of coca in a different way revealing a very different story under the surface.[52]

5.5   Analysis and Reporting Qualitative Research

Analysing qualitative research is not a precise, numerical process. The task is to take all the data – video or audiotapes, transcripts, notes and any written or pictorial work done by the interviewees – and try to make sense of it and produce a summary that will attempt to answer the issues posed in the particular research brief. The process involves a thorough review of all the material, structuring it in a relevant and ordered way, identifying those things that are of greater importance and drawing significant conclusions. The qualitative researcher should also keep in mind at all times the purpose of the research and ensure that where possible the report answers the research brief.

There is often a lot of work to do. Tapes need to be transcribed or at least summarised and the significant quotes collected. The researcher should look for what findings there are in common between the various focus groups, and where there are differences. Some of this analysis can go on while the project is proceeding. Good qualitative research is usually a dynamic process involving the continuous testing and modification of hypotheses.

One way to organise the data is to create a matrix on which to sort the various topics to come out of each of the groups. This could have the group or individual characteristics on one axis and the topics on the other. This is a good way to see an emerging picture with clear comparisons between the different participants.

The qualitative researcher requires certain professional skills to assist in this process. A qualification in psychology is a good basis for qualitative research. So also is knowledge of anthropology and sociology. It is unusual to find someone who has all the skills and knowledge that might be required. This is why agencies that specialise in qualitative research usually employ people with a range of these and related skills. As I noted in the previous section on reliability and validity it is good practice to have more than one person doing the analysis and comparing their findings and conclusions.

A final point about qualitative research within the field of audience research is that creative people like it. It is more highly valued by producers, writers, journalists and artists working in the media than quantitative research. They value the insights that qualitative research can give into motivations and individual response to media content. When it is used to develop ideas and draws on the creativity of people either individually or in groups, it can also be of great value and stimulation to creative people.

Desk Research

6

What can be learned about the audience from existing data? Do we make sufficient use of data already available, from the census, from departments of agriculture, health, housing etc. Sometimes new field research may be unnecessary because the work has already been done. It can be a very useful exercise simply to carry out an audit of what is available and of what research has been done. Although I have put this section after those on quantitative and qualitative research, as an activity it almost always comes first.

In multilingual countries there is usually a good deal of very valuable data on language use, comprehension and ability, of enormous value to press journalists and broadcasters. Production and/or import figures for TV and radio sets may be obtainable. Readership figures for the press may exist. Research may have been done into leisure, education and other aspects of daily life or any other aspect of daily routines that would be useful when planning broadcasts or press and advertising campaigns.

Universities can be a very useful source of research and I believe it is a great pity that there is not more co-operation between the academic community on the one hand and press, advertising and broadcasting research communities on the other. Media researchers tend to look askance at the academics, accusing them of far too much theory with little empirical evidence, whilst academics tend to scorn media researchers' apparent lack of theoretical understanding and their apparent attachment to numbers and the single-minded pursuit of ratings or readership figures. In fact each has a lot to offer the other. There is a wealth of important data in broadcasting organisations that is often not fully analysed because full use for broadcasting planning purposes has been made of the significant parts. For broadcasters, yesterday's data are history. At the same time we see a lot of academic work which uses little or no empirical data in reaching conclusions about radio and television viewing. The freedom academic researchers have from the day-to-day constraints and demands of a broadcasting organisation or advertising department could give them the ability to discern trends and other information from the data collected by media research departments. Both the academic and media organisation research communities would benefit greatly from working together.

111

Sometimes television and radio audience research departments become quite closely involved in desk research for programmes. For example, Indian state television Doordarshan's audience research department did a study of a medical and social research institute at Karigiri on which an award-winning programme was made. The project gave birth to a new concept and philosophy for audience research, ie. to provide direct support and input and become an integral part of programme development. The orientation changed from merely evaluating (or crudely speaking, auditing) the programmes as an outsider to a more active role of a constituent in the production team.[53]

Listeners' Viewers' and Readers' Letters, Phone Calls and other Personal Communications from the Audience

All media receive letters. Increasingly these days they also receive faxes, email and phone calls as the facilities for these grow, even in less developed areas of the world. Personal communications like these are often greatly valued as a source of feedback and knowledge about the audience. But how reliable are they? How reliable are letters, faxes, emails or word-of-mouth communications to broadcasters or journalists? What do they represent? Is an over-reliance on letters and similar communications dangerous? Can a systematic study of the mail be a useful guide to programme makers, press journalists and media and campaign planners? As we have shown already when we were looking at ways to investigate listener behaviour and attitudes, listeners' letters can provide us with addresses for the despatch of postal questionnaires. But are the letters themselves and statistics compiled from them of value to audience research? And can any sample chosen in this way be regarded as a safe source for information?

Letters take on an added importance when research is not very regular, or where there is little or none at all. In these cases letters can be highly misleading. Sometimes they are used as if they were a barometer of listener opinion or even a meter of audience size. But letters can tell you very little, if anything, about general listener opinion or the number of listeners.

I lose count of the arguments I have had with producers about this! Many research projects in Britain and elsewhere have shown conclusively and consistently that those who write do not represent the generality of opinion. A letter represents the person who wrote the letter and no one else. The opinion expressed may be the opinion of many others. It may be a minority view. You have no way of telling without research. You may get thousands of letters of complaint about something and only a few letters of praise or contentment about the same thing. The latter may represent the majority opinion!

Reliance on letters can be very misleading. This makes reliable audience and readership measurement research so important – to show producers what their audience is really like – because there is always a tendency to take too much notice of opinions in letters or phone calls and other personal communications.

None of this is to suggest that letters, phone calls etc. are unimportant and should be dismissed. My former department in the BBC World Service employs more people to handle listener's letters than to do research. This is not because letters are more important but because handling letters in more than thirty languages is a labour-intensive activity. Letters are valuable for their individuality. Broadcasting is about addressing large numbers of individuals and the spontaneous responses of those people are of great value, not least to the creative broadcaster. But they should not be used for purposes for which they are not suitable.

The most absurd use of letters is when a station attempts to make as estimate of its

7

audience size by multiplying every letter received by 100 or 200 and claiming this as a true audience estimate! I know of at least two international radio stations that have used this spurious method! This leads to another rule to remember. There is no relationship between numbers of letters and numbers of listeners, viewers or readers The BBC Arabic Service audience grew in 1990-91 during the war in the Gulf. The number of letters fell. The BBC Hindi language service has about 20 times as many listeners as the Tamil language service. But it receives about the same number of letters.

However, letters can stimulate research. When producers receive letters that tend to reflect one view, research in the field among a representative cross-section of listeners or viewers can reveal the true state of opinion on the matter. Letters can be a useful source of feedback for educational programmes – that is in the broad sense of education. Later we will look briefly at a project in Tanzania that looked at the impact of a 'soap' radio serial which carried family planning and other health themes. One of the techniques employed to assess impact and effects was content analysis of responses. This analysis was used to see if messages contained in the programmes were being reflected in the letters. In other words, did the serial's message seem to have an impact on what people who responded wrote? Content analysis is beyond the scope of this book. But it is a widely used and valuable research technique, not of audience research but of communications research, more used in the academic world than in any actual media business.[54]

Research to Improve and Test Effectiveness

The promotion of commercial products and services using the modern techniques of advertising can be very successful. The objective of advertising may be to achieve any of a number of things, including the following:

1. *Promote a new product or service*

2. *Retain customer loyalty and market share for an existing product or service*

3. *Increase market share*

4. *Increase sales, subscriptions, use etc. (not always the same as increasing share)*

5. *Change existing public attitudes towards a product or service*
   – shifting the image of a brand perhaps

6. *Increase awareness of a product or service*

7. *Inform the public or some target within the public of a change in the product or service*

A campaign may be designed to achieve any one or several of these and perhaps others. What happens then and what part does research play in the whole process? Advertisers, who spend so much money on advertising in the media, nowadays look for solid and dependable evidence that they have spent their money effectively. They want to know what advertising medium has worked best. They may also want to know how it has worked. They will probably also want to know which message had the greatest impact. Nowadays more money is spent by advertisers than anyone else on researching media consumption in order to provide answers to these and similar questions. It is important to remember this. Audience research in the world is very largely driven by the demands of the advertising industry.

Those who sell advertising time and space in the media, as they become increasingly dependent on advertising revenue, need also to know more about audience behaviour. They have the problem of selling airtime or advertising space in a market that, almost everywhere in the world, is becoming more competitive. For as the media grow in number and spread, the amount of advertising space and time on offer in the advertising market place is forever rising. Media salespeople have to work ever harder to make sales. One of the tools that can help the better sale of advertising time and space is adequate market and audience research. Usually when you sell any product it helps to know something about it! The TV or radio advertising sales person who does not know in some detail about the audience size and profile for the station or stations whose advertising space he or she is selling, is at a considerable disadvantage. In many cases the companies buying advertising space or time will be in a stronger position because they will have this information from research. In my experience, and especially where

8

radio and television stations are monopolies run by the state, the advertisers often know much more about audiences for radio and television stations than the stations know themselves.

Both buyer and seller of advertising time or space need to know what they are buying or selling. Research is an essential prerequisite. As we have seen earlier in this book, audience measurement data, obtained through the different methods described, will inform both the seller and buyer about what they can expect. Will these data not also be useful, if not essential, for others interested in using the media to put over messages to audiences? It is my argument here and elsewhere that the same techniques and methods can be used to serve social and development purposes. Research used to test the effectiveness of advertising can therefore be used to test the effectiveness of any communication activity and also to understand how communication works.

Research plays a central role in modern marketing, and in three consecutive phases.

1. Providing information about existing customers and markets.
Those developing new commercial products and services usually make extensive use through desk research of existing sources of data. They may also carry out research among potential users of a new product or service in which they find out about customer needs, desires and perceptions. Research, both qualitative and quantitative, is also often used to look at existing customer behaviour, consumption patterns etc.

2. Research to inform communication, including pretesting messages.
Guidance on the best way to communicate any new product or service can also be sought from research. Existing media data are consulted to find out how different media outlets reach different segments of the population, thus enabling those running campaigns to chose the most suitable and cost-effective channels to be used. Research is also often used to pretest advertising, using some of the qualitative techniques described earlier. Hall tests can also be used. These involve a technique described below in which potential consumers are asked to test new products or, in this case, to respond to or comment on radio or television, press or other advertisements.

3. Testing Effectiveness – Did the message work?
Research is used after a campaign to test the effectiveness of the advertising in communicating the message about the new product or service.

What is true for commercial products and services can also be true for radio and television programmes, editorial material in newspapers and magazines and for any communication of social, educational and health information, for the communication of new ideas and much else besides. Indeed it is the belief of many in the field of marketing that the methods used are applicable across a wide range of human activity. What makes the marketing of Coca-Cola or Gillette so successful can and should be used in the promotion of more socially beneficial and developmental goals. Often this wider role for marketing is referred to as *social marketing*.[55]

In this section I am going to look briefly at some of the methods used in the commercial world of market research to improve the effectiveness of advertising and ways in which the effectiveness of messages via the media can be tested. Can we improve the chances of a TV or radio programme being successful? Can we improve the content and presentation of an advertisement? Can we ensure that we have worded and designed a campaign in the most appropriate way? Can we be sure that we are not about to say something that will be misunderstood? How can the effectiveness of advertising or similar attempts at communication be tested? How can we find out about the impact of a radio or television programme?

The various research methods described in this book can in various ways be used to provide the kinds of answers required by advertisers and the sellers of advertising capacity. But there is a method used to test advertising (among other things) which needs to be described here.

Hall Tests – or Similar Ways of Pretesting Advertising etc.

The most usual use of hall tests in market research is in the testing or trying out of new products. New processed foods, hot or cold drinks, household electrical equipment and furniture are just a few examples of items that are usually subjected to hall tests before they are made fully available in the marketplace.

Hall tests are so called because they usually involve renting a suitable large hall in which the tests can take place. Usually such halls are rented near shopping centres where respondents can be recruited. Interviewers are given instructions on the kinds of people who are being sought to take part. Quota samples are normally employed in recruitment for hall tests. If a new food product is being tested, the quota could be constructed to create a sample of people who normally do the shopping for food. Structured questionnaires are used to record the interviewee's response to or opinion of the product or products involved in the test.

Hall tests need not be carried out in halls! Nor need they be always be carried out indoors. The climate in many countries may require their use. Also a degree of privacy and security may be essential. However there is no other reason why successful hall tests should not be conducted in the open air.

Hall tests are a well tried and relied on way of testing new products. They can also be used to pretest such things as packaging, advertising and television and radio programmes. The tests need not involve a finished production. Concepts and ideas for advertising or for radio and television programmes can be tested. These could consist of sketches and outlines of what is proposed or of a completed execution. Sometimes hall tests can be used to test the effectiveness of advertising or the impact of programmes in the ways described in the next section.

Hall tests can be used to measure response to a new advertisement or a new radio or television series. Responses could be measured according to criteria such as understanding, enjoyment, persuasiveness, memorability, acceptability and information value. This list could be longer; it is not intended to be comprehensive.

A use of hall tests sometimes encountered in European audience research is when TV programmes or series from one country are tested to see if they are likely to be successful in another. It is not unusual, for example, for TV series from the United States to be pretested in this way in some European countries. Viewing facilities are made available; people are invited to watch programmes and to answer a few questions to measure their reactions and opinions. Sometimes each invited viewer may be provided with a handset linked to a computer on which they can record their impressions and reactions as the programme is in progress.

Research into the Effectiveness of Advertising and Other Media Messages

In order to find out if programmes, advertisements or any other communication are effective and make the desired impact we obviously need to look beyond measurement data. We may find from research that a particular advertisement, radio or television programme, or a particular edition of a magazine reached a very large number of people. But did it make any difference? Did those who saw, heard or read the item remember anything? Did it make any difference to them? Were there any consequences that flowed from receiving this communication?

These are important questions. They are also among the most difficult for researchers to answer! The reason for this is because it is so difficult to establish and prove a link between cause and effect. A new product is advertised widely. It sells very well. How do we know whether it would have sold equally well even without advertising? More crucially, we might well want to know how many resources to put into a campaign. We may accept that some publicity and promotion is essential. But how much is required? Is there any provable link between the amount of advertising and the results achieved? If we increase the number of advertisements will sales increase also, and if so, by how much? These same questions can be posed about any form of communication in which one is trying to inform, educate, persuade, change perceptions or change behaviour.

Let us suppose that there is a campaign to make people aware of the dangers of AIDS. (We will look at a real campaign shortly.) The intention of the campaign would probably be twofold – to inform people about how the AIDS virus is transmitted and to persuade those in the most vulnerable groups to change their behaviour in such a way as to reduce or eliminate the possibility of contracting the disease. We could, after a campaign, test these two aspects. How much was people's *knowledge* of AIDS changed by the campaign? And how much was their *behaviour* changed. Both are important but they are different. Some campaigns will bring about changes in knowledge and awareness without changing behaviour. People may remember advertising campaigns and be very familiar with the name and even the qualities of the product on offer. They may not buy it however. We need to keep these two aspects of effectiveness in mind.

The two major kinds of change we need to look for are known as *cognitive*, that is to do with people's knowledge, and *behavioural*, that is to do with what people actually do. It could be argued that there is a third type that comes between these two, which is *attitudinal* change. People's opinions and views, much more than their knowledge, are greatly influenced by other people. I will treat attitude change as part of a change in their behaviour because the two go very closely together. But they are not the same. If we take the example of AIDS, people may learn from a campaign about its causes and how to prevent its spread. They may even change their sexual behaviour. But their basic and more deep-seated attitudes and beliefs may change very little, at least in the short term.

There are hundreds of studies in the academic literature on the subject of communication and change, a few of them listed in the bibliography. One of the main methodological problems in proving the effectiveness of any communication in making a difference to people's knowledge or their actual resulting or consequential behaviour is that it is difficult, and very often impossible to separate out the influence that the media may have from all other influences. The media do not operate on their own in communicating ideas and information. How people actually learn new ideas, obtain new information or are influenced to buy a new product, change their farming methods or adopt new practices in personal health and hygiene, are not at all easy to discover. Often we can do little more than say that this or that influence was *probably* the major factor. What very often happens is that several influences are playing a part. Indeed several research projects have shown that messages via the media probably are most powerful when other influences tend to be in harmony and point in the same direction. That is to say, messages via the media probably have the most effect on knowledge and behaviour when other influences are pointing in the same direction.[56] The converse is also true, that the media are least effective when their content is different from and may be in conflict with the prevailing cultural and social ethos and influences.

How then do we test effectiveness? We do not need to devise immensely complex methods that might be required if we were demanding a complete proof of effectiveness. In audience research we should be content with results that strongly suggest or point to linkages between exposure to communication and changes in recipients' knowledge and/or attitudes and behaviour.

In audience research we can learn a lot from the allied field of advertising research. Advertisers have always tried to evaluate advertising, but the link between advertising and sales performance used to be made on judgement that was not systematic or precisely measured. Nowadays advertisers tend to demand more definite data on the link between advertising spend and product sales. Much depends on what the objective of the advertising is, and this in turn will depend upon the product or service and the market in which they are available. Often advertisers are not seeking, nor do they expect, advertising to result in increased sales. The objective may, in the case of some fast moving consumer goods, be simply to retain market share. That is to say that advertising is known by experience to be necessary to maintain brand awareness and loyalty of existing customers. Sometimes the objective may be to increase awareness of the brand or product. At other times it might be to shift opinion about the brand or product – to change the product's 'image' in the minds of the public. It might be to inform the buying public that the product has been improved in some way. These and similar objectives can be tested.

Questions can be asked in quantitative surveys that will provide measures of use, opinion, awareness and knowledge of product and service attributes. Changes in these can be measured over time by successive studies. (See *tracking studies* described below.)

If the objective is simply to increase sales, the research needed may be relatively simple. With a manufactured product where sales have been at a certain known level it is a simple matter to record the change in the level of sales and demand following an advertising campaign. The only major problem with this approach is that it makes no allowance for anything else that might be taking place in the market that might also influence demand. We must not assume that it is only advertising that influences sales or demand. But in practice you usually know about other likely factors such as competitor activity, changes in demand caused by weather or other factors and can make allowance for these.

Sometimes it is possible to test the effectiveness of advertising by making comparisons between different areas of a similar kind – one where the advertising has taken place and the other where it has not. Such so-called *area tests* can provide a good basis on which to evaluate the sales effectiveness of advertising.

Sometimes *tracking studies* are used to monitor advertising performance. These are continuous surveys in which samples of 100 or thereabouts are taken each week among the target groups (housewives, motorists, beer drinkers etc.) and data on aspects of a product or brand's performance can be presented and compared or tracked over time and, where appropriate, compared with advertising activity. Tracking studies are a regular feature of market research in several industrialised countries and are being used increasingly in developing economies also. Typically a series of core questions are asked about ten or so products and these will normally include spontaneous and prompted awareness of advertisements, products or brands, detailed recall of the content of advertisements and responses to and attitudes towards the advertising. Questions are usually also asked about purchase or use of the products.[57]

Measures of 'spontaneous' and 'prompted' awareness are often taken in research, including audience research. We often want to know how well known something is. If we ask the question in a survey "Can you name all the radio stations that can be listened to here on your set?" the results will give you the spontaneous awareness figures for all radio stations available. This can tell you a lot about the prominence and fame of each station. If you then ask "Which of these other radio stations have you heard of?" and then read out a list of those radio stations that the respondent has not named, you will obtain the *prompted awareness* figures for all stations. Both sets of data will be useful in telling radio stations more than just their respective popularity. A station with low spontaneous awareness may need to spend money on promotion to its target groups. If prompted awareness is also low it may have to engage in more general promotion to ensure that the public as a whole become more aware of its existence and what it has to offer. Questions like these are used in market research for all kinds of product and can tell us a lot about the place of a product or service in public perceptions.

There are several published examples of research into the effectiveness of advertising campaigns. Each year the British Institute of Practitioners in Advertising (IPA) publishes a collection of recent research showing the impact of campaigns. I have chosen two examples that seem relevant to the purpose of this book. The first is a campaign between 1988 and 1993 about AIDS.[58] The objective was twofold:

1. *To keep the issue from slipping off the public agenda, and*

2. *To encourage the use of condoms among young heterosexuals.*
   (There was a separate campaign aimed at homosexuals.)

I will briefly outline what the research showed. The UK Government through its Health Education Authority (HEA) funded the advertising campaign. To prevent the transmission of the HIV virus, the HEA wanted sexually active young people to use condoms. But experience in health campaigns had shown that if there were to be a change in behaviour, people had to have sufficient concern about their own health, believe that they were at risk of illness, believe that a change in behaviour was possible, would avoid infection and would not cost too much. A major problem with HIV/AIDS is that individuals can be HIV positive for a long time without knowing it. And even when the sufferer knows, the disease is not apparent to anyone else. Moreover, in Britain, the incidence is relatively low. The advertising had to get over the message to the general public that AIDS remained a serious ongoing threat to heterosexuals as well as homosexuals and that one could be HIV positive without showing any of the symptoms of AIDS. Advertising was also aimed at young people who were sexually active and likely to have more than one partner. It was designed to convince them that they could be at risk. It sought to promote condom use as the primary means of preventing the disease being spread, and to reduce some of the barriers to the use of condoms. These barriers were known, through research, to be the emotional 'cost' of condom use – they were viewed as a contraceptive device rather than a way of preventing disease. Moreover, the widespread use of contraceptive pills by women had largely made the condom redundant as a contraceptive device.

National advertising was used via the television, radio, cinema, posters and press. Some of this was in media designed to reach the entire population. Other advertisements were placed in media aimed at young people. The total cost of the campaign between 1988 and 1993 was over £15 million ($25 million). The campaign had to contend with counter messages in the media. For example, public concern about AIDS waned in 1989 and 1990 when press stories suggested that there was little or no risk of heterosexuals catching HIV. There were even headlines in the British press that spoke of 'the myth of heterosexual AIDS'.

Research was carried out throughout the period to track changing views among the general public and among young people about HIV/AIDS. Before the campaign, at the end of 1988, only 24% of the public could spontaneously name HIV as the virus that led to AIDS. By the end of 1993 this figure had increased dramatically to 90%. Other results showed that over the whole period AIDS had been retained as a key health concern in the mind of the public. More crucially, research also showed that there had been a significant increase in the use of condoms among sexually active young people. The data also showed that concern about AIDS in the public mind fluctuated primarily in response to advertising or the lack of it. The conclusion is that advertising was a key factor in maintaining "an appropriate level of public concern regarding AIDS and against this backdrop encouraging condom usage amongst young people at risk".

The other piece of research showing the effectiveness of advertising also showed how advertising worked. In 1989 a British advertising agency, BMP, took over responsibility for advertising for the National Dairy Council, the body which promotes dairy products in the UK. It ran a campaign specifically aimed at encouraging children to drink more milk.[60] Over the next five years the advertising campaign was successful in increasing per capita milk consumption by 12%. It generated extra income worth nearly three times the cost of the advertising campaign.

Per capita milk consumption had fallen by 30% between 1979 and 1988. It was known also that children aged 2 to 15 years old accounted for 50% of milk drinking, even though they formed only 20% of the population. It was also known that while their milk drinking was in decline, their consumption of other drinks, especially fizzy drinks, was increasing.

The next task for the advertisers after learning all they could about the state of the market in terms of sales and consumption was to find out about children's attitudes towards milk. Focus groups with children showed that while they believed that milk was nourishing and refreshing, there was a problem inherent in these qualities for children. Children can tend to be put off something that is good for them. They make decisions about what they want or do not want for other reasons. Milk is one of those 'good' things that mothers tell you to drink. This did not as a result make it something they wanted. Children prefer sweets and biscuits to healthier brown bread and vegetables. The advertisers realised that they needed to "overturn milk's worthy, dull and 'mumsy' image into one that kids would find admirable".[61] Milk's perceived core qualities did not appeal to children.

Advertisements had to put over a message other than the simple one that milk was good for you. The advertisers found an opportunity to do this by associating milk with sporting success, linking it with well-known and popular sporting heroes. A short drama of two boys discussing what to drink when they were thirsty was made. It was funny and entertaining and quickly became a favourite with children who had seen it on television. In focus groups, the advertising agency found that many children could act out the lines and actions in the advertisement perfectly. Lines from the advertisement became catchphrases in the playgrounds of Britain. The witty drama had started a craze. Its characters "seemed to reflect exactly the sort of people children wanted to be".[62]

Advertising was further refined to target older children. The idea was that they were most likely to regard milk with disfavour. And by targeting older children it was hoped that if their opinions and outlook towards milk could be changed, younger children would follow by the fact that in many respects they tend to copy their older brothers and sisters. Two further advertisements were created, one associating milk with the top sprinter Linford Christie. The other was comic creation with some novel and startling animation. Qualitative research showed that these advertisements had also entered playground culture. The Linford Christie ad was especially popular with boys and it was very much in harmony with the emerging craze for athletics gear and trainers.

In a number of different ways the authors of the article from which I have taken these findings prove that it was the advertising that changed children's perceptions of milk and their consequent consumption of it. Among other things, they prove this by showing that adult consumption over the same period remained constant. They also showed how the 'craze' started by the ads worked. After the initial showing of the advertisements, milk drinking increased and then fell off. It is known that ads make an impact and then the effects wear off. But they noticed that there was a later peak that was not related directly to the showing of advertisements. What could be causing this? The conclusion was that one of the advertisements, the Linford Christie one, was having a double effect. The craze started among the older children and then filtered down through personal influence to the younger children. They show how children see and then adapt ads to their culture.

> 'Kids are very prone to crazes. They live in a world where social acceptance is very important. All sorts of things from their everyday experiences of life form a kind of social currency: from pop music and fashion through to TV programmes and adverts.
>
> Kids copy things they admire and in their social world, this escalates into a craze.'[63]

The main problem with these finding for the National Dairy Council was to sustain something that was based on a children's craze. The solution is that such advertising has to be recreated and repeated frequently if the effects are to be sustained.

Other content than advertisements may be designed to have intended effects. Even entertainment programmes may have a secondary purpose. The long-running daily 'soap' radio serial on radio in Britain, *The Archers*, now in its 49th year, had as one of its original purposes to improve the flow of agricultural information. It was devised and for many years directed by someone from the BBC's agricultural programmes department. To this day it has an agricultural story editor.[63] The same idea has been tried in many countries. Radio Tanzania has been broadcasting a 'soap' since 1993 called *Twende na Wakati (Let's Go with the Times)*. The idea was based on similar *telenovelas* designed both to entertain and promote socially beneficial change in Mexico. There are two half-hour episodes weekly. The format is a continuing drama serial with characters who become well known. The story line is realistic and set in a familiar Tanzanian context. Social and educational messages included in the drama cover family planning, the prevention of HIV infection, economic development, maternal and child health, recognition of the equal status of men and women and environmental conservation. Funding has been provided by various aid agencies, including the United Nations Family Planning Association.

Research was carried out to determine the effects of the broadcasts and focused on the period 1993 to 1995 but also drew data from before and after this period. Because not all areas were able to receive the programme well, it was possible to do area tests, comparing results in areas of good reception to one where it was difficult or impossible to listen. The research, which focused on family planning, used eight different and independent methods.

1. *Annual surveys involving 3,000 respondents*

2. *Attendance at family planning clinics was monitored and measured*

3. *A survey of new adopters of family planning methods to discover their sources of referral to the family planning clinic*

4. *Condom distribution data were collected*

5. *National data from the government's ongoing health surveys were collected*

6. *Content analysis of listeners' mail to the programme*

7. *Content analysis of Twende scripts*

8. *Focus group discussions with Twende listeners*

The government's health surveys showed an increase in exposure to family planning messages on radio from 22% in 1991/2 to 45% in 1996. Exposure to *Twende* reached 23% of the population by 1996. The majority of listeners found the programme entertaining and nearly everybody thought it was realistic. Listeners identified with the role model character. Almost 90% of the listeners, a very high figure, identified family planning as one of the educational themes of the programme. There was a significant increase over the period in knowledge of family planning methods, but this happened both in areas where the programme could easily be heard and the area where it could not. However, the programme seems to have been effective in increasing the belief that one can control family size, one of its main objectives. Exposure to the programme was also positively correlated with a growth in approval of family planning methods. There was also a significant effect in promoting discussion about family planning between couples. Other measures also showed that the programme had an impact on knowledge about HIV/AIDS and the study showed that there was a significant effect on behaviour and attitudes.[65]

123

Data Analysis

The rapid advances of computer technology have opened up enormous opportunities for all kinds of research. The task of data analysis was previously a very complex and time-consuming activity. Completed questionnaires had to be hand counted. The answers had to be coded and data written onto large sheets of paper, not unlike doing accounts by hand. The early computers, from some fifty years ago, made a lot of this work easier. But it was still quite time consuming. And there were limits on the analysis one could do. This was because researchers did not usually have direct access to computers. The results from the questionnaires had to be coded onto punched tape or cards, but at that point the computer specialists took over. Let me describe how I analysed the results of my first survey. This was of newspaper readership and radio listening in Tanzania in 1968. I returned to Manchester in July of that year. After the questionnaires were all coded and the data punched onto cards, I then had to go to the Manchester University Computer Centre to arrange for my cards to be read and analysed. I could not do the work myself. Instead I had to explain very carefully and precisely what analyses I wanted – how I wanted the results to be tabulated, what demographic breaks I required, whether any weighting was required etc. The computer staff then wrote computer instructions and my project was run on the famous Atlas computer at some date booked several weeks in advance.

Everyone who used that computer spoke in almost hushed and awe-struck tones about what was then one of the most powerful machines of its kind in the world. Now, only thirty years later, computers of far greater capacity than Manchester University's famous Atlas which, incidentally occupied quite a large building, can be bought for a few hundred pounds and taken around in a small hand-held case.

The personal computer has meant a revolution in market research. All researchers can now do their own analysis. What is more, they can do several repeat analyses of the same data without difficulty. When I took those Tanzanian results to the Manchester computer in 1968 I had to know exactly what I wanted. I could go back later and run the data again to look at things in a different way. But this was not something I could do very often. It was not just that computer time was expensive. This computer like the few other computers in use at that time was in constant demand running for 24 hours every day.

Personal computers speed up and simplify research analysis and report writing. They have also made possible the development of databases for the continuous analysis of market trends as well as many more powerful facilities relevant to all aspects of media research. Formerly research was reported in long and comprehensive papers and documents. This is still done but it is not always necessary or desirable. Data can be stored and information provided on request when it is needed. Surveys almost always provide far more information than can be digested in a single report. A comprehensive database can be maintained and kept up-to-date and be used to answer questions as they occur.

9

9.1   Interpretation and Terminology

Most audience research activity is quantitative. The same goes for a lot of other media research as well. Many figures are produced. What do they mean and what do we do with them? If we say that the evening news on television's main national channel had a 20% audience, what does this mean?

The first point to be clear about is the coverage - what is the universe? 20% of what? It could be the population aged 4 and over, 12 and over, 15 and over, depending on the age covered by the research method. Is it 20% of everyone over that age, or 20% of people in TV households? Figures are usually given for whole populations, over a given age, but one must make this clear. The figure could mean 20% of those watching any TV at that time. 20% of those watching TV is a very different thing from 20% of the population over the age of 15.

There are other things we need to know about the meaning of this 20%. Does it mean that 20% watched the entire news programme? Or does it mean that 20% watched any part of the programme? Or is it the average audience for the programme?

As you can see, there are rather a lot of things we need to know about the meaning of any data. It is a good discipline whenever dealing with any market research data to make sure that nothing is taken for granted. Make sure always that the bases to which the data relate are clearly stated. If you are given data by others that do not provide this information make sure you demand it. Quantitative research data are not really useable unless you know precisely what they mean and on what they are based.

Let us suppose that in the above hypothetical case the data mean that 20% of the population aged 15 and over watched at least some of the particular news bulletin. Is this enough information? Are there any further things we need to ask? What do we mean by 'watch'? What do we mean by 'at least some'?

If the data have come from a peoplemeter system, 'watch' probably means presence in the room where the television was switched to this particular channel at this time. If the data has come from a self-completion diary it means that this percentage reported watching this channel at this time. But if someone watched for only one minute a news programme lasting half an hour, did he or she 'watch' the programme? What if he or she watched for ten minutes? What about fifteen minutes? At what stage do we admit the person to membership of the audience to the programme? These are important questions for which answers must be given. Once again, there is no correct answer; the users of research need to say what they want to be measured and reported.

Try this. One might ask the question, "How many people in Zambia listen to Radio Four?" What is meant by this question? What would it mean if we said that half the adult population listens to Radio Four? We might mean that on an average day, half the population listens to at least one programme on Radio Four. Or we might mean that on average, each week half the population listens. Or we could mean that of all the radio listening that occurs, half of it is to Radio Four. Or we could mean that on average, at any time, about half the radio listening is to Radio Four.

All these measures, and there are more, mean different things. They are all used at various times and they have different uses. They are very different. A TV station may reach at least half the population in a week but only 20% of them on an average day. It may reach less than 5% of the TV audience at any time and have an even smaller overall share of all TV viewing. Note the uses of these words 'reach' and 'share'. They are used a lot in audience research and we will see how they are calculated shortly. Other measures exist and new measures could still be devised for new requirements, especially in underdeveloped regions where special audience research needs may emerge.

Different kinds of people in broadcasting organisations and different kinds of broadcasting organisations require different kinds of information for different purposes. Producers of programmes require different information from those who plan the schedules. Those responsible for raising advertising revenue will have special data requirements. Services funded by advertising or sponsorship need audience measurement data for their advertising sales teams to show potential customers what audiences are reached at different times of the day by different networks. Those who buy and sell advertising time on radio and television are especially interested in Share, Ratings (and Gross Rating Points) and Demographics. Publicly funded public service broadcasting organisations like the BBC are more interested in Reach, Demographics and, to a lesser extent, Share.

9.2 Ratings and Gross Rating Points

Ratings and Gross Rating Points are widely used by those who buy and sell TV and radio time for advertising. Most American literature on audience research tends to concentrate on ratings when covering the quantitative aspects of the subject.[66] *Ratings* are obtained in the same way as *Reach* (see below) but the word is usually used to describe what happens at a particular time of day, or in the word often used in advertising, 'daypart'. An audience rating is usually given as an average percentage of people in a given population listening or watching a TV or radio station within a given time period. The rating is calculated by dividing the estimated number of people in the audience by the number of people in the population and multiplying the result by one hundred. The process depends, of course, on the assumption that in quantitative research our sample represents the population as a whole and the sub-samples who listen or watch represent the respective audiences. Let us take the following hypothetical example to illustrate:

We have data for a country that has six main television channels. The audience measurement system uses a representative sample of households and covers individuals in those households aged 4 and over. The population thus covered is 12 million. The sample used for the research is 2,000 individuals. (The measurement methods used, whilst very important, do not substantially affect the point I am demonstrating here. These data could come from diary, face-to-face interview or meter methods.)

Let us suppose that we want to provide ratings for a Monday evening at 2100. Looking through the analysed data we find that out of the 2,000 sampled, the following numbers were viewing TV at that time, broken down by the different available channels:

Channel 1	*305*
Channel 2	*298*
Channel 3	*236*
Channel 4	*132*
Channel 5	*15*
Channel 6	*34*
Other channels	*20*
Total viewing any TV	*1040*
Not viewing any TV	*960*
Total	*2000*

The sample represents the population. Therefore each sub-sample of the viewers of each channel represents all those listening to each channel in the population. We calculate the rating by the following formula:

$$Rating = \frac{Number\ listening\ to\ the\ channel}{Population} \times 100$$

So the rating for Channel 1 is calculated as follows:

$$\frac{305}{2000} \times 100 = 0.1525 \times 100 = 15.25$$

And for Channel 2:

$$\frac{298}{2000} \times 100 = 0.149 \times 100 = 14.90$$

Continuing with the same formula, we obtain the following ratings for each channel:

	%
Channel 1	*15.25*
Channel 2	*14.90*
Channel 3	*11.80*
Channel 4	*6.60*
Channel 5	*0.75*
Channel 6	*1.70*
Other channels	*1.00*
Total viewing any TV	*52.00*
Not viewing any TV	*48.00*
Total	*100.00*

Note the total rating – all those viewing any television – is 52. This means that just over half the population in the area of our survey was watching television at 2100 on the Monday in question.

As we should expect (and it is always wise to check to confirm the accuracy of ones calculations!) the ratings, together with the figure for non-viewers add up to 100. A rating is actually a percentage figure and each rating represents the percentage of the population (in this case everyone aged 4 and over in the coverage area). Therefore these ratings percentages can be used to calculate estimates of the numbers of people who were watching each channel at the time in question. This is done by the following formula:

Numbers of People = Network Rating × Population ÷100

Channels 1, 2 and 3 are in fairly close contention for being the leading channels at 2100 on Monday evenings. Using this formula we can estimate their audiences.

Channel 1: 15.25 × 12,000,000 ÷100 = 1,830,000

Channel 2: 14.90 × 12,000,000 ÷100 = 1,788,000

Channel 3: 11.80 × 12,000,000 ÷100 = 1,416,000

Advertisers use ratings to work out how much it costs to reach their target audience. They need to be able to work out the efficiency of an advertising placement on radio or TV to determine which selected spot is the most cost effective. One way to do this is to compute the *Cost per Thousand* – ie. what it costs the advertiser to reach one thousand people. It is calculated as follows:

$$\textit{Cost per Thousand} = \frac{\textit{Cost of Advertisement}}{\textit{Audience Size (in Thousands)}}$$

Exercise

If on Channel 1 the cost of a 30-second advertising spot is $20,000 and on Channel 3 $15,000, which channel has the lower cost per thousand? Calculate, using this formula, the cost per thousand of each channel. What is the difference between them?

Comment

You may think that the difference is small, but often this can be enough to switch a lucrative media campaign from one channel to another. If you enjoy calculations, you might like to look at what the cost of advertising on the other channels would need to be to compete with Channels 1 and 3 on cost per thousand criteria alone. You might draw the conclusion that Channels 5 and 6 would need to offer fairly low costs for advertisers. But this may not necessarily be the case. This is where demographic analysis comes in and can be so important. If the audience, although small, is nonetheless made up of a high proportion of a particularly attractive target group, the TV company may be able to attract advertisers seeking to reach such people and charge a premium rate. All media can do this. Their audience or readership may not be very large but they may still be successful at attracting advertising revenue at a relatively high rate. This is because they are reaching audiences defined by characteristics attractive to certain advertisers. For example sports equipment manufacturers might well be attracted to place advertisements on a sports channel, arts publishers on an arts channel, financial services companies in a financial weekly paper, farm equipment dealers in a commercial farmers' magazine, and so on.

A term often used in the buying and selling of advertising spots is *Gross Rating Point* or *GRP*. An advertiser or an advertising agency or 'media buyer' typically does not buy single advertising spots, but many at a time for a product campaign. An advertiser may want, for example, to buy 15 placements for an advertisement on a radio channel. He/she will want to know the gross audience they are likely to reach. Ratings data for past weeks will be used to calculate what can be expected.[67] The rating is multiplied by the number of advertising spots in each time period to give the Gross Rating Points or GRP in the last column.

Daypart	Number of advertisements	Rating %	GRP %
Weekday 0700-0800	5	8.6	43.0
Weekday 0800-0900	5	6.7	33.5
Weekday 0900-1000	2	4.1	8.2
Saturday 1200-1300	1	2.1	2.1
Sunday 1200-1300	2	3.0	6.0
Totals	15	(Avg) 6.19	92.8

These give a total GRP for the 15 advertisement campaign of 92.8 (the total in the right-hand column). This does not mean, of course, that nearly 93% of the population will hear at least one commercial. Many will hear the advertisements more than once and many others not at all. But it is a measure by which advertisers can get some idea of the overall exposure achieved by a campaign. There are other ways of making estimates of how many people are likely to actually hear at least one advertising spot, but those are beyond the scope of this manual.

9.3   Amount of Listening or Viewing, and Share

We can also use the figures from the imaginary TV market shown previously to compute the share of viewing at this particular time. For convenience I repeat the ratings chart here.

	%
Channel 1	15.25
Channel 2	14.90
Channel 3	11.80
Channel 4	6.60
Channel 5	0.75
Channel 6	1.70
Other channels	1.00
Total viewing any TV	52.00
Not viewing any TV	48.00
Total	100.00

First we have to exclude the non-viewers and recalculate the percentages. Note that share is defined as a measure of viewing or listening. The measure is derived from the commercial world where, for example, we might speak of the market share of soft drinks and mean by this the proportions of sales of soft drinks by each brand name or manufacturer. What we attempt to do here is to compute what share of all viewing is accounted for by each channel, just as we might use sales figures to work out what share of the soft drinks market was accounted for by Fanta, Pepsi Cola and so on.

With television and radio this is how we calculate share for viewing at a particular time:

$$Share = \frac{Channel\ Rating}{Total\ Rating} \times 100$$

So Channel 1's share would be:

$$\frac{15.25}{52} \times 100 = 29.3$$

You can work this out in another way and get the same result.

$$Share = \frac{Number\ Viewing\ Channel}{Number\ Viewing\ any\ TV} \times 100$$

In our sample representing the entire population, 305 people were watching Channel 1 and 1,040 people (2,000 less 960) were watching TV.

$$\frac{305}{1040} \times 100 = 29.3$$

Doing the same calculation for all the channels we get the following result:

	%
Channel 1	29.3
Channel 2	28.7
Channel 3	22.7
Channel 4	12.7
Channel 5	1.4
Channel 6	3.3
Other channels	1.9
Total	100.0

In the example I have used here, share has been worked out by using data from a particular time of day or *daypart* (a word often used in the advertising industry when talking about radio or television use). In this hypothetical case the time used was 2100 or 9p.m. But share is more often used as a measure of channel use over a longer period of time, usually a day or a week.

To illustrate this and to show how share can be calculated I will take the figures produced for television in the United Kingdom for the week ending 26 April 1998. BARB, the Broadcasters' Audience Research Board produces these figures every week. BARB is a joint company of the BBC and the Independent Television Association. The data are supplied by two research companies, RSMB and Taylor Nelson Sofres and are obtained from a representative sample of households where all the televisions are fitted with the TV meters described earlier.

UK Weekly Viewing Hours (including timeshift[69]) in April 1998

Avg Weekly Viewing (Hrs:Mins) per Person	
BBC1	7:13
BBC2	3:22
Total / Any BBC	10:35
ITV	7:56
Channel 4 or S4C	2:30
Channel 5	0:59
Total / Any commercial TV	11:25
Other channels	3:11
Any / All TV	25:11 [70]

It is important to note what these figures mean. It is rather unlikely that this represents any individual's viewing behaviour! The figures are obtained by adding up all the viewing to each channel and dividing the total by the number of individuals. They tell us that the average person in the UK living in a home with TV watched for 25 hours and 11 minutes in April 1998. Some watched a lot less and by the same token some a lot more. Some people devoted most of their viewing to one or two channels. Others watched several. All this table tells us, and it is quite a lot, is that this is what British TV viewers as a whole do.

We can use these average weekly viewing times to work out share. This is done by calculating each channel's viewing hours and minutes as a percentage of all viewing. This is done by converting each figure into minutes – remember that time is not decimalised!

The total amount of viewing, 25 hours and 11minutes becomes for our calculations 1,511 minutes. Let us take BBC1 in order to calculate its share. 7 hours and 13 minutes becomes 433 minutes.

$$\frac{433}{1511} \times 100 = 28.7$$

BBC1's share of viewing is 28.6. This means that of all viewing in that week, BBC1 accounted for 28.6%. The following table gives the results for all the channels.

UK Share of TV Viewing by Channel (including timeshift) in April 1998

	Share of Total Viewing %
BBC1	28.6
BBC2	13.4
Total / Any BBC	42.0
ITV	31.5
Channel 4 or S4C	9.9
Channel 5	3.9
Total / Any commercial TV	45.3
Other channels	12.6
Any / All TV	100.0

9.4 Reach

This measure is used to refer to the percentage of the population (aged over 4 or 12 or 15 or whatever) who listened to or watched at least some of a programme, or a network, or service or group of services during a day or week. Thus we have three common uses:

Programme Reach: The percentage who watch or listen to at least some of a programme (A minimum period needs to be defined. It could be a minute, or it could be at least five minutes. Practice varies.)

Daily Reach: The percentage of the population who watch or listen at least once to the network in question in a day. Sometimes a group of services or networks may be taken together. We might produce a figure giving reach for all or any BBC radio or TV service.

Weekly Reach: The percentage who watch or listen at least once in a week.

132

Note, that we can use reach to refer also to any use of TV or radio. We might want to know what the weekly reach of radio is in Nigeria – that is what percentage of the adult population listen to at least some radio, no matter what network, within an average week. In 1996, the weekly reach of radio among the adult population in Nigeria was 62%. But this hides a wide range of difference within the population. The following chart shows how uneven the weekly reach of radio is in Nigeria.

Weekly Reach of Radio in Nigeria among Adults (15+) in 1996

Sex	Men	72
	Women	55
Educational	No education	39
Achievement	Primary	62
	Secondary	78
	Tertiary	92
Age	15-29	70
	30-44	63
	45-59	57
	60+	42
Area	Urban	75
	Rural	57

A marked bias towards male, better-educated, younger and urban Nigerians is obvious from these data. Note that Nigerians without education are the least likely, from this analysis, to be radio listeners. Weekly reach among them is only 39%. Or to put it another way, 61% do not listen in an average week.[71]

Reach is a measure used in a variety of ways. Some public service broadcasters view it as particularly valuable and important. They need to know if their services are reaching the majority of the population who pay for them. They will usually also want to see if their reach is satisfactory among all segments of the population. Publicly funded broadcasters need to be able to show that they are serving all sections of the society. It may be that no single programme on a public service network enjoys the largest audience figures. But if a network or perhaps a group of networks run by the same company are appealing to many different tastes and interests they can, across a day or, even more so, a week, have an impressive reach. Thus, if we take BBC Radio Four in the United Kingdom, we find that at no time does its audience rating exceed 5%. That is to say that at no time is more than 5% of the population listening. However, it has a weekly reach of 17% of the population. In fact no BBC Radio network normally reaches an audience higher than about 5% at any time, but the weekly reach of each network as well as the commercial competition is shown in the following table.

133

Weekly Reach of Radio Stations in the UK in millions and percentage of population aged 15+ in 1st Quarter of 1998

	%	millions
BBC Radio 1	20.5	9.72
BBC Radio 2	18.8	8.95
BBC Radio 3	5.5	2.61
BBC Radio 4	17.2	8.16
BBC Radio 5	11.7	5.55
BBC Local or Regional Radio	18.7	8.89
Any BBC Radio	57.1	27.11
Classic FM	10.6	5.03
Talk Radio	4.8	2.27
Virgin Radio	8.8	4.21
Atlantic 252	6.5	3.10
Any Local Commercial Radio	50.1	23.82
Any Commercial Radio	60.5	28.74
Any Radio	85.5	40.64 [72]

We can compare these figures, for the first quarter of 1998, with the equivalent figures for 1991. Between these two dates, commercial, independent radio has enjoyed considerable growth, both in the number of stations operating and in their audiences.

Weekly Reach of Radio Stations in the UK percentage of population aged 4+ in 1991

	%
BBC Radio 1	28
BBC Radio 2	13
BBC Radio 3	5
BBC Radio 4	15
BBC Radio 5	4
BBC Local Radio	18
BBC Regional Radio	3
Any BBC Radio	58
(Commercial) Independent Local Radio	36
Other (Commercial)	8
Any Radio	76 [73]

There are some difficulties encountered in comparing the two figures. First, the data are reported in a slightly different way. The latest data do not include those aged between 4 and 15. The earlier data are reported only in whole numbers. But more importantly, the research methods changed between the two dates. Until 1992, radio audiences were measured by face-to-face interviews in which the respondent was asked to recall his or her listening. The *Daily Survey*, used for over sixty years was replaced by a diary system and it is on this that the first table here is based. However some things can be said with some certainty. The first is that although the BBC's share of listening has fallen, as one would expect with the growth in the availability of new radio networks, its reach among the population has hardly changed. Radio One's reach is substantially down, but Radio Two has increased by almost the same amount. Radio Five has increased its reach.

This is not the whole story of course. We also need to see who is reached and whether the service provided by the BBC is uneven across different sections of the population. But before doing that let us look at UK television figures.

The following chart shows daily and weekly reach figures for the main TV channels in the UK. The source of data is the same as for the previous charts showing share. These data are for the same week in April 1998. The figures for BBC2 are worth a second look. BBC2, the second publicly funded channel in Britain, tends to carry more minority interest programmes than BBC1, the mainstream popular channel. BBC2's largest audiences are about 10%, whereas the popular channels, BBC1 and ITV regularly achieve over 30% ratings. Yet BBC2's weekly reach – the percentage of the population who watch any of the channel's programmes – is an impressive 82%.

UK Reach of TV Channels (including timeshift) April 1998

	Daily reach %	**Weekly reach** %
BBC1	64.2	91.8
BBC2	42.8	82.2
Total / Any BBC	70.4	93.2
ITV	62.5	91.1
Channel 4 or S4C	37.6	79.7
Channel 5	15.6	39.7
Total / Any commercial TV	69.5	92.9
Other channels	19.5	28.7
Any / All TV	81.4	95.3

These data show that most TV viewers in the UK watch the four main channels, BBC1, BBC2, ITV and Channel4 (or S4C in Wales) in an average week. Rather fewer watch Channel 5, which is a relatively new channel and which, unlike the four main national channels, cannot be seen everywhere in the country. But the main point of interest to note here is that while a majority of the population view BBC1 and ITV on an average day, the same is not true of either BBC2 or Channel 4. They reach a majority of the population not within an average day but over seven days.

It is important for a broadcasting institution, funded by the public, to show that it serves all sections of the public. The following table shows the demographic profile of BBC TV channels and radio networks in 1997 together with the overall performance of the commercial competition, with the overall demographic profile of the UK population aged 4 years and over for comparison.

United Kingdom: TV and Radio Services:

Profiles of Audiences of Radio and TV, BBC and Commercial, by Age, Sex and Social Grade 1997

	Radio								Television						UK population
	Radio 1	Radio 2	Radio 3	Radio 4	Radio 5	LR/NR	Any BBC	Commercial	BBC1	BBC2	ITV	Channel 4	Channel 5	Sat/Cable	
Age															
4-15	7	1	2	1	3	2	3	8	11	13	11	11	11	22	18
16-24	31	2	2	1	6	3	9	16	7	7	7	9	11	10	11
25-34	32	5	6	8	16	7	13	23	14	13	14	15	17	19	15
35-44	15	9	8	15	21	10	12	20	13	14	13	13	14	18	15
45-54	8	20	18	23	21	17	17	15	14	13	14	13	14	14	14
55-64	4	28	27	22	17	23	20	10	14	13	14	13	13	9	11
65+	3	35	37	30	16	38	26	8	27	27	27	26	21	8	17
Sex															
Male	61	46	53	44	73	48	51	51	44	50	40	45	48	53	47
Female	39	54	47	56	27	52	49	49	56	50	60	55	52	47	53
Social grade															
AB	15	19	42	41	26	13	23	13	18	18	13	15	12	13	19
CI	30	33	32	34	32	26	31	27	26	27	24	25	23	24	27
C2	32	26	11	13	22	27	24	31	23	22	23	23	23	26	23
DE	23	22	15	13	20	34	22	30	33	33	40	37	42	37	31

BBC channels are shaded.   LR/NR = Local/National Regional Radio.   All figures are %.

Each of these columns gives what we call the demographic profile of the weekly audience to each network or channel. To achieve these figures we take the weekly reach data for each channel or network and break it down into the different categories. This is a tried and tested way of showing the characteristics of audiences, readerships, consumers or users of many services and products. Other categories could be added as appropriate – ethnic origin, language group, region, education, household size etc.

Demographic profiles need to be read with care. In each column the audience for each channel or network is broken down into its demographic components in order to compare it with the population as a whole. This is given here in the last column and is essential for comparative analysis.

There are many things we can learn about the BBC's audience from this chart. If we begin by looking at the Radio 1 column it can be seen that 31% of its audience is aged between 16 and 24. But in the column showing the composition of the UK population (aged 4 and over) we find that only 11% are in this age group. Radio 1 is attracting over twice as many people in this age group than it would if its audience matched the age composition of the population as a whole. The character of the Radio 1 audience as a 'pop' music station mainly targeted at young people is clearly reflected in its audience profile.

Note the very high male (73%) proportion of Radio 5's audience. Radio 5 carries a lot of sport. Sport is also a major attraction of satellite TV and this is probably the reason why satellite and cable TV has a high (53% compared to 47%) proportion of males. The higher social class of the audience profiles of both Radio 3 and Radio 4 reflects those networks' appeal to better educated listeners and the high correlation of educational achievement with social class in the UK.

Audiences for the BBC's Radios 2, 3 and 4 all have an older profile than the population as a whole. But note also that children of 15 and under are very under-represented in the radio audience, especially that of the BBC. Only 3% of the BBC's total weekly radio audience is in this very young age group compared with 18% of the population. Note that although commercial radio had a much higher proportion of children using it (8% of its listeners are children) this is still well short of 18%. The fact is that at present, children in Britain listen to radio much less than adults do. The difference is less with TV. Between 11 and 13% of terrestrial channels' audiences are made up of children. Note also that children are especially well represented (22%) in the audience for satellite and cable TV.

Readership Research

This book is primarily about how to do research into radio and television audiences. However, I believe audience researchers need to know about readership research and how to do it. They may have occasion to include some research into the use of newspapers and magazines in research about TV and radio. Moreover, there is a danger in always treating radio and TV consumption and use as something entirely separate from other media. Reading, listening and viewing are different activities, but they do overlap. People read newspapers, watch television and/or listen to the radio to be informed, entertained, follow their favourite football team, learn about new films, follow fashion or popular music and much else besides. There is much in common between the various media. They each may carry news, comment, entertainment, sport and a lot of other popular content. Some carry material designed to appeal to minority interests and tastes. Most of them carry advertisements.

They also have in common the demand for audience readership data. Who reads what, when, how often and what do they think of what they read? This demand comes mainly from the advertisers but newspaper and magazine writers, journalists, editors and managers are also interested in the behaviour, reactions and motivations of readers.

When there is no research into readership of magazines and newspapers, the only way an advertiser can evaluate a purchase of space for an advertisement is from publishers' claims. In some countries this is still all that there is. Publishers will usually tell advertisers how many copies they print. But there is often a large gap between what is printed and what is sold. And publishers are in no position to tell us anything about how many people read the paper or magazine or what kinds of people they are.

This is not to say that print and sales figures are of no value. Publishers usually keep a good record of how many papers they print and how many they sell. They can usually also show you something about the geographic distribution of sales. They will also know how sales can rise and fall with changes in content. For example, in some countries the publication of examination results at certain times of the year substantially increases sales, as also may a major news story or a special popular feature. Publishers usually have enough experience from the past to be able to anticipate such occasions and increase the print run. This kind of information can be useful but it is neither reliable nor comprehensive. Publishers will often claim how many readers per copy they have. But without reliable and regular research such claims are suspect.

Exercise

Contact local magazine and newspaper publishers and find out what they say about their publications. What claims do they make about sales and distribution and on what do they base these claims? Ask for an advertising rate sheet and note what it says about sales and readership.

10

The main method used to measure readership is the face-to-face interview in a general adult population survey. The measure in most common use in many countries is Average Issue Readership (AIR) which is an estimate of the number of people who will have read on average an issue of a newspaper or magazine.

Various methods are used to achieve this. The more common approach is to read out a list of magazine or newspaper titles, sometimes with a show card reproducing images of the title or front pages. Respondents are then asked when they last looked at or read any issue. Michael Brown, a leading expert in this field, describes how an AIR estimate is then made:

> *'The number claiming contact within a period of time preceding the day of the inter-view and equal in length to the interval between successive issues (the previous seven days, for example, in relation to a weekly magazine) is taken as an estimate of AIR. This technique is usually referred to as the recent reading (RR) method.'*[74]

This system is in widespread use in many parts of the world. The main problem is that people may not always remember accurately what they read or when they last read it.

Another method is to ask respondents about what they read yesterday. This method enables comparisons to be made with other media contact, including radio and television use. It does not make such great demands on memory as the previous method described here. It also fits in well with radio and television measurement and enables a fair comparison to be made between different media. However it does require very large daily samples to be taken for accuracy, especially if we are measuring readership of weekly and even more so of monthly publications and it probably causes under-estimates of readership of non-dailies.

Reading frequency is also often measured in surveys. Respondents are asked to estimate how often they read a particular publication by asking them to answer a question which gives a scale with labels such as 'most issues' or 'at least once per week' (for a daily paper) or 'occasionally'. Questions may be phrased to pick up habitual behaviour or they may relate to a fixed period such as 'within the last month'. The problem with such questions, like the same questions with radio and television, is that people can tend to over-estimate their frequency of readership. There is no equivalent with readership research to the peoplemeter method now extensively used to measure TV viewing in most developed markets. These measure not what people say they watch but what actually happens with TV sets in people's homes.

Just as questions about both broadcasting and print media may be asked in face-to-face interviews, both media may be included in a self-completion diary. Indeed it is quite common for a diary primarily used for radio or TV audience measurement to include questions which ask the respondent to record his or her newspaper or magazine readership each day. The main purpose is to compare the use of different media.[75]

Adapting Audience Research to Different Cultures

Audience and market research have developed in industrialised countries and many of the disciplines and procedures, as well as many of the assumptions on which research is based, are derived from the West. There is a strong emphasis on the individual in a lot of the research methods and processes I have described. This derives from the importance industrialised, liberal democratic systems place on individual choice and decision. Some cultures, especially in Africa and Asia, place significantly more emphasis on group responsibilities and decisions. It is therefore important to be ready to adapt research methods accordingly. But how can this be done? To adapt appropriately requires a thorough understanding of how different societies operate. But thorough studies by anthropologists may not exist already and can take a long time to complete.

A leading advocate of the cultural adaptation of market research methodology in less developed, non-industrial societies is Scarlett Epstein who has offered a very useful, practical and relatively simple approach. She provides a valuable checklist of what she calls *Key Cultural Variables*. I have reproduced it in the following chart together with, first, her explanation.

> *'[The Chart] sets out some of the most important cultural variables together with the extremes of possible options. It must be stressed here that this is not meant to represent an exhaustive list nor is it an attempt to predetermine cultural responses. All the list tries to do is to provide a set of key cultural variables that need to be considered when tackling the cultural adaptation in the limited time allocated to [market research]. With experience this list will of course be refined'.*

Key Cultural Variables

Cultural Variable	Extremes of possible options	
Unit of decision-making	individual	group
Ethos of social organisation	egalitarian	hierarchical
Patron-client relationships	situational	continuous
Allocation of status	achieved	ascribed
Prestige criteria	behaviour	expenditure
Kinship structure	patrilineal	matrilineal
Family organisation	nuclear	extended
Marriage arrangements	monogamy	polygamy
Residence pattern	patrilocal	uxorilocal
Gender relationship	equality	subordination
Land tenure	individual	group
Factionalism	interest-based	kin-based
Colonial experience	enlightened administration	exploitative administration [76]

11

Not all of these are of major importance in relation to the way media area used. However you cannot make that assumption without some investigation and enquiry. The checklist is not comprehensive; there may be other aspects of culture that have some impact and importance. I reproduce the list in order to remind us that societies can vary greatly. Market research, especially quantitative research, tends to consider the individual consumer as a separate decision-making unit. Equal weighting is given to each individual response. But we know that even in the most egalitarian, democratic societies, things are not in reality like this. People often defer to others, within families as well as other social groups. In some societies decisions are made jointly after discussion. It is fairly obvious that relationships between roles in the household can profoundly affect the way the media are used in the home. I told the story of the locked-away radio set in the Moroccan household. BBC research among Afghan refugees in 1986 found that many husbands prevented their wives from independently listening to the radio because, as one man put it "I do not wish my wife to listen to a strange man without me being present".

Traditional patron-client relationships, criteria for status and prestige and kinship structures can also have a considerable influence on the ways in which media are used within a household and within a social situation. For example, patron-client relationships and ascribed social status in some societies cut across linguistic and ethnic divides. You may also find that the connected power relationships in that society are reflected in what is and is not available through the media. The subordinate group may be left out of the media or served only inadequately.

Family organisation can be another important variable in understanding the way the media are used. In many societies, the care of the aged is a family responsibility. The elderly do not as a consequence, live alone. In other societies, older people tend to be independent and to live alone. Media access and use will be much affected by these differences. Extended families have an even greater impact. When in 1970 I was carrying out a survey of Lusaka, Zambia, the number of poor and ill-educated people who were claiming to watch television at least once per week seemed rather too high. On further examination – follow-up interviews with some of the people concerned – we discovered how some of this was happening. Television sets in those days were almost entirely confined to the homes of expatriates and wealthy Zambians. Wealth in Zambia was and is strongly correlated with education. But educational achievement was not closely related to caste, family or ethnicity. People with a university degree or other higher education with well-paid jobs always had relatives, sometimes quite close ones, with no education. The extended family would almost always include some who were very poor. Under the traditions of most Zambian ethnic groups, members of an extended family felt entitled to visit and watch television at the home of a better-off relative, and many did so.

The colonial experience of different countries had great influence on the development of modern media, an influence that continues today. Countries with French and Portuguese connections tended to give less importance to indigenous languages in their media. This is because under the French and Portuguese, indigenous languages tended to be neglected in favour of French or Portuguese. The British system of indirect rule tended (not in all cases) to give greater emphasis to indigenous languages.

Research should always have the purpose of enlightenment – to throw light on a subject – not to obscure things. And yet, if we use research tools in a mechanistic way and do not make the necessary adaptations that are called for in different circumstances we will not be doing our work professionally. The good audience researcher is always alert to the cultural and social realities of the societies he studies and is always ready to adapt his research methods and approaches accordingly. The exciting thing about audience research is that you are always breaking new ground. Nothing is the same everywhere. All social situations are different. People are wonderfully different and never stop being so. Your task is to use your skills to understand and, through research, help others also to do so.

How Research is Used

12

Research in the communications business – whether in advertising, press, radio or television, is not done for its own sake. It must have a purpose. All research costs money. If research is done very thoroughly and well, it can be quite expensive. How can we ensure that when we do research or use it we get good value for money?

12.1 Meeting the Challenge of Competition

We can look at a number of examples. Over the past few years, several public or state funded broadcasters first in the industrialised and now increasingly in less developed countries have faced the arrival of competition from new commercially funded independent broadcasters. Many of them, although not all, have seen the need for research to help them meet the challenge of competition by seeking to understand viewer and listener behaviour better so as to maintain audience loyalty. Research has also been an essential element in seeking to demonstrate publicly the value of continued support from public funds (licences, taxes or other) for publicly funded, public service broadcasting. Research can determine the use made by the public of various services which may not have high levels of overall popularity but which serve separate minority interests and tastes.

Commercial broadcasters usually target audiences with spending power in order to attract advertisers wishing to sell their goods and services. Public service broadcasters may do much the same. Many of them raise funds through advertising in precisely the same way. Both need audience research data to demonstrate to advertisers what kinds of people and how many are 'delivered' by different programmes or networks and at different times. But public service broadcasters have a wider mandate. Their purpose has to be to serve all the people of a country or region. They may seek to raise levels of cultural awareness and to produce programmes that are challenging, or educational or in other ways worthwhile in quality and content. Many public service broadcasters are major sponsors of the arts, employing orchestras and drama units, commissioning new examples of creative writing and new music. Many of these activities cost much more than some more popular entertainment programmes. Moreover, they may attract little advertiser interest and usually need public funding or subsidy. Audience research can be used to determine the level of public support that is not just a matter of numbers in the audience.

We find here that the concept of separate and distinct minority interests is important. Public service broadcasters can, through surveys and qualitative research, demonstrate support from those who appreciate the cultural fare on offer, even though quantitatively the audiences may not be large. They may seek to serve various minority interests through specially targeted programmes. The BBC in Britain, the CBC in Canada and many other public service broadcasting corporations have programmes for ethnic minorities, for farmers, for school leavers, for people interested in photography, antiques, philosophy or history. Sometimes such programmes can and do have a wider, even mass appeal. But support for such programming can come from those with strong attachments to these subjects. Specially targeted research can be designed to discover if the intended audiences of farmers, teachers or subject enthusiasts are being reached and, if so, what they think of the programmes.

More or less the same considerations apply in less developed countries, especially when commercial competition arrives to challenge the state-funded monopoly broadcasters. Commercial channels tend to do little or nothing for the very poor. They tend not to carry much programming for development, health, education and other services for the public good. To remain competitive, public service broadcasters may feel compelled to increase their production or purchase of popular entertainment programmes and at the same time reduce their commitment to and involvement in more developmental programming. Research can be a vital tool in efforts to find the right balance between the different objectives of entertainment, information and education that can ensure a maximisation to audiences for popular material at the same time as a continuing commitment to minority interests and education.

Public service broadcasting stations want to attract general audiences through making popular programmes of wide appeal, while retaining a commitment to quality in cultural output and good national and international news coverage. Audience research is an essential part of any strategy to do this. New Zealand's National Radio, reorganised and renamed recently to meet the intense competition of private stations, has made substantial use of audience research in this process. Research provided detailed information about the times of day different age groups listened and the different interests and preferences of these groups. For example, older listeners who were prominent among the afternoon audience, preferred European light classical music and wanted more of it. The network carried a lot already but this was not the perception of the listeners who like this kind of music. It was decided to devote an hour of classical music between 3 and 4 pm. After the change, research showed a favourable reaction. There was an increase in listening.

National Radio in New Zealand broadcasts a lot of news and current affairs especially during the morning peak when a news programme *Good Morning New Zealand* runs from 6 am to 9 am. Audience measurement, which in New Zealand is done by the diary method, showed a declining audience. Further investigation showed the audience loss was to a commercial competitor at 7 am. Some qualitative research through focus groups (group discussions) was commissioned. Some of these were conducted among existing listeners while others were from among those who had stopped listening to the programme. The research focused on four issues:

The morning routines of listeners and lapsed listeners and how these influenced listening habits

The characteristics of those who listen to National Radio and those who had lapsed

The characteristics of occasional and potential listeners

Reaction to the content and format of Good Morning New Zealand *and competitor stations' breakfast programmes, especially at 7 am.*[77]

When the groups met, extracts from both the National Radio and the competitor in the period 7 to 7.14 am were played. The results showed that National Radio's presentation at 7 am made it sound to listeners like the beginning of an hour long programme of in-depth interviews. By contrast the competitor provided a news summary with a roundup of local, national, international, sports, financial and weather news. National Radio's offering was not perceived as a news bulletin at all. It started with a bulletin at 7 am. but it was not clearly differentiated in the listeners' mind from what followed. As a result of this research, New Zealand's National Radio made changes to its *Good Morning New Zealand* running order.

Similar research in other industrialised or urbanised parts of the world into radio listening before work in the morning shows that listeners appreciate fairly rapid and concise summaries of the main news items, weather, traffic news and so on, interspersed with related reports and interviews. Usually, few people listen at this time to more than 30 minutes and the programme or sequence structure needs to take account of this. Most listeners will join and leave the programme at various points between its beginning and end. This is obviously because people get up at different times and leave for work, shopping, school etc. also at different times. Their radio listening (and television viewing routines also) is governed by these and other individual factors. If programme producers don't structure their programme accordingly, listeners may be lost, especially in an intensely competitive environment.

In RAI, the national public service broadcasting network in Italy, audience research took on a considerably enhanced role when, in the 1980s, the Italian broadcasting environment was transformed by competition. Hundreds of private TV and radio stations appeared during the period. Most of these new stations were small and lacked financial power to challenge RAI's dominance. However, there soon developed a large commercial radio and TV company, now one of the largest anywhere in Europe, Berlusconi's company Finninvest, which linked up many of these small stations into a major network and thus began to have the financial and organisational strength to make inroads into RAI's audiences. RAI has used audience research to meet this challenge.

RAI's audience research department, Servizio Opinioni, has used TV meter data to look in the minutest detail at the channel switching behaviour of viewers. When they switch from RAI1, RAI2 or RAI3, the three public service TV channels, where do they go? What is on the other channels and what are they switching away from? Through a detailed analysis of the data, the audience research department was able to answer these questions and the programme schedulers were able to make changes accordingly. As a result, and unlike many other public service channels in Europe, RAI has retained a share of around half the available audience. Critics argue that it has done so at the expense of quality in programmes. They point to the absence of documentaries on Italian TV and the higher level of what is seen as rather trivial light entertainment. However, RAI has used audience research also to segment its audience, that is to identify different tastes and interests and, most importantly, different lifestyles and times of viewing. It is this sort of research, using the now very detailed data available from electronic meters, which

145

can help public service or commercial broadcasters achieve their objectives better – of targeting different interests or groups with the material in which they are interested.

In Italy new RAI programmes are often pre-tested. Going back a stage, sometimes even before a pilot programme is made, a new concept or idea will be submitted for research. What do potential viewers or listeners think of the idea? RAI has also re-introduced the technique used in the United States in the 1930s and 1940s, of coincidental telephone inter-view, but not for audience measurement. Viewers or listeners have been asked for their opinions of what they have just heard or watched. One of the consequences of this research has been a strengthening of those aspects about which respondents have been positive.

As one of RAI's researchers explains, "RAI presents live broadcasting as its hallmark – both in news reporting and in light entertainment shows hosted by well-known personalities – and thereby creates an image of being constantly in touch with the real world. This is the result of a precise strategy."[78]

12.2   Understanding Audiences

The Ghana Broadcasting Corporation has a small audience research department which is there to "determine whether GBC is achieving the stated aims of broadcasting, namely to inform, educate, entertain and activate". It points out that Ghana has a particular need for audience research. The people who make the programmes "are usually people who have had a Western-oriented education. They live in urban areas and their cultural values and outlook may in some ways have alienated them from the relevant environments in which they operate. [They] cannot claim to have sufficient knowledge of their audience's habits, tastes, needs and aspirations".[79]

The attitude of both management and production staff is not always positive and helpful. Often audience research departments are bearers of bad tidings or report things that contradict or question existing assumptions. GBC's Audience Research Department warns new staff not to expect to be popular. There is an important task to be done to help prod-uction staff understand audience research and help them to produce better programmes.

Audience research can help broadcasters improve their capacity to raise revenue. Even in relatively poor countries it is necessary to obtain accurate audience data so as to determine appropriate prices for advertising at different times of the day on TV and radio. This has been one important function of the Ghana Broadcasting Corporation's small research unit since it was established in the mid 1950s.

Despite its modest facilities and budget, GBC's audience research has been able to show that a morning transmission on TV would be viable and that there was popular demand for football commentaries in indigenous Ghanaian languages. When research showed that schools were not using educational broadcasts intended for them these broadcasts were stopped and the problem was investigated before they were restarted. It was found that school timetables did not fit in well with the broadcast schedules. The subjects did not harmonise with what the schools were doing. Many schools did not have listening facilities; others had problems getting sets repaired and so tried to use them as little as possible! Some schools were not served by electricity and could not afford to buy dry cell batteries. Some of these problems have been overcome and, since the transmissions restarted, take-up has improved.[80]

Many TV stations pre-test films and imported programmes to find out beforehand what viewer reaction is likely to be. It may be that unanticipated reactions will be discovered. For example, it may be found that a particular series is appreciated more by older people but less by the generality of viewers. Such a programme might be placed at a time especially suitable for older people.

Many radio and television stations have meetings to review programmes. These programme review boards, as they are often called, usually include someone from the audience research department. He or she can perform a number of important and useful functions. Programme makers need advice on interpretation of whatever audience research data are available for the programmes being reviewed. Or it may be that the timing of the programme is being discussed. The researcher can come with evidence about audiences at the time of day when the programme is broadcast. Producers are often fond of quoting from listeners' and viewers' letters or phone-calls. "This programme series has been immensely popular. I have had a sack-load of mail" is a not uncommon boast. But it is an inadequate and unsatisfactory way of measuring popularity! Alternatively another person present at the meeting may say of a programme, "it's not very popular and we do seem to have had a lot of complaints". This is a no more reliable way to assess the true picture. Producers engaged in creative work pay a good deal of attention to the views of colleagues. These views are important and should be given proper consideration. But they are insufficient. We need to know in some detail what the listeners or viewers think and how they respond to the programme in question. The representative from the audience research department has the important and heavy responsibility of speaking for the listener and viewer. What validity do the letters have? Is the programme as popular as the producers' boast? Do the complaints or appreciative comments received from the audience reflect a general view?

The research expert won't always have answers to all the questions. Almost always there will be some things unknown or only partially covered by research. Programme reviews can have the vitally important role of linking research to the production process and of making a systematic and on-going study of the audience an integral part of the creative process in broadcasting and of the planning that goes into the commissioning and scheduling of programmes.

But the research department's members need to use great sensitivity. The former head of research at Czech Radio explained it to me in this way. "Radio employees consider themselves to be creative personalities and therefore they do not like to confess any outside influence at all." He went on to point out that audience research is only one of many influences on broadcasting decisions and it is not easy to separate one from another.[81]

Audience researchers need to have humility and common sense to accept that programmes should never be entirely led by audience research. But what is to be done when it appears that no notice is taken of their efforts? It is unprofessional for audience researchers to attempt to interfere; the task is to go on with the work of providing accurate, reliable and useful information, even when it appears that little use is being made of it.

A senior person in the BBC once told me he took no notice of the audience measurements and audience reaction data we provided for him. I later discovered that he wasn't telling the truth, for when I asked him about some schedule changes he had made and some revisions to programmes, he admitted, rather sheepishly, it was because of what he knew about audiences from our research! This story might be dismissed as a case of awkwardness on his part. I don't think that this was so. Audience research data tend to be absorbed by most people who see them. Often what happens is that people then forget where audience information came from. It becomes part of the intelligence along with much else besides, which they carry with them when making programmes, creating schedules, starting new initiatives and so on.

Interestingly, I find producers often much more interested in qualitative research than audience measurements. Watching video recordings or hearing audio cassettes made of group discussions about their programmes often fascinates them. It is the kind of feedback they get from no other source. Conversations they have with listeners or viewers tend to be coloured by politeness. Listeners' and viewers' letters are useful, even stimulating or infuriating. But nothing is the same as comments of members of the audience obtained in a neutral situation using professional researchers.

Some producers, not surprisingly, like to boast of the millions of viewers or listeners to their programmes. But there can be an unhealthy obsession with numbers. Audience researchers know that a change in audience from one week to the next of one percentage point is probably not statistically significant and may be within the margin of error inherent in all sample surveys. This is a dilemma for the researcher. He or she has to speak up and explain that the increase may not be real. But this would seem to be casting doubt on the value of the exercise among people who have a secret belief, perhaps, that surveys are a bit doubtful anyway! Sensitivity, a thick skin and persistence are all qualities needed in our profession!

Research by itself neither achieves nor improves anything. It is the intelligent use of data from research, combined with other relevant information and the creativity of the programme makers that have impact. Research doesn't make decisions or changes, although sometimes the results of research point firmly in a certain direction. Usually in my experience information about audience behaviour or response will enable programme makers, schedulers, planners, announcers and many others in the industry, to make more informed choices and decisions in their work.

It is difficult to prove a link between improved broadcasting performance and audience research. One audience research executive told me that over the past few years his management has paid increasing attention to research. Audience sizes had increased and audiences were a little more satisfied than previously but they could not prove that these outcomes were due to research or to taking notice of it.

What matters most are high standards in research and a commitment by management to the activity and to the use of the results. Research, supported by management, will address the concerns of the organisation and, if professionally and thoroughly carried out, research can only enhance the ability of the organisation to meet objectives, to grow, to improve and to change when change is necessary. Any business enterprise or public service requires accurate and relevant information. In a broadcasting organisation, audience research supplies an essential area of information about broadcasting activity.

Audience research can have a very important role in the development of broadcasting. In India, research has been used to provide information to guide decisions about the new television and radio services of the state broadcasters, All India Radio and Doordarshan. In the last few years many new local radio services have been started. In each case, surveys of radio listening habits in the locality were conducted at the planning stage.

Television development in India has been guided by audience research since 1982 when national television began in India. Doordarshan has gradually been extended to all main urban centres and into rural areas. Audience research was used to plan this development in a very mixed and large country. Research provided information on timing, content and language for the new programmes. Research showed, for example, that television in India would succeed more if it made full use of the visual aspect of the medium and less reliance on the spoken word. Research also enabled the planning and development of successful new programme series.[82]

149

12.3   Strategic Research – Seeing the Big Picture

The global and economic context of the media is undergoing rapid change. Even in the relatively short period of five years between the first and this edition of this book, there have been some far-reaching changes in media in many parts of the world, not confined to the highly developed industrialised countries.

The changes have been both in technology and in the regulatory environment. Consumer behaviour is also changing. Indeed, I find it helpful to think of the changes in media environments as having these three characteristics:

1. *Technological*
2. *Regulatory*
3. *Behavioural*

The technological changes are easy to see all around us, although things can happen with such bewildering speed that it is difficult for one to keep up-to-date with what is happening. One major development is in satellite delivery of television direct to homes or to cable-heads for onward transmission to homes. The arrival of satellite and cable has, over the past few years, transformed entirely the mass media environment in India (as well as other parts of South and East Asia). From the situation that existed until 1990 – a single state-run television monopoly alongside a state radio monopoly – we now see a situation in which millions of households have a choice of many TV channels, both Indian and foreign. Until the arrival of satellite and cable, the number of television channels available was restricted by a combination of political regulation and the physical limitation on the amount of terrestrial spectrum (ie. the Hertzian frequency bands available for use by TV, after reserving other parts of the spectrum for radio, for mobile phones, for the police, emergency services, the defence forces and much else besides). In most countries it is not possible to provide more than five or six TV channels by terrestrial means to any one area. Satellite transmission uses an entirely different part of the spectrum, delivering new capacity. And cable does not use any Hertzian spectrum at all.

Satellite and cable are greatly increasing the number of channels available in many countries. Digitalisation of transmission and reception, of both TV and radio, takes the process much further and allows several times as many channels in the same spectrum used by existing analogue services. But not only can the digital 'revolution' increase the number of channels, it can also transform the way we use both media. This was explained recently by Johann Rupert, managing director of Richemont, one of the largest groups in the world's rapidly developing pay-TV industry. Richemont is joint owner with the South African group, MultiChoice, of the Nethold Corporation which provides satellite TV services to Europe, the Middle East and Africa. It was the first to introduce digital television by satellite to Africa and Europe in 1995. Without going into too much technical detail, the main point to remember about digitalisation of radio and TV is that it enables not only many more channels to be carried (as well as providing the opportunity of inter-active services and much more) it also allows the services to be 'packaged' in an entirely different way from what we have been accustomed to over the past eighty years of analogue radio and sixty years of analogue TV. Digitally delivered TV can offer to subscribers 150 or more channels. This is what Rupert said:

> *"With such a variety of choice it is clear that consumers will approach the media differently. For instance, the navigation system is based on menus classifying the content in specific categories: cinema, sport, art, music, and so on. Then through the use of the remote control one can select an item, sport for instance, and other sub-menus will appear allowing more detailed choices, a game of golf, or whatever. There would then be five or more tournaments to choose from. Such changes in the architecture of choice will make irrelevant what particular network one is watching. Tomorrow we will not be able to tell whether we are watching NBC or CBS, or at least this could be one of the possible outcomes."* [83]

The last sentence hints at a wise caution. Neither Johann Rupert nor Rupert Murdoch nor any other major media tycoon knows what consumers will do, although they will make some intelligent and quite well informed guesses. Of course, they will also seek to influence consumer behaviour. But merely because a technology can do something does not mean that this is how it will be used. The analogy of the marketplace helps us here. No one knows how viewers with a new array of choice of networks and programmes, presented in a different way, will actually behave. We have seen this with a previously introduced new technology. The VCR or video recorder is capable of recording TV programmes so that they can be watched later. But relatively little viewing is accounted for by 'time-shift' viewing. Most use of the VCR in most countries, although this varies a good deal between them, is for watching purchased, borrowed or rented videos. Audience research tells us how people use their VCRs and their TV sets. In the same way it will also be used to show the owners and planners in TV companies like Nethold and its many affiliates, just how its new digital services are actually being used. And from this information will come decisions on future marketing strategies, what networks and programme streams will be offered, and so on.

Optical fibre, replacing traditional cables, is also making major changes to the media situation by providing greatly expanded capacity. Optical fibre cables are already delivering telephone and computer services to houses and businesses at the same time and in the same way as they deliver television. Writers on the media speak of the *convergence* of the technology and the services they provide – convergence that is between point-to-point and broadcast communications. It should also be noted that digitalisation also substantially increases the capacity of ordinary copper telephone lines which can be used not only to link up computers as on the Internet, but also to carry television and radio channels.

It is sometimes argued that new technologies are less relevant to the poorer majority in the world. This is actually not true. The transistor radio, developed from the discovery in 1948 of the semi-conducting properties of silicon by the Nobel Physics Prize winning team of Bardeen, Brattain and Shockley, transformed radio into a truly global mass medium. Its impact was far greater in the less developed world than in the developed, because the transistor liberated the radio from reliance on electricity supply which was, and still is, unavailable in many millions of households. The transistor was a technology that met the needs of the relatively poor. Today, satellite phones and fax machines can be found in Somalia, mobile phones are in extensive use in Lagos, Nigeria, and cable and satellite television thrives throughout India. War, crime and a state monopoly of terrestrial television have made each of these three new technologies of particular relevance and attractiveness in each case respectively.

No part of the world is unaffected, but a lot of people are unaffected. It is often pointed out that there are more telephones on New York's Manhattan Island than in all of Africa. There are more radio sets in Britain than in the whole of sub-Saharan Africa. Developments in technology are often very uneven and audience research can throw up some surprising and thought-provoking data. A few years ago would anyone have supposed that today there would be more households in most Indian states with a television set than with a radio? What has happened in India has shown that a new technology will succeed when it meets demand, perhaps in unforeseen ways.

Everyone said radio would be the most important medium in India. It is often said that despite the growth of television, radio will go on reaching the poor. But this is not the case. Radio has reached a peak in India, reaching less than half the population. And television now reaches more people in India than radio.

The following data are taken from surveys between 1995 and 1998 in eight states and the capital New Delhi. The states – Madhya Pradesh, Bihar, Maharashtra, Tamil Nadu, Uttar Pradesh, Punjab, Haryana and Himachal Pradesh, together with the capital city Delhi, represent an adult population of 339.6 million people – about 54% of India's population aged 15 and over. These state-wide surveys used representative samples of the entire adult populations in each, so we are dealing here with very comprehensive and widely representative data.

What I have done here is to combine the data from each of these states. This has to be done carefully and with proper attention to the respective size of each state. For example, Uttar Pradesh has a population that is nearly thirty times as large as that of Himachal Pradesh. Obviously I cannot just add together the results equally from each state. What one does when adding different survey results together is to weight each according to the respective population size.

The table shows how analysis of data like these can give us a picture of the spread and use of the media and how they highly correlated with such things as educational achievement, age, sex and area. The table shows how radio and television reach, or do not reach different population groups.

Media Access and Use in India – Analysis from Eight States

	All	Sex		Age			Education				Area	
		Male	Female	15-29	30-44	45+	No formal	Primary	Secondary	Tertiary	Urban	Rural
All adults (age 15+)	100	100	100	100	100	100	100	100	100	100	100	100
Media equipment												
Have a Radio	35	39	31	38	34	32	20	38	58	72	49	30
Have a Television	33	34	32	34	33	31	14	36	63	79	70	19
Have both Radio & TV	18	20	16	19	18	17	6	18	40	61	40	10
Have Neither	50	47	54	47	52	54	71	44	20	9	21	61
Weekly audiences												
Radio	33	40	25	38	32	27	18	39	54	57	37	31
Television	48	54	41	55	47	38	24	57	80	88	78	36
Radio but not TV	12	13	10	12	11	12	12	14	10	7	5	14
TV but not Radio	27	27	26	29	27	22	17	32	36	39	46	19
Both Radio & TV	21	27	15	26	20	15	6	25	44	50	32	17
Either Radio or TV	60	67	51	67	59	50	35	71	90	95	83	51
Neither	40	33	49	33	41	50	65	29	10	5	17	49 [84]

152

There is a wealth of data here for you to study. Note just a few of the outstanding pieces of information supplied by this table. The first is that although there are still slightly more people with radio than television sets at home, more people watch TV than listen to radio, or to be more precise, more people are reached weekly by TV than by radio. Radio reaches fewer people in all demographic groups used for analysis here.

I did the same analysis with data from several Indian states three years ago. At that time I found that it was only among those with no formal education and in rural areas that radio continued to reach more people than television, but the margin was small. These latest results show that TV now reaches more illiterate people than radio.

But note how many people are left out entirely. While many Indians now have access to multi-channel television, half the population has no access at home to either television or radio. Note also the large proportion reached by neither radio nor TV in an average week. 40% overall and 49% in rural areas. 65% of those with no formal education are reached by neither radio nor TV in an average week.

Exercise

Take some time just to study the table more closely. What other facts about radio and television in India do they reveal apart from what I have already noted above? I have provided only a limited analysis here showing results cross-tabulated by sex, age, education and urban/rural area. What other analysis might you want to do in order to learn something more about the media in India and the way in which they are now being used?

These results were obtained from eight separate surveys conducted face to face with 5,000 or more adults aged 15 and over in each of eight states. The samples were selected in each case to represent the entire adult populations of each state. Fieldwork was conducted between the beginning of 1995 and the end of 1997.

Television in India has grown very fast in the last few years, especially since 1991 when satellite television services began to become available, mainly via cable, and broke the state monopoly of terrestrial TV held by Doordarshan. Doordarshan has responded to the challenge and has successfully held on to a high audience share by diversifying the appeal of its programmes and by offering more entertainment and choice. Radio in India, by contrast, has continued to enjoy (if that is the word) a state monopoly and this fact may be a major reason for the decline in radio use. Some privately run entertainment radio services have been started in some larger cities, but radio in India remains a very poor cousin of television and the decline in listening is not really surprising.

In India, as elsewhere, we are seeing changes in technology, economics and culture interweaving in the mass media in a fascinating way. Quantitative research can show us how media are actually used and measure the changes accurately. But different methods are needed to understand what is happening. Those numbers from India tell us nothing at all about what people are doing with the new television services they are now enjoying. Other methods, mainly of a qualitative nature, are required to help us to understand how media are used. We must beware of making assumptions from quantitative data. Viewers and listeners interact with the media they use. They do not merely 'consume' them. .

One thing however needs to be remembered at all times by anyone involved in using audience research. It is never the whole story and can never provide all the answers. It does not substitute for imagination and creativity. Audience research cannot tell if a new idea will translate successfully into a programme or series. It can only, with considerable difficulty, tell if a new series or programme type is likely to be popular. What it can do is to provide the kinds of information, both of a quantitative and qualitative kind, which will enable creative programme makers to make decisions and give those decisions a better likelihood of success.

The death in 1991 of radio producer and writer Andrew Boyle reminded me of one such case. Before 1965 at 1.00 pm. there was a news bulletin on the BBC's Home Service (later renamed Radio Four), followed by various programmes, not of current affairs. Audiences were small. Andrew Boyle, then in charge of some existing current affairs programmes on BBC radio, was convinced that a large audience could be built for an extended news magazine programme at this time. Another idea he had was that instead of using a trained BBC newsreader as presenter to employ a Fleet Street journalist (and one whose spoken style made most BBC voice specialists wince!) The programme, *The World at One* was very successful, both in gaining audience and in enhancing the BBC's public service position. The successful programme team put together by Boyle went on to add two other similar programmes with similar degree of success. Audience research can supply some information to help decisions of this kind. It can show low audiences at a time when they could be higher. It can even research what people might be interested in hearing. It can even try our new programme ideas by using test or pilot programme material in discussion groups. But all this effort works best in harness with the creative energy and ideas of talented and imaginative programme makers.

Appendices

Appendices

List of 396 random numbers between 1 and 1000

885 277 506 74 975 411 335 358 157 615 524 699 464 577 597 59 453 88
272 396 902 895 696 180 613 813 721 576 824 16 66 610 15 403 148 950
470 224 187 718 353 159 384 371 411 786 622 104 675 196 818 554 885 525
851 613 158 942 464 233 589   6 52 724 951 314 338 784 333 878 496 477
583 236 627 341 528 992 91 305 369 817   8 803 230 859 618 415 745 309
710 37 679 828 684 341 555 128 903 909 126 311 686 458 193 676 741 332
566 437 415 169 775 345 164 304 900 347 936 426 32 280 355 524 136 309
933 367 368 786 783 392 681 538 883 896 375 781 696 998 967 420 215 195
 68 348 515 709 557 569 461 639 781 898 415 464 995 326 992 499 168 264
199 852 959 966 338 248 734 106 472 879 385 671 759 374 89 869 422 43
242 193 166 589 919 283 377 911 827 17 320 612 189 978 765 862 834 910
803 351 83 608 939 858 700 977 30 932 496 737 283 241 448 72 205 839
220 586 635 190 646 556 131 796 118 877 151 961 528 52 687 466 135 24
106 817 915 86 299 956 24 258 652 662 679 401 522 308 11 307 134 373
717 61 731 86 195 807 521 232 964 387 25 780 244 929 403 357 832 126
486 893 862 136 525 683 196 540 321 644 773 710 863 410 509 681 155 907
559 851 359 320 117 124 173 451 334 515 822 510 711 92 250 320 669 272
964 750 793 814 37 465 426 56 482 605 684 320 35 997 850 414 444 661
 66 131 645 247 919 375 884 634 833 72 896 929 745   1 979 858 351 191
338 228 950 643 214 416 541 879 452 44 548 783 937 435 534 992 115 44
894 422 171 71 330 737 238 533 604 993 388 785 93 478 141 388 408 134
704 927 570 646 571 601 934 124 219 550 937 526 311 314 300 846 300 842

Many computer programmes can generate random numbers. They are also printed in some books on statistics.[85] Or you can create random numbers yourself. This is how PG Moore describes the process of creating random numbers, in his excellent book on statistics, now unfortunately out-of-print.

A table can be constructed with two ordinary dice, one red and one black, as follows. The two dice are thrown simultaneously. If the black die turns up 1, 2 or 3, then the red die gives a random digit from 0 to 4 as shown in [the table]. A red 6 is ignored and a re-throw of the dice takes place. Similarly, if the black die is 4, 5 or 6, then the value of red die indicates the random digit between 5 and 9 (again a red 6 is ignored and a re-throw follows).

Table Construction of Random Digit

Black	1 or 2 or 3					4 or 5 or 6				
Red	1	2	3	4	5	1	2	3	4	5
Random digit	0	1	2	3	4	5	6	7	8	9

For example, if a four-digit random number were required the dice will be thrown four or more times. Suppose the results were:

Throw	Black	Red	Random digit
1	3	5	4
2	5	4	8
3	1	1	0
4	2	6	(re-throw)
		2	1

The corresponding number is 4,801.[86]

Reliability of Estimates

The following two tables, derived from well-established statistical formulae, should be used to help you and those who use your quantitative results to determine the strength and reliability of the data. The first table helps you to estimate the sampling error for any single result – that is the likely true figure within a probable range of numbers.

Confidence Levels for a Single Percentage Result for Different Sample Sizes at the 95% Level.

Sample size

%	50	100	150	200	250	300	400	500	700	1000	1500	2000	3000	5000	%
50	14.1	10.0	8.2	7.1	6.3	5.8	5.0	4.5	3.8	3.2	2.6	2.2	1.8	1.4	50
60	13.9	9.8	8.0	7.0	6.2	5.7	4.9	4.4	3.7	3.1	2.5	2.2	1.8	1.4	40
R 70	13.0	9.2	7.5	6.5	5.8	5.3	4.6	4.1	3.5	2.9	2.4	2.0	1.7	1.3	30 R
E 80	11.3	8.0	6.5	5.7	5.1	4.6	4.0	3.6	3.0	2.5	2.1	1.8	1.5	1.1	20 E
S 85	10.1	7.1	5.8	5.0	4.5	4.1	3.6	3.2	2.7	2.3	1.8	1.6	1.3	1.0	15 S
U 90	8.5	6.0	4.9	4.2	3.8	3.5	3.0	2.7	2.3	1.9	1.5	1.3	1.1	0.9	10 U
L 92	7.7	5.4	4.4	3.8	3.4	3.1	2.7	2.4	2.0	1.7	1.4	1.2	1.0	0.8	8 L
T 94	6.7	4.7	3.9	3.4	3.0	2.7	2.4	2.1	1.8	1.5	1.2	1.1	1.0	0.7	6 T
95	6.2	4.4	3.6	3.1	2.8	2.5	2.2	1.9	1.6	1.4	1.1	1.0	0.9	0.6	5
96	5.6	3.9	3.2	2.8	2.5	2.3	2.0	1.8	1.5	1.2	1.0	0.9	0.7	0.6	4
97	4.8	3.4	2.8	2.4	2.2	2.0	1.7	1.5	1.3	1.1	0.9	0.8	0.6	0.5	3
98	4.0	2.8	2.3	2.0	1.8	1.6	1.4	1.3	1.1	0.9	0.7	0.6	0.5	0.4	2

[87]

For any percentage result you wish to check, you obtain the confidence interval or margin of likely error with a 95% degree of confidence by reading off the figure against the column with the appropriate sample size.

Exercise

Your survey of 1,000 randomly selected adults produces a figure of 10% for household ownership of at least one colour television set. What is the confidence interval and what does this mean?

Comment

We can be 95% confident that the true picture lies somewhere between 8.1% and 11.9% because the confidence level for 10% (or 90%) with a sample of 1,000 is 1.9.

Remember that the sample size you should use when employing this table will not in all cases be the entire sample. Let us suppose that you are dealing with a sub-sample. Of those with a colour television, 40% have the capacity to receive the new digital transmissions. What is the probable range of the true figure now? The sub-sample size is 100 – those with at least one colour TV – 10% of 1,000. The chart shows you that the probable margin of error is much larger, at 9.8%, so that we can say that the 'true' figure for colour set owners with digital capability lies somewhere between 30.2 (40 – 9.8) and 49.8 (40+9.8).

When we want to compare two results taken from different samples of the same or different sizes we can do two things. You could use the above table and use it for each result. The test is simple. Is the margin of error you obtain with each greater or less than half the difference between the two results? If it is greater then we have to say that the difference between the two results may not represent any real change. If however the two figures we get from the table are less than half the difference between the results then we can be 95% sure that the difference represents a real one.

Let us try this with the real example used in the text. The radio station's weekly reach had fallen from 43% to 37%. Both samples were 2,000. I have not produced a full set of possible percentage results on this table, not even of whole numbers because there is no space for such detail. However, this does not matter very much. We choose the nearest percentage: 40%. The plus or minus margin of error for this result with this sample size is 2.2. This is less than half the difference between the two results (half of 6 is 3) so we can be 95% confident that this radio station's weekly reach really has fallen. If the sample size were only 1,000, the margin would 3.1% – greater than half the difference, although only just – and we could not then say that the change was significant.

If the sample sizes are different, proceed in the same way but remember to use the different columns for the different sample sizes. If with our radio station example the first sample had been 1,000 and the second 2,000, we would obtain two margins of error – 3.1 and 2.2 respectively. The average of these two is 2.65, less than half the difference between the results so we would be able to say that the change in audience figures is significant.

Another way to discover whether any difference between two results is significant is to use the χ^2 or chi squared test. There are several uses of this formula but one of the most common is in the analysis of survey data. The chi-squared test is used to determine whether one result differs from another more than is likely to be the result of chance. There is not the space here to explain the chi-squared formula, but below is a much-simplified table derived from it. It is not possible in limited space to give more than a few sample combinations. Choose the ones nearest that apply.

The formulae used to create these tables, and other formulae like them for calculating confidence levels, margins of error and significance, are to be found in any good book on statistics. There are some suggested titles in the bibliography.

	RESULT				
	10 or 90	20 or 80	30 or 70	40 or 60	50
4000 and 4000	1.3	1.8	2.0	2.1	2.2
2000 and 2000	1.9	2.5	2.8	3.0	3.1
S 2000 and 1000	2	3	3	4	4
A 2000 and 500	3	4	4	5	5
M 1500 and 500	3	4	5	5	5
P 1000 and 1000	3	4	4	4	4
L 1000 and 500	3	4	5	5	5
E 1000 and 100	6	8	9	10	10
750 and 750	3	4	5	5	5
S 750 and 250	4	6	7	7	7
I 500 and 500	4	5	6	6	6
Z 500 and 250	5	6	7	7	8
E 500 and 100	6	9	10	11	11
S 250 and 250	5	7	8	9	9
250 and 100	7	9	11	11	12
100 and 100	8	11	13	14	14 [88]

Examples of Audience Research in Action

On the following pages I have used examples from audience research practice around the world, first to give some examples of questionnaires that have been used and then to give some examples of the presentation of results. The focus is on quantitative research.

MEDIA QUESTIONNAIRE IN ZAMBIA

SELECTION PROCEDURE

SPEAK TO ANY RESPONSIBLE MEMBER OF THE HOUSEHOLD
I am working for a group of radio and television companies. We are conducting a survey of radio, TV etc.and would like to ask you a few questions. (Or an alternative, introduction.)

S1   May I know the name of the head of this household? Please tell me the full address of this house.
Name
Address
Telephone

S2   How many members are there in your household? Please include children and lodgers and anyone who shares your kitchen, but exclude guests and servants who have their own homes

S3   Among these members, how many children are there below 15 years of age?

S4   Please tell me the names and ages of all males/females who are 15 years
Enter the names and ages of people in the household aged 15 years and over starting with the oldest and working down to the youngest. Look along the row of the last person in the list. Where this meets the column of the last digit of the questionnaire number is the number of the person in the list to be interviewed.

Name	Age	1	2	3	4	5	6	7	8	9	0
1		1	1	1	1	1	1	1	1	1	1
2		2	1	2	1	2	1	2	1	2	1
3		3	1	2	3	1	2	3	1	2	3
4		2	3	4	1	2	3	4	1	2	3
5		1	2	3	4	5	1	2	3	4	5
6		4	5	6	1	2	3	4	5	6	1
7		7	1	2	3	4	5	6	7	1	2
8		5	6	7	8	1	2	3	4	5	6
9		4	1	2	3	4	5	6	7	8	9
10		1	2	3	4	5	6	7	8	9	10

The rest of the questionnaire is to be administered to the selected member.

If selected member not available, two more attempts are to be made at times when he/she is likely to be at home.

If you are not able to interview the selected member note the reason below and substitute with a new household.

Respondent's name (Original/substitute)
Address of substitute

Reason for substitution:
Could not contact   1
Away from home   2
Refused   3
Other   4

1. Media Survey Questionnaire in Zambia
This was used in an *ad hoc* survey conducted face-to-face with a sample of adults throughout Zambia in 1995. I have reproduced the first five pages. Note the grid method of choosing the respondent at each household (S4). Note the clear interviewer instructions which say where to go next when there is a Yes/No question or one with alternatives requiring different questions to follow (Qs. 5, 8, 11, 14). Note with Q15, three questions are asked about yesterday radio listening – two linked questions about times of listening, and the station(s) listened to. Note that in this survey the intervals are of 30 minutes.

ASK ALL RESPONDENTS

Q1   What is your main source of entertainment?
DO NOT READ OUT LIST – MULTIPLE ANSWERS POSSIBLE – CIRCLE ALL CODES WHICH APPLY
IF RESPONDENT SAYS THEY ENJOY LISTENING TO RADIO, ASK THEM WHETHER THAT IS ZAMBIAN OR
FOREIGN RADIO AND CODE ACCORDINGLY

    Visit friends/relatives' houses.................1
    Go to the local pub/bottle store............ 2
    Watch television.....................................3
    Watch video...4
    Listen to ZNBC radio.............................5
    Listen to foreign radio stations.............. 6
    Go to the cinema.....................................7
    Visit night clubs/discos..........................8
    Read books/newspapers........................9
    Play sports...A
    Listen to records or cassettes...............B
    Other (Write In)..................................... C

Q2   I am going to read to you a list of topics, for each one please tell me if you are interested in it or not.
CIRCLE CODE FOR EACH ONE INTERESTED IN. READ OUT LIST ROTATE START OF LIST FOR EACH
INTERVIEW AND MARK WHERE YOU BEGIN – MULTIPLE ANSWERS POSSIBLE

    Football commentaries.. 1
    Other sports 2
    Medicine/Health 3
    Political events in Africa 4
    Political events in Zambia.. 5
    Economic issues in Zambia... 6
    Relationships between men and women
    (eg problems in marriage, at work etc.) 7
    Relationships between generations
    (eg problems between youth and elders)... 8
    Scientific/technological advancement... 9
    Agriculture .... A
    AIDS .... B

Q3   I am now going to read to you a list of different types of music. For each one, please tell me if
you enjoy listening to it or not.
CIRCLE CODE FOR EACH ONE ENJOYED. READ OUT LIST ROTATE START OF LIST FOR EACH INTERVIEW
AND MARK WHERE YOU BEGIN – MULTIPLE ANSWERS POSSIBLE

    Zambian music...1
    Reggae.. 2
    Calypso... 3
    Disco... 4
    Pop.. 5
    Rhumba... 6
    Rock..7
    Classical.. 8
    Soul... 9
    Country.. A
    Gospel... B
    Jazz... C
    Traditional music...D
    Other music (specify)...E

Q4   Have you ever heard of any of the following magazines (It does not matter whether you have read
them or not) ?
CIRCLE APPROPRIATE CODE. READ OUT LIST

Magazine	Aware of magazine?	
	Yes	No
Newsweek	1	2
Jeune Afrique	1	2
Time	1	2
Focus on Africa	1	2
Economist	1	2

161

Q5   Have you read any newspapers or magazines in the last 12 months?

Yes....................1 → *CONTINUE*
No ....2 → *GO TO Q11*

Q6   Which, if any, of the following newspapers or magazines have you read in the last 12 months
READ LIST

Q7   When did you last read..............................*(MENTION EACH NEWSPAPER OR MAGAZINE READ IN THE
LAST 12 MONTHS)? FIT ANSWER TO CODES IN GRID BELOW*

Names of newspapers/magazines 12 months	Q6 Read in last		Q7 Last read			
	Yes	No	Y	7D	P4W	12M
Times	1	2	1	2	3	4
Daily Mail	1	2	1	2	3	4
Financial Mail	1	2	1	2	3	4
The Post	1	2	1	2	3	4
The Chronicle	1	2	1	2	3	4
The Sun	1	2	1	2	3	4
Focus on Africa	1	2	1	2	3	4
The National Mirror	1	2	1	2	3	4
Beauty/fash!on magazines	1	2	1	2	3	4
Other (Please specify)	1	2	1	2	3	4
Other (Please specify)	1	2	1	2	3	4
Other (Please specify)	1	2	1	2	3	4
Other (Please specify)	1	2	1	2	3	4

Key
Y=Yesterday
7D=Within last 7 days
4W=Within last 4 weeks
12M=Within last 12 months

Q8   How do you get to read newspapers? Do you buy your own, borrow from friends or
available at work? *MULTIPLE ANSWERS POSSIBLE CIRCLE ALL CODES WHICH APPLY*

I buy my own.. 1 → *ASK Q9*
I borrow from friends....................................... 2 → *GO TO Q10 IF CODE '1' NOT CIRCLED AS WELL*
I read newspapers available at work.............. 3 → *GO TO Q10 IF CODE '1' NOT CIRCLED AS WELL*

Q9   How many other people read your newspapers after you have finished?

No-one eise.. 1
One or two others... 2
Three or four others.. 3
Five or more others... 4

Q10   Which sections of the newspaper do you pay particular attention to?
MULTIPLE ANSWERS POSSIBLE CIRCLE ALL CODES WHICH APPLY

Front page... 1
Sports.. 2
Business section... 3
Features.. 4
Classifieds.. 5

Q11   Now I will ask you some questions about radio listening. Have you listened to the radio in the last
12 months? It does not matter whether you listened to it at home or somewhere else.

Yes....................1 → *CONTINUE*
No ....2 → *GO TO Q11*

162

Q12   Where do you usually listen to the radio?
       MULTIPLE ANSWERS POSSIBLE CIRCLE ALL CODES WHICH APPLY

       At home... 1
       At friends, relative's house............. 2
       At work (office, field etc.).................3
       At school/college........................... 4
       In a bar/restaurant.......................... 5
       In a car.. 6
       On a bus.. 7
       Other (write in)............................... 8

Q13   How often do you listen to the radio? Would you say.....?
       READ LIST AND FIT ANSWER TO CODES BELOW

       Almost everyday (6 or 7 days a week).......................... 1
       Most days..2
       At least once a week.. 3
       At least once every 4 weeks...4
       Less often than that..5

Q14   Apart from today, when did you last listen to the radio?
       FIT ANSWER TO CODES BELOW

       Yesterday...................................... 1 ➞ *ASK Q15*
       Within the last 7 days.................... 2 ➞ *GO TO Q18*
       Within the last 4 weeks................ 3 ➞ *GO TO Q18*
       Within the last 12 months............. 4 ➞ *GO TO Q18*

YESTERDAY RADIO LISTENERS ONLY

Q15   Please think about the times you listened to the radio yesterday. At what time did you first begin
        listening to the radio yesterday and at what time did you stop listening?
        ONCE THE RESPONDENT HAS GIVEN THE FIRST TIME THEY LISTENED ASK:

        When did you next listen to the radio yesterday? And when did you stop listening?

        *REPEAT UNTIL THE RESPONDENT HAS GIVEN ALL THE TIMES THEY LISTENED TO THE RADIO YESTERDAY
        AND WRITE '1' NEXT TO ALL TIMES GIVEN EY RESPONDENT UNDER FIRST COLUMN 'ALL LIST'.*

        You said you listened to the radio at..............*(GIVE FIRST DME LISTENED TO)* yesterday.
        Can you remember which station or stations you were tuned in to at the time?

        *MARK THE COLUMN OF THE,STATION OR STATIONS NAMED REPEAT FOR EACH TIME THE RESPONDENT
        LISTENED TO THE RADIO YESTERDAY.*

	All listeners	ZNBC1	ZNBC2	ZNBC4	BBC	Phoenix	Icongelo	Christian Voice	Channel Africa	Other	Don't know
0500-0530											
0530-0600											
0600-0630											
0630-0700											
0700-0730											
0730-0800											
0800-0830											
0830-0900											
0900-0930											
0930-1000											
1000-1030											
1030-1100											
1100-1130											
1130-1200											
1200-1230											
1230-1300											
1300-1330											
1330-1400											
1400-1430											
1430-1500											
1500-1530											
1530-1600											
1600-1630											
1630-1700											
1700-1730											
1730-1800											
1800-1830											
1830-1900											
1900-1930											
1930-2000											
2000-2030											
2030-2100											
2100-2130											
2130-2200											
2200-2230											
2230-2300											
2300-2330											
2330-2400											
2400-2430											
2430-0500											

zaterdag

avond/nacht

18:00-0600

Wanneer u vandaag helemaal niet heeft
geluisterd, dit hokje aankruisen ───▶ ☐

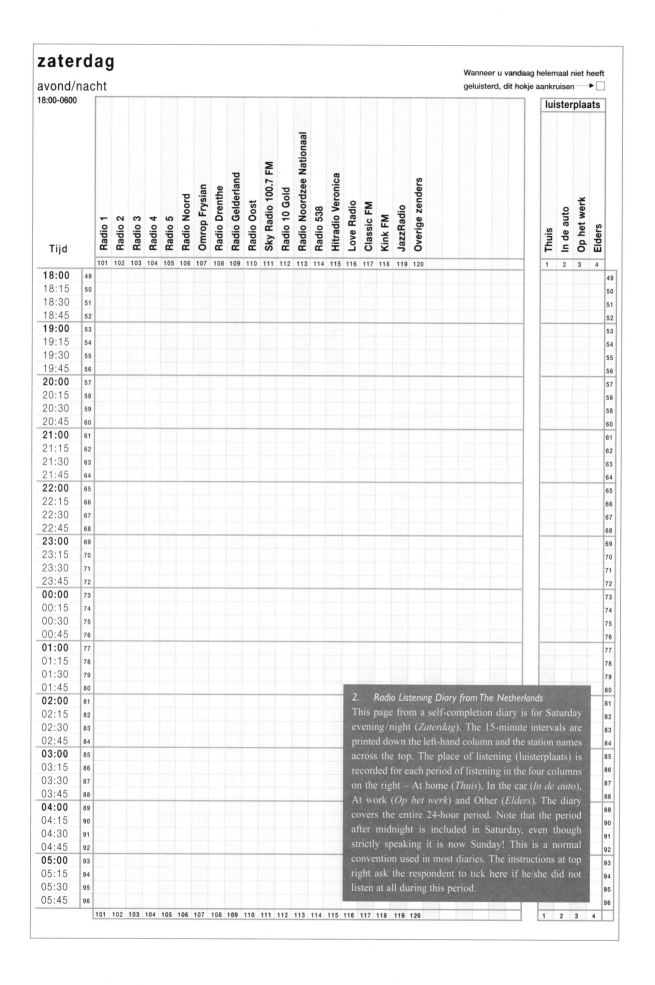

Tijd		Radio 1	Radio 2	Radio 3	Radio 4	Radio 5	Radio Noord	Omrop Frysian	Radio Drenthe	Radio Gelderland	Radio Oost	Sky Radio 100.7 FM	Radio 10 Gold	Radio Noordzee Nationaal	Radio 538	Hitradio Veronica	Love Radio	Classic FM	Kink FM	JazzRadio	Overige zenders			**luisterplaats**				
																								Thuis	In de auto	Op het werk	Elders	
		101	102	103	104	105	106	107	108	109	110	111	112	113	114	115	116	117	118	119	120			1	2	3	4	
18:00	49																											49
18:15	50																											50
18:30	51																											51
18:45	52																											52
19:00	53																											53
19:15	54																											54
19:30	55																											55
19:45	56																											56
20:00	57																											57
20:15	58																											58
20:30	59																											58
20:45	60																											60
21:00	61																											61
21:15	62																											62
21:30	63																											63
21:45	64																											64
22:00	65																											65
22:15	66																											66
22:30	67																											67
22:45	68																											68
23:00	69																											69
23:15	70																											70
23:30	71																											71
23:45	72																											72
00:00	73																											73
00:15	74																											74
00:30	75																											75
00:45	76																											76
01:00	77																											77
01:15	78																											78
01:30	79																											79
01:45	80																											80
02:00	81																											81
02:15	82																											82
02:30	83																											83
02:45	84																											84
03:00	85																											85
03:15	86																											86
03:30	87																											87
03:45	88																											88
04:00	89																											89
04:15	90																											90
04:30	91																											91
04:45	92																											92
05:00	93																											93
05:15	94																											94
05:30	95																											95
05:45	96																											96
		101	102	103	104	105	106	107	108	109	110	111	112	113	114	115	116	117	118	119	120			1	2	3	4	

2.   Radio Listening Diary from The Netherlands

This page from a self-completion diary is for Saturday evening/night (*Zaterdag*). The 15-minute intervals are printed down the left-hand column and the station names across the top. The place of listening (luisterplaats) is recorded for each period of listening in the four columns on the right – At home (*Thuis*), In the car (*In de auto*), At work (*Op het werk*) and Other (*Elders*). The diary covers the entire 24-hour period. Note that the period after midnight is included in Saturday, even though strictly speaking it is now Sunday! This is a normal convention used in most diaries. The instructions at top right ask the respondent to tick here if he/she did not listen at all during this period.

165

3. *Estonian Radio and TV Diary*

These two pages are from the self-completion diary used by the Estonian research agency Baltic Media Facts. They cover Wednesday (*Kolmapäev*) from 0530 to 1730. The next two pages, not reproduced here, cover the remaining twelve hours. Radio and TV use are separately recorded on opposite pages. Note the use of a final column on each page to record listening to audiotapes (*Kuulasin magnetofoni*) and videotapes (*Vaatasin videot*). This diary is capable of recording listening to 19 radio stations and viewing 16 TV channels. If the number of channels increases further, as it probably will, there may not be room to continue with this format.

Estonian Radio and TV Diary — self-completion diary pages for Wednesday (Kolmapäev) covering 05.30–17.30, showing radio stations (RAADIOJAAMAD) and television channels (TELEKANALID).

1. PONDELOK 7.12.1998   Nesledoval: ☐   Sledoval - Nevyplnil: ☐

4.00-15	....	1	12.00-15	....	33	20.00-15	....	65
4.15-30	....	2	12.15-30	....	34	20.15-30	....	66
4.30-45	....	3	12.30-45	....	35	20.30-45	....	67
4.45-00	....	4	12.45-00	....	36	20.45-00	....	68
5.00-15	....	5	13.00-15	....	37	21.00-15	....	69
5.15-30	....	6	13.15-30	....	38	21.15-30	....	70
5.30-45	....	7	13.30-45	....	39	21.30-45	....	71
5.45-00	....	8	13.45-00	....	40	21.45-00	....	72
6.00-15	....	9	14.00-15	....	41	22.00-15	....	73
6.15-30	....	10	14.15-30	....	42	22.15-30	....	74
6.30-45	....	11	14.30-45	....	43	22.30-45	....	75
6.45-00	....	12	14.45-00	....	44	22.45-00	....	76
7.00-15	....	13	15.00-15	....	45	23.00-15	....	77
7.15-30	....	14	15.15-30	....	46	23.15-30	....	78
7.30-45	....	15	15.30-45	....	47	23.30-45	....	79
7.45-00	....	16	15.45-00	....	48	23.45-00	....	80
8.00-15	....	17	16.00-15	....	49	0.00-15	....	81
8.15-30	....	18	16.15-30	....	50	0.15-30	....	82
8.30-45	....	19	16.30-45	....	51	0.30-45	....	83
8.45-00	....	20	16.45-00	....	52	0.45-00	....	84
9.00-15	....	21	17.00-15	....	53	1.00-15	....	85
9.15-30	....	22	17.15-30	....	54	1.15-30	....	86
9.30-45	....	23	17.30-45	....	55	1.30-45	....	87
9.45-00	....	24	17.45-00	....	56	1.45-00	....	88
10.00-15	....	25	18.00-15	....	57	2.00-15	....	89
10.15-30	....	26	18.15-30	....	58	2.15-30	....	90
10.30-45	....	27	18.30-45	....	59	2.30-45	....	91
10.45-00	....	28	18.45-00	....	60	2.45-00	....	92
11.00-15	....	29	19.00-15	....	61	3.00-15	....	93
11.15-30	....	30	19.15-30	....	62	3.15-30	....	94
11.30-45	....	31	19.30-45	....	63	3.30-45	....	95
11.45-00	....	32	19.45-00	....	64	3.45-00	....	96

Zoznan stanic: 66-video   77-teletext STV   78-teletext -ostatne stanicé

1-STV 1	25-VOX	49-Kabel 1	*/ 88-ostatné stanice
2-STV 2	26-DUNA TV	50-NBC	/okrem uvedenych/
3-MARKIZA	27-ZDF	51-TV 2	
4-VTV	28-ARD	52-Club RTL	
5-(Not in use)	29-3 SAT	53-mdr	
6-CT 1	30-POL SAT	54-TV Turiec	**/ 90-Rozne stanice
7-CT 2	31-TV POLONIA	55-Hallmark	/prepinanie stanic/
8-NOVA	32-SUPER CHANNEL		
9-CABLE PLUS	33-ARTE		
10-prima	34-CNN		
11-MTV 1	35-TV5 EUROPE		
12-MTV 2	36-VIVA		
13-ORF 1	37-VIVA 2		
14-ORF 2	38-SUPER RTL		
15-PRTV 1,2	39-TV NASA		
16-PRO 7	40-FILMNET		
17-RTL	41-HBO		
18-RTL 2	42-MAX 1		
19-RTL PLUS	43-Super MAX		
20-SAT 1	44-Kinder Kanal		
21-EUROSPORT	45-wdr		
22-MUSIC-TV	46-VH-1		
23-CARTOON-TNT	47-Discovery Channel		
24-DSF	48-Animal Planet		

4. Slovakian Television Diary

This is one solution to the problem of how to accommodate several channels. This one page from Slovakia's current self-completion television diary covers Monday (*pondelok*). Note that it has only one column in which all television viewing is to be recorded, broken into three for the whole day from 0400 to 0400. The respondent is instructed to write in a code for each station viewed and these are listed at the bottom. There are codes for 'other' stations – 88 (*ostatné stanice*) and for channel hopping or 'grazing' – 90 (*rôzne stanice*). There are also codes for video recorder – 66, teletext from Slovak TV – 77, and other teletext – 78.

Questionnaire for survey at Phoum Kroum, Cambodia, August 1998
(English version: original in Khmer)

"Good day. I am...............from the Regency College. We are doing a survey, and I'd like to ask you a few questions."

1. "Do you have a radio at home?"

Yes ❑   No ❑   Other ❑

2. "Which radio stations do you listen to at least once a week?" ... "Any others?"

FM95 ❑   FM97 ❑   FM98 ❑   FM99 ❑   FM103 ❑   FM105 ❑
NRC ❑   BBC ❑   Other....   None ❑ (if none, go to Q6)

3. "Which one radio station do you listen to most often?"

FM95 ❑   FM97 ❑   FM98 ❑   FM99 ❑   FM103 ❑   FM105 ❑
NRC ❑   BBC ❑   Other

4. "At what times of day do you listen to radio"

"Before 6am? ❑   "Noon to 3pm? ❑
"6am to 9am? ❑   "3pm to 6pm? ❑
"9am to noon? ❑   "After 6pm? ❑

5. "Which types of radio program do you prefer...

"News? ❑   "Requesting songs? ❑
"Traditional music? ❑   "Stories? ❑
"Modern music? ❑   "Education? ❑
"Talkback? ❑   "General knowledge?" ❑

6. "Do you have TV at home?"

Yes ❑   No ❑   Other ❑

7. "Which TV stations do you watch at least once a week?" ... "Any others?"

TVK ❑   Channel 3 ❑   Channel 5 ❑   Channel 9 ❑   Channel 11 ❑
Other.......   None ❑ (if none, go to Q15)

8. "Which one TV station do you watch most often?"

TVK ❑   Channel 3 ❑   Channel 5 ❑   Channel 9 ❑   Channel 11 ❑

9. "At what times of day do you normally watch TV...

"Before 12 noon? ❑
"12 noon to 4pm? ❑
"4pm to 6pm? ❑
"6pm to 8pm? ❑
"8pm to 10pm? ❑
"After 10pm?" ❑

5. Media Survey in Phoum Kroum, Cambodia
This very short and simple two-page questionnaire for face-to-face use is a typical example of something to use in an immature market, where audience research is still in its infancy and when resources are very limited. This was devised with assistance from Dennis List from Australia. Note that the time periods for recording listening and viewing are long ones (three hours) and that habitual rather than yesterday listening or viewing is recorded. Analysis of this questionnaire will be simple and straightforward but it will give adequate information in a market where previously little or nothing was known.

10. "Which types of TV program do you like to watch...

"News? ☐	"Traditional arts? ☐
"Films? ☐	"Karaoke music? ☐
"Comedy? ☐	"Romantic films? ☐
"Human rights? ☐	"Violent films? ☐
"Documentaries? ☐	"Khmer films? ☐
"Sports?" ☐	

11. "Which is the best TV station for entertainment?"

TVK ☐   Channel 3 ☐   Channel 5 ☐   Channel 9 ☐   Channel 11 ☐   Can't say ☐

12. "Which is the best TV station for news?"

TVK ☐   Channel 3 ☐   Channel 5 ☐   Channel 9 ☐   Channel 11 ☐   Can't say ☐

13. "Which is the best TV station for Khmer cultural identity?"

TVK ☐   Channel 3 ☐   Channel 5 ☐   Channel 9 ☐   Channel 11 ☐   Can't say ☐

If they do not watch TVK (in Q7-8) go now to Q15.

14. "Here are some ways that people have suggested to improve TVK. Please tell me if you agree with any of these suggestions...

"More entertainment programs? ☐	"Fewer repeated programs? ☐
"Less political news? ☐	"Fewer long speeches? ☐
"A more regular timetable? ☐	"Shorter news?" ☐

"Is there anything else you can suggest to improve TVK?"
....
....

15. Age group...

15-24 ☐	25-34 ☐
35-54 ☐	55 or over ☐

16. Sex

Male ☐   Female ☐

17. "What is your occupation?"

Student ☐	Housewife ☐
Retired ☐	Unemployed ☐

Worker —> Occupation...

18. "How many people live in this house?"
Write number of people: . . .

"That is the end. Thank you for your co-operation."

169

Issues survey 1997
Interviewers' instructions

Selecting the respondent

Only people aged 18 and over are to be interviewed, and only one person per household. And only people living in the household are to be interviewed. By 'living' is meant that this household is their main home for at least the next week.

When you reach each household, ask to interview the person aged at least 18 who last had a birthday. There is no replacement for a refusal or somebody judged unsuitable. If you can't interview the selected person, don't interview anybody else in the household. When the person you want to interview is not home but is expected before 9pm, make an appointment to ring back on a later night.

The survey area
This survey covers the whole of Australia, divided into 12 regions:

S Sydney	P Perth	4 Regional Queensland
M Melbourne	C Canberra, ACT	5 NT and regional SA
B Brisbane	2 Regional NSW	6 Regional WA
A Adelaide	3 Regional Victoria	7 Tasmania

Beginning the interview

Dial a number from a call sheet. Introduce yourself by saying:

"Hello, I'm Bertha Blowfly from Media Scan Research. We're doing a survey about radio and media use, and I need to speak to the person living in your household who last had a birthday, not counting children under 18."

When you ring a number, write in the result of that call, using these codes:

If the call wasn't answered by a live person:
G = gave up after 10 rings
E = engaged
D = disconnected
A = answering machine (don't try to leave a message)
X = fax machine (high-pitched squealing)

If the call was answered by a real live person, use these codes:
B = business number
W = wrong number
F = foreign languages
R = refusal
U = unsuitable to interview
  (eg. deaf, senile write in a brief note)
L = selected person not available, ring back
  (note name/day/time to ring)
Z = other result
  (write in a brief explanatory note)
S = started interview
M = mobile phone,
  but also have a phone at home

6. Telephone Recruitment Questionnaire from Australia: Issues survey 1997
The following example shows how listeners were recruited by telephone to take part in a survey that the Australian Broadcasting Corporation wanted to conduct. The survey sought to discover attitudes towards speech-based radio and the ways in which it was used. The survey used a postal questionnaire. The purpose of the telephone questionnaire was to find respondents. Note the very detailed instructions for the interviewer. Note the method of randomising respondents in each household by selecting the person with the most recent birthday, a simple alternative to the Kish Grid and other more complex methods.

If the number you dialled was a mobile number (beginning with 014, 015, 018, 019, or 041) ask **"Is this your only number, or do you also have another phone at home?"** If they have another phone at home, don't interview them, as this would give them two chances of being included in the survey. Code the result M. If they do not have another phone, they are eligible to be interviewed. If a call to a mobile produces the message 'switched off, or out of range', code this as G.

If the last result was W, G, E, or A, try the number again; also if it was L (an appointment), at the appropriate time. It's best to try an engaged number about 10 or 15 minutes later, a number that doesn't answer an hour or more later. If you get an answering machine, don't try again that day. After 6 unsuccessful attempts to ring a number, don't ring again unless there is an outstanding appointment.

If you get a refusal, try to get a reason for this, and note it down. Likewise if you judge the person unsuitable to be interviewed (this should be very rare) write in the reason – eg. 'deaf', 'drunk', 'senile'. If the person you have asked for is not there, get their first name and a suitable time and day to ring back, and note this.

For most respondents, the interview will take about five minutes. If people cannot spare the time to answer when you first ring, arrange to ring back later.

The questionnaire
As you read out question 2, copy from the call sheet:
• Your initials
• Today's date, eg. 3/11 for 3 November.
• The letter or number for the region code - at the top of the sheet in parentheses after the area name, eg. SYDNEY (S)
• The phone number from the call sheet. Don't copy the dash, which is only to make it easier for you to read.

Q1 We've put this first, so that you'll be less likely to forget to circle the gender code.

Q2 If the respondent doesn't listen to the radio at all, circle the 0 code, and also the 1 code in Q6. That's all.

Q3 Note that three answer codes are followed by an asterisk. Only people who give these asterisked answers will be asked to accept a mail questionnaire.

Q4 Read the first three answers from the first column, then jump up to the top of the second column and keep reading from there.

Q5 A little bit different from usual, combining employment status and occupation in a single question.

Q6 If you don't ask this question circle the 1. Otherwise read out Q6 and invite them to accept a questionnaire. If they're doubtful, don't try and talk them into it, because they probably won't return the questionnaire.

If they agree to take a questionnaire, get their name and address. Make sure you print it clearly. To help with the spelling, the call sheet contains the postcode, surname, and locality name (which will usually be right, but not always). Only fill in the phone number if it's different from the one at the top of the page.

If they ask about the questionnaire, tell them it's 4 pages long, usually takes about 10 minutes to fill in, and most people find it very interesting.

Tell them we'll send out their questionnaire within a few days, and that if they have any queries they can ring the free-call number on 1800-819-602.

ISSUES 1997 SCREENING: RADIO

Initials __ __   Date __ / __   Area __   (0_)__ __ __ __ – __ __ __ __

Q1. Note their sex:
Male 7   Female 8

Q2. **About how many hours in a typical day would you listen to radio?**
Not at all 0 __, *Finish & circle 1 in Q6*
Half an hour or less 1
About one hour 2
About 2 or 3 hours 3
About 4 or 5 hours 4
About 6 hours or more 5

· Q3. **When you're listening to radio, do you like to hear**
nearly all music, with a minimum of talk 1
or mostly music 2
or music and talk about equally 3 *
or mostly talk 4 *
or nearly all talk? 5 *
Can't say - it varies, depends on mood etc. 6

Q4. **Which of these age groups are you in:**
18 to 24? 1   **45 to 54?** 4
25 to 34? 2   **55 to 64?** 5
35 to 44? 3 ...... or /   **or 65 or over?** 6

Q5. **What is your occupation?**
If not working circle a code from 5 to 8
If working, write in occupation; only circle codes 1-4 if you are certain of the category
....

Professional, managerial 1   Student 5
Other white collar 2   Home duties 6
Blue collar, trades, manual 3   Retired 7
Farming, fishing, forestry, etc. 4 Unemployed etc. 8

End interview now (and circle code 1 in Q6) unless answer to Q3 is 3, 4, or 5 ***

Q6. **Based on the answers you've given, you're eligible to take part in our**
survey on the issues or topics covered on radio. What I'd like to do is to
post you a questionnaire covering a number of different issues. You can
fill it in when you have a moment, and post it back in our business reply
envelope. May I send you a questionnaire?
Not asked 1
Don't send questionnaire 2
Send questionnaire 3

Could I have your name and address, please?

Name *(print clearly!)*..

Postal address ....

.... Postcode ....

Phone number (0............)...

Questionnaire no. _____   sent on: _____

TV5
LA TÉLÉVISION
INTERNATIONALE

CPY 04/98

QUESTIONNAIRE TÉLÉSPECTATEURS
Cochez la ou les case(s) correspondant à votre réponse

NOM :...

Adresse :..

....

Pays :..

Êtes-vous originaire de ce pays ? ❏ Oui ❏ Non
Si non, de quel pays venez-vous ?

❏ France ❏ Belgique ❏ Suisse

❏ Maghreb ❏ Afrique Noire ❏ Québec-Canada ❏

Autre(précisez)..

Avez-vous déja répondu à un questionnaire TV5 ? ❏ Oui ❏ Non

Q 1: Quel est votre âge ?

❏ Moins de 15 ans
❏ 15 à 24 ans
❏ 25 à 34 ans
❏ 35 à 49 ans
❏ 50 à 64 ans
❏ 65 ans ou davantage

Q 2: Quel est votre sexe ?

❏ Homme ❏ Femme

Q 3: Quelle est votre situation professionnelle ?

❏ Cadre supérieur, profession libérale,
  haut fonctionnaire
❏ Cadre moyen
❏ Enseignant
❏ Employé
❏ Artisan, commerçant
❏ Ouvrier
❏ Étudiant
❏ Retraité
❏ Femme au foyer
❏ Sans profession
❏ Autres

Q 4: A quel âge avez-vous arrêté vos études ?

❏ Moins de 15 ans
❏ 15 à 17 ans
❏ 18 à 22 ans
❏ 23 ans ou plus
❏ Je suis encore étudiant(e)

Q 5: Le français est-il votre langue maternelle ?

❏ Oui ❏ Non

Q 5b: Si non, vous comprenez la langue française...

❏ Couramment
❏ Assez bien
❏ Avec difficultés

Q 6 : Choisissez la phrase qui décrit le mieux votre rapport avec TV5 :

❏ TV5 me permet d'améliorer ma
  connaissance du français

❏ TV5 est utile pour mon activité
  professionnelle

❏ TV5 me permet de mieux connaître la
  culture et le monde francophone

❏ Quand je voyage, j'aime bien regarder TV5
  pour me tenir informé

❏ TV5 me permet, grâce à ses rediffusions, de
  regarder les émissions que je n'ai pas pu
  voir sur les chaînes nationales

❏ Vivant à l'étranger, je regarde TV5 pour
  rester en contact avec ma langue ou mon pays

❏ Il m'arrive de regarder TV5 par hasard ou par
  curiosité et de m'y arrêter quelques minutes

❏ Je regarde tout simplement TV5 par plaisir,
  parce que certains programmes m'intéressent

Q 7 : Comment recevez-vous TV5 ?

❏ Par le réseau câblé de la ville
❏ Par antenne parabolique individuelle
❏ Par antenne parabolique collective
❏ Autre moyen.......................................

173

7. Postal Questionnaire used by TV5, France
TV5 is an international francophone TV channel. Its target audience is francophone people wherever the channel is shown and others interested in French language and culture. This questionnaire is sent to viewers of the channel in several countries, seeking their evaluation of TV5 programmes. It is a good example of a method of obtaining feedback from a thinly and widely scattered audience. Note that with a postal questionnaire the layout has to be more immediately attractive and less technical looking.

Q 8: **Que pensez-vous de la qualité de réception de TV5 ?**

Image ❑ Satisfaisant ❑ Pas satisfaisant

Son ❑ Satisfaisant ❑ Pas satisfaisant

Q 9: **Avez-vous accès au service télétexte TV5 ?**

❑ Oui ❑ Non

Q 10: **Vous arrive-t-il de consulter le site internet de TV5 ?**

❑ Souvent ❑ Parfois ❑ Jamais

Q 11: **En général, combien de fois par semaine regardez-vous les programmes de TV5 ?**

❑ Tous les jours ou presque

❑ Quelques fois par semaine

❑ Moins souvent

Q 12: **A quelle(s) heure(s) regardez-vous habituellement TV5 ?**

❑ 6h-10h30   ❑ 18h30-20h
❑ 10h30-12h30 ❑ 20h-22h
❑ 12h30-14h30 ❑ 22h-minuit
❑ 14h30-18h30 ❑ minuit-6h

Q 13: **Vous arrive-t-il de regarder TV5 en dehors de votre domicile ?**

❑ Oui ❑ Non

Q 13b: **Si oui, où ?**

❑ Chez des amis
❑ A l'hôtel
❑ Autre (précisez)...

Q 14: **Quel(s) genre(s) de programmes aimez-vous plus spécialement regarder sur TV5 ?**

❑ Information
❑ Musique
❑ Magazines & documentaires
❑ Films et téléfilms
❑ Jeux / divertissement
❑ Théâtre
❑ Programmes jeunesse
❑ Sport
❑ Cours de français

Q 15: **Quelles sont les émissions que vous appréciez le plus sur TV5 ?**

....
....
....

Q 16: **Quelles émissions appréciez-vous le moins sur TV5 ?**

....
....
....

Q 17: **Avez-vous récemment remarqué des changements sur TV5 ? Lesquels et qu'en pensez-vous ?**

....
....
....
....
....
....
....
....
....
....
....
....
....
....
....
....
....
....
....
....
....
....

Q 18: **Comment vous informez-vous le plus souvent sur nos programmes ?**

❑ Par la presse nationale quotidienne
❑ Par un magazine de programmes TV
❑ Par l'hebdomadaire de programmes TV5
❑ Par le télétexte de TV5
❑ Par les bandes-annonces diffusées à l'antenne
❑ En téléphonant à TV5
❑ En consultant le site internet TV5

Merci de nous avoir accordé un peu de votre temps et à bientôt...sur TV5 !

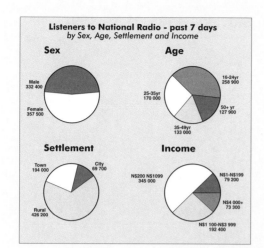

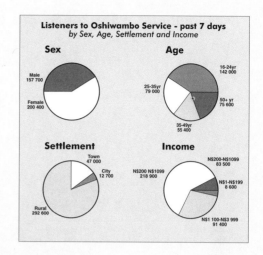

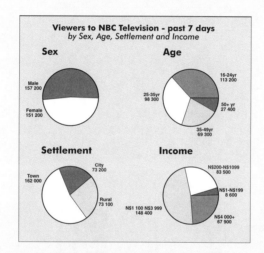

1. *Namibian Broadcasting Corporation Audience Data*
These 'pie charts' compare the profiles of the three of its networks with the greatest weekly reach – the National Radio in English, NBC Television, mostly in English and the Oshiwambo language radio service. Note that projected numbers in the population are used here rather than the percentages on which they are based. There are no rules in this matter; all is a matter of preference and practice.

Development of Market Shares in Slovakia 1995, 1996, 1997

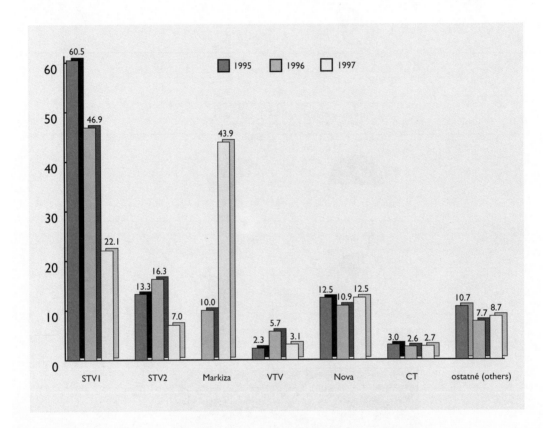

2. *Slovakia – Trends in TV Shares*
This chart, produced by Slovak TV's Research and Inform-ation unit, uses bar charts also known as histograms. It shows the steep loss of share by the main public TV channel, STV1 as the new private channel Markiza rapidly built up its share soon after its launch in 1996. The other private channel VTV has had much less impact. Nova is the main private Czech TV channel and CT is the public one. (Ostatne means 'other'). VTV began terrestrial broadcasts on 22 April 1995 and Markiza began on 31 August 1996.

EBU	EURO-FACTSHEET	GEAR
	MEDIAFACTS - AUSTRIA	AUT/media/9.97

	1997
Adult Population (in millions, age basis 10+)	6,984
Private Households (in millions)	3,131
Gross Domestic Product (US $/month/capita)[1]	2,440
Knowledge of English (in % of adult population)	53
CONSUMER ELECTRONICS (in % of households)	
Telephone	95,7
Mobile Telephone[2]	8,6
At least 1 TV-Set	96,3
At least 1 Colour TV	95,7
Multiple Set Households[2]	46,5
TV with Stereo Sound[2]	49,0
Wide-Screen Receiver (16:9)[2]	5,0
Teletext	60,5
At least 1 Videorecorder	65,7
Videogames Console[2]	12,3
At least 1 Personal Computer	31,3
CD-ROM Equipped Personal Computer	21,1
Compact Disc Player	70,2
At least 1 Car Radio	74,0
Car Radio Having RDS Capability	N/A
Modem	8,8
Access to the Internet or Other On-line Services	4,5
MULTI-CHANNEL-HOMES (in % of TV-HH)	72,4
Cable-Households (in % of TV-HH)	37,5
Households with Private Satellite Dish (in % of TV-HH)	26,9
Satellite Master Antenna Households (in % of TV-HH)	8,1
Percentage of Households Subscribing to at least 1 Pay-TV Service (See Attached Definitions)	3,0
Percentage of Households Subscribing to at least 1 Pay-per View Service (See Attached Definitions)	–

3. Austria – Euro Factsheet
Data can be shown in simple table or list format rather than in charts. These Factsheets produced by ORF's audience research department, are in a standard format developed by and for the Group of European Audience Researchers, (GEAR), which links together audience research professionals from all over Europe. Standardised data enable meaningful comparisons to be made between countries. ORF audience research department, which produces these figures for GEAR and the European Broadcasting Union, also adds in data for other countries where these are available. I have included these pages because I believe the Factsheets are an excellent model for wider international use.

ADVERTISING LIMITS	public	commercial
TV	30 min/day for each ORF channel	max. 12 min/h, max.90 min/day
Radio	115 min/day for all nat. ORF channels together; 5 min/day for each reg. ORF channel	max.12 min/h, max.90 min/day

ADVERTISING GROSS REVENUE[3]	1.519
TV	23,02%
Radio	10,70%
Papers	39,03%
Magazines	17,67%
Outdoor	7,01%
Others	2,56%
Licence Fee (Colour TV + Radio p.a. in US $)[4]	226

[1] 1996 data, US$ exchange rate as of 31.12.1996
[2] In % of population 14+
[3] 1996 data, in million US $, US $ exchange rate as of 31.12.1996
[4] US $ exchange rate of 25.9.1997
ORF/Audience Research, Wurzburgasse 30, A - 1136 Vienna, Tel: +43/1/87878/2264, Fax: +43/1/87878/2743, E-mail: judith.stelmach@orf.at

(c) GEAR 1997

177

EBU   **EURO-FACTSHEET**   **GEAR**
AUT/tv/9.97

TELEVISION DATA - AUSTRIA
(Ranked by 24 Hrs. Share)

TV Households (in millions): 3,005

Adults in TV-Households (in millions, age basis 12+): 6,660

1. Cable-Households (in % Of TV-Households): 37,5
2. Households with Private Satellite Dish (in % Of TV-Households): 26,9
3. Satellite Master Antenna Households (in % Of TV-Households): 8,1
4. Multi-Channel-Homes (=1+2+3): 72,4

Name of TV-channel	P or C [1]	Channel profile [2]	National data							Multi-channel-HH 24 Hrs. share (in %)
			Coverage (in % of TV-HH)	Min. of daily Viewing	Daily share (in %)	Weekly reach (in %)	24 Hrs. share (in %)	Prime time share (in %)	Max. 1/4 hr. (in %) [3]	
ORF 2	P	G	100	53	50.1	N/A	36,3	44,0	19,6	29,0
ORF 1	P	G	100	37	45,8	N/A	25.3	23.8	10,1	19,6
RTL	C	G	66	9	18,0	N/A	5,9	4,5	2,1	8,1
PRO7	C	G	64	8	16,6	N/A	5,4	4,5	2,1	7,4
SAT.1	C	G	66	8	16,5	N/A	5,3	3,9	1,9	7,2
RTL2	C	G	64	4	12,7	N/A	2,9	2,6	1,2	4,0
ARD	P	G	69	4	13,8	N/A	2,8	2,9	1,3	3,3
ZDF	P	G	69	3	11,4	N/A	2,3	2,4	1,2	2,7
Kabel 1	C	G	50	3	7,4	N/A	2,2	1,8	0,8	3,0
VOX	C	G	60	3	8,9	N/A	1,9	1,5	0,6	2,6
BFS	P	G	63	2	8,7	N/A	1,3	1,3	0,7	1,5
Super RTL	C	G	37	2	5,6	N/A	1,2	1,2	0,6	1,6
Eurosport	C	S	59	2	6,6	N/A	1,1	0,7	0,3	1,4
3sat	P	C	63	1	7,1	N/A	0,9	0,8	0,5	1,2
DSF	C	S	47	1	4,8	N/A	0,6	0,4	0,2	0,8
DRS	P	G	36	*	2,1	N/A	0,3	0,3	0,1	0,3
VIVA	C	MU	16	*	1,5	N/A	0,2	0,1	*	0,3
MTV	C	MU	25	*	1,3	N/A	0,1	0,1	*	0,2
n-tv	C	N	43	*	1,9	N/A	0,1	0,1	*	0,2
CNN	C	N	39	*	0,5	N/A	*	*	*	*
All Domestic Public TV	P	G	100	91	62,1	N/A	61,6	67,8	25,0	48,6
All Domestic Comm. TV	C	-	-	-	-	-	-	-	-	-
All Foreign TV	P/C	-	72	56	41,4	N/A	38,2	32,1	14,1	51,2
TV total / Any TV	P/C	-	100	147	68,0	N/A	100,0	100,0	38,5	100,0

Age basis	-	-	-	12+	12+	12+	12+	12+	12+	12+
Reference Period	-		January - June 1997							

[1] P = Public TV, C = Commercial TV

[2] Code for channel profile - see diagrams

[3] Maximum average rating per quarter hour (in %)

(c) GEAR 1997

ORF/Audience Research, Wurzburgasse 30, A - 1136 Vienna, Tel: +43/1/87878/2264, Fax: +43/1/87878/2743, E-mail: judith.stelmach@orf.at

EBU

EURO-FACTSHEET

GEAR
AUT/radio/9.97

RADIO DATA - AUSTRIA
(Ranked by 24 Hrs. Share)

Radio Households (in millions): 3,131

Adults in Radio-Households (in millions, age basis 10+): 6,984

Name of radio channel with short description (Only national radio channels)	P or C 1)	Daily national reach (in %)	Min. of daily listening	24 hrs. national share (in %)	Max. 1/4 hr. (in %) 2)	Avg. 1.4 hr. 6,00-18,00 (in %)
O2 - family and regional programme	P	38,6	77	43	15,0	9,5
O3 - news, pop music, sports	P	37,8	73	41	12,4	8,6
Antenne Steiemark - commercial regional radio in Styria	C	4,5	9	5	1,4	1,0
O1 - serious music, literature, science	P	5,2	6	4	1,6	0,7
Blue Danube Radio/FM4 - programme in + F/ programme for young people	P	2,3	3	1	0,4	0,3
Radio Melody - commercial regional in Salzburg	C	1,7	3	2	0,5	0,3
Bayern 3 - public from Germany	P	0,8	1	1	0,2	0,1
Antenne Bayern - commercial from Germany	C	0,6	2	1	0,3	0,2
Radio Uno - commercial from Italy	C	0,6	1	0	0,2	0,1
Radio Lindau - commercial from Germany	C	0,1	0	0	0,0	0,0
SWF 1-3 - public from Germany	P	0,1	0	0	0,0	0,0
DRS 1-3 - public from Switzerland	P	0,1	0	0	0,0	0,0
All Domestic Public TV	P	73,6	159	89	29,1	19,1
All Domestic Comm. TV	C	6,2	11	7	N/A	N/A
All Foreign TV	P/C	4,6	8	4	N/A	N/A
TV total / Any TV	P/C	78,8	178	100	31,6	21,3

Age basis	-	10+	10+	10+	10+	10+
Reference period	-	January - June 1997				

1) P = Public TV, C = Commercial Radio
2) Maximum average rating per quarter hour (in %)

(c) GEAR 1997

179

ORF/Audience Research, Wurzburgasse 30, A - 1136 Vienna, Tel: +43/1/87878/2264, Fax: +43/1/87878/2743, E-mail: judith.stelmach@orf.at

EBU **EURO-FACTSHEET** **GEAR**

AUT/general/9.97

Country: AUSTRIA

Number of domestic radio channels

National		Regional		Local	
Public	Commercial	Public	Commercial	Public	Commercial
3	0	9	2	3	~10

Number of domestic television channels

National		Regional		Local	
Public	Commercial	Public	Commercial	Public	Commercial
2	0	9	0	0	16

Continuous radio research

Method	Name of operation	Sample / Panel size	Date of introduction	Main contractor	Period of contract
Telephone	Radiotest	24.000/year	1993	Fessel	1996-1998

Continuous television research

Method	Name of operation	Sample / Panel size	Date of introduction	Main contractor	Period of contract
People meter	Teletest	1200	1991	Fessel/ifes	1996-2000

(c) GEAR 1997

ORF/Audience Research, Wurzburgasse 30, A - 1136 Vienna, Tel: +43/1/87878/2264, Fax: +43/1/87878/2743, E-mail: judith.stelmach@orf.at

EBU   EURO-FACTSHEET   GEAR

DEFINITIONS

PAY-TV:
A televised programme service, normally of a specialised nature (eg feature, sport, etc.) available on payment of an additional subscription.

Pay-per-View
A payment system allowing the purchase of access to individual programmes selected in advance.

Channel codings:

A - Adult
C - Cultural
CH - Children's
D - Documentary
E - Entertainment
ED - Educational
ET - Ethnic
G - Generalist
M - Movies
MU - Music
N - News/Information
R - Religious
S - Sport
SE - Series
SH - Shopping
T - Travel
Y - Youth

181

Brazil Urban Areas 1993
Average Daily Listening and Viewing Times (n=4,031)

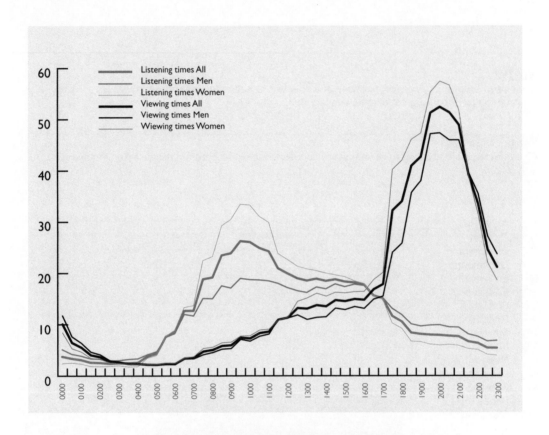

Legend:
- Listening times All
- Listening times Men
- Listening times Women
- Viewing times All
- Viewing times Men
- Wiewing times Women

4. Viewing and Listening Times – Chart from Brazil
This chart was taken from a national survey of Brazil's urban areas commissioned by the BBC World Service in 1993. The sample was designed to represent about 80 million people. It shows how times of viewing and listening can appear in chart form. This 'line chart' is the generally preferred method. Note the typical patterns of listening and viewing found in many parts of the world. Radio listening peaks in the morning – but at 1000, rather later than in most other countries. Television viewing peaks in the evening at between 2130 and 2200, also rather later than in most countries. It demonstrates data separated to show behaviour by demographic group and the difference between Brazilian men and women. We could also look at difference in age groups, occupation or social class, etc. Another useful analysis would be to compare listening and viewing times for the different stations.

Bibliography

Ang, Ien, *Desperately Seeking the Audience*, London and New York: Routledge, 1991.

This book is highly regarded by many scholars in the study of mass communications. It is a good antidote to a lot of what is written today about television. She reminds those of us who talk about 'the audience' that it is really not something that has much meaning! This very readable book, which is required reading on many university communications studies courses, points out that numbers and ratings hide the realities of how people actually view television. Viewers in the real world are active, social human beings with a wide variety of different ways of using and relating to the medium.

Bell, Judith, *Doing Your Own Research Project*, Buckingham: Open University Press, 1987

A rarity for this kind of research – a best seller! A brilliantly clear, concise and readable study book for students doing sociological or educational research for the first time. Full of practical advice and common sense. It is also inexpensive.

Berger, Arthur Asa, *Media Research Techniques*, Thousand Oaks, London and New Delhi: Sage, 1998.

Relates a whole range of research techniques to their use in studying the media. Written mainly for students of communications it has especially good sections on qualitative research with some good examples and exercises.

Beville, Hugh Malcolm, *Audience Ratings: Radio, Television and Cable*. Hillsdale, NJ: Lawrence Erlbaum Associates, 1988.

Traces the origin and development of radio and TV ratings in the United States and describes how it is done today, with a (now somewhat dated) look to the future. This book is a standard audience research teaching book in the United States, where audience research is almost entirely dominated by the needs of commercial advertisers.

Birn, Robin, Hague, Paul and Vangelder, Phyllis, *A Handbook of Market Research Techniques*. London: Kogan Page, 1990.

A comprehensive guide to the whole field of contemporary commercial market research. It focuses on the industry as it is in Britain, but there are many useful descriptions of how market research is done, including some of the most recent developments.

Breen, George and Blankenship, AB, *Do-It-Yourself Marketing Research*, New York: McGraw-Hill, 1989.

A business-oriented guide for companies without the resources to commission agencies to do their market research. It is useful for anyone else in this position.

Buttle, Francis (ed.), *Relationship Marketing*, Thousand Oaks, London and New Delhi: Sage, 1996

A description of this new development in marketing which places great emphasis on developing and maintaining relationships between the supplier of goods or services and the customers. It has special relevance I believe for broadcasters in an increasingly competitive market.

Casley, DJ and Lury, DA, *Data Collection in Developing Countries*, Oxford: Clarendon Press, 1981

An account of some of the problems of research in non-industrialised countries, this book provides solutions, with many examples from research experience.

Duverger, Maurice, *Introduction to the Social Sciences*, London: George Allen and Unwin, 1961

A classic originally written in French and in my view one of the very best basic books on the main methods of social investigation on which all market research is or should based.

Epstein, T Scarlett, *A Manual for Culturally Adapted Market Research (CMR) in the Development Process*,
Bexhill-on-Sea: RWAL Publications, 1988

A short but convincing argument for the use of market research to improve the performance of development projects and a concise outline of how to do it.

Epstein, T Scarlett, Gruber, Janet and Mytton, Graham, *A Training Manual for Development Market Research (DMR) Investigators*, London: BBC World Service, 1991,

A short and inexpensive training manual designed to be used to teach market research methodology in a way that is suitable in a variety of different cultural situations. The authors view is that market research techniques when suitably adapted to local conditions would assist the development process in poor countries. The book's dedication is 'to those who, in serving the poor, seek first to find what they want and need.' Copies may be obtained by post by writing to the BBC World Service Shop, Bush House, London, WC2B 4PH at a cost of UK£8 (US$14) including airmail postage.

ESOMAR, International Codes and Guidelines. (These are published in English, French and German, unless otherwise stated.

ICC/ESOMAR *International Code of Marketing and Social Research Practice* (Also in Spanish).
ESOMAR *Guide to Opinion Polls (Including the ESOMAR International Code)* (English only).
Guideline *Interviewing Children.*
Guideline *Selecting a Research Agency.*
Guideline *Tape and Video-recording and Client Observation of Interviews and Group Discussions* (Also in Spanish).
Guideline *Harmonisation of Fieldwork Standards* (English only)
Guideline *Standard Demographic Classification: A System of International Socio-economic Classification of Respondents to Survey Research* (English Only).
All the above are available free of charge from ESOMAR, JJ. Viottastraat 29, NL 1071 JP, Amsterdam, The Netherlands. Email: publications@esomar.nl and on the Internet at http://www.esomar.nl/codes_1.html

Fink, Arlene, *The Survey Kit*, Thousand Oaks, London and New Delhi: Sage, 1995 (9 volumes).
All you probably ever need to know about doing surveys, from planning to reporting. Each of the volumes is also available separately. One of the volumes *How to Measure Survey Reliability and Validity* by Mark Litwin is a valuable and inexpensive short guide to this subject.

Fink, Arlene, *How to Conduct Surveys*, Thousand Oaks, London and New Delhi: Sage, 1998.
An up-to-date outline of methodology with a good account of the latest computer-assisted methods, new data analysis techniques and ways of testing reliability.

Gordon, Wendy and Langmaid, R, *Qualitative Market Research: A Practitioner's and Buyer's Guide*, Aldershot: Gower, 1988.
One of the best and most comprehensive accounts of commercially oriented qualitative market research.

Hague, Paul and Harris, Paul, *Sampling and Statistics*
A basic and inexpensive guide to the subject by two market research practitioners specially for the market research profession.

Hague, Paul and Jackson, Peter, *Do Your Own Market Research*, London: Kogan Page, 1998.
A business-oriented manual with good practical advice for the non-specialist. Similar to the Breen and Blakenship book listed above.

Klapper, Joseph T, *The Effects of Mass Communication*, New York: Free Press, 1960.
A classic in the field of books on the effects of modern media.

List, Dennis, *Radio Survey Cookbook*, Adelaide: Australian Broadcasting Corporation, Audience Research Department, 1990.
An excellent, inexpensive, practical manual on audience research, with many practical tips from many years experiences in Australia and also some developing countries. This book can easily be purchased by post. For details see footnote 35.

McCrossan, Liz, *A Handbook for Interviewers*, London: HMSO, 1991.
A short and inexpensive guide to interviewing techniques and best practice, this book is written from the perspective of the British Government's Social Survey Division within the Office for National Statistics. It is one of the best available publications on this topic written by someone who knows from personal experience.

McDonald, Colin, *How Advertising Works*, Henley: NTC Publications, 1992.
An excellent account for the non-expert of how advertising works. It is mainly drawn from UK experience but has a wider relevance.

McKee, Neill, *Social Mobilisation and Social Marketing in Developing Communities: Lessons for Communicators*, Penang: Southbound, 1992.
A challenging and very readable argument for the use of marketing in promoting solutions to the widespread problems in developing countries of poverty, ignorance and disease. McKee works for UNICEF and his wide experience of training and advocacy in this field makes him a valued and respected authority whose case for the greater use of social marketing deserves to gain wider currency and acceptance.

McQuail, Denis, *Audience Analysis*, Thousand Oaks, London and New Delhi: Sage, 1997.
Like Ien Ang's book, this is an academic, scholarly study of the relationships between people and modern media. McQuail questions, as do many, the concept of audience and whether it will continue to have any relevance as the media undergo even greater changes.

Moores, Shaun, *Interpreting Audiences*, Thousand Oaks, London and New Delhi: Sage, 1993.
A book written within the academic field of communication studies looking at media consumption ethnographically. The book draws mainly on qualitative research and provides valuable insights into cultural aspects of the way that modern media are consumed in the home.

Morgan, David L and Krueger, Richard A, *Focus Group Kit*, Thousand Oaks, London and New Delhi: Sage, 1997. (6 Volumes).
Like The Survey Kit by Arlene Fink listed above, this is a multi-volume boxed set giving a comprehensive explanation of how to run focus group qualitative research. Each of the volumes is also available separately.

Morgan, David L, *Focus Groups as Qualitative Research*, Thousand Oaks, London and New Delhi: Sage, 1997.
An academic book on the theory and practice of focus groups, with many examples from best practice in the field. Examples are mostly from non-commercial research.

Morse, Janice M (ed.), *Completing a Qualitative Project*, Thousand Oaks, London and New Delhi: Sage, 1997.
The writer collaborated with 21 others in the production of this book. She is a professor of nursing and draws on experience of the use of qualitative research in that field. There is a valuable section on reporting the findings of qualitative research to the public arena, including the media. This book was actually produced with the assistance of focus group discussions on the topic.

Moser, Claus A and Kalton G, *Survey Methods in Social Investigation*, London: Heinemann Educational Books, 1971.
Like the Duverger book, a classic in this field and is still relevant and valid today. Claus Moser's great strength is in quantitative analysis. But he is a man of many skills and talents and this shows in his ability here to make complex and technical matters make sense.

Silvey, Robert, *Who's Listening?* London: George Allen and Unwin 1974., p14.
This account of the early history of audience research is long out-of-print. I have included it here because it is an outstanding example of how audience research was developed for what I believe is its most vital and worthwhile function, that of understanding audiences and improving the programmes and services made available to them, not for profit or the benefit of the broadcaster but as a public service.

Robson, Sue and Foster, Angela (eds.), *Qualitative Research in Action*, London: Edward Arnold, 1989.
One of the most authoritative books on qualitative research edited by (and some of it also written by) two of Britain's leading practitioners.

Rogers, Everett M, *Modernisation Among Peasants: The Impact of Communication*, New York: Holt, Rinehart & Winston, 1969.
A rare academic work on the topic – one that actually uses plenty of strong empirical evidence from field research to show the impact of media among the rural poor. The book uses much evidence from Colombia with some comparative data from Kenya, Turkey, India and elsewhere. This book, written thirty years ago, is still one of the best in this academic field.

Søgaard, Viggo, *Research in Church and Mission*, Pasadena: William Carey, 1996.
A book written with churches and Christian organisations particularly in mind, encouraging them to use survey research. It gives a comprehensive and well-explained outline of methods and guidance on analysis and presentation.

Twumasi, PA, *Social Research in Rural Communities,* Accra: Ghana Universities Press, 1986.
An account of actual research activity in poor rural areas with some case studies.

Vogt, W Paul, *Dictionary of Statistics and Methodology*, Thousand Oaks, London and New Delhi: Sage, 1993.
A non-technical guide for the non-specialist, and written with people doing social and market research especially in mind.

Weisberg, Herbert F, Krosnick, Jon A and Bowen, Bruce D, *An Introduction to Survey Research, Polling and Data Analysis*, Thousand Oaks, London and New Delhi: Sage, 1997.
A good basic textbook on the subject with a good outline of the problems that can be encountered.

Wimmer, Roger D and Dominick, Joseph R, *Mass Media Research: an Introduction*, Belmont, California: Wadsworth, 1991 (3rd Edition). Like the similar book by Beville, an account of methods used in the United States to research media audiences.

185

Glossary of Terms

Ad Hoc

Describes single research projects designed for a specific purpose in contrast to continuous or repeated projects.

Agency

Market research companies that carry out market / media / audience research for clients. Often known as research agencies.

Aided Recall

A way within a questionnaire of assisting respondents to remember things that may not be at the front of their minds, by reminding them through associated events or items. See also Awareness. In audience research aided recall is used to assist people to remember what radio or TV programmes and networks they have listened to or viewed. In readership research it is used to assist respondents to remember what they have purchased and/or read.

Area tests

A term used in research when the effects of a campaign through the media is tested by comparing behaviour, knowledge, awareness, response etc in an area where the messages have been communicated with one where they have not.

Attitude

Reacting or responding in a favourably or unfavourably to given objects. In the field of audience research this usually means networks, programmes, presenters of programmes, personalities on screen or in sound, styles of presentation, types of content, etc.

Awareness

Awareness of products, services, networks, programmes, personalities, magazine or press titles, advertisements and so on, can be measured through surveys using structured questionnaires. Often changes in awareness are tracked over time in tracking studies. Awareness can be measured spontaneously and/or with prompting.

Back Check

A check by the supervisor in a quantitative survey that an interview has taken place and was properly carried out. Checks can be done by telephone or personal visit to the respondent. Usually a percentage of back checks is routinely carried out by research agencies.

Base

The base number used in calculating percentages shown on a typical table of the results of quantitative research. When weighting has occurred, the weighted base is the number used to calculate percentages whereas the unweighted base is the actual number of respondents in the sample or sub-sample being analysed.

Brand

A product or service which has an identity and a name that is consistently used. The brand name can take on attributes in the minds of the public. In the field of the media, branding becomes increasingly important as the number of available channels, especially in radio and television, increases.

Breakdown

Sub-groups used in analysis. These are usually based on demographic data collected during a survey which are used to 'break down' results into different social or other categories.

Brief

A research brief is a statement of what is required from the research. It forms the basis for the contract between the commissioner and the supplier of the research. The subsequent research and any reports written should at all times be guided by and refer back to this initial brief.

Briefing

Research projects usually involve many people and briefing them – explaining to them very thoroughly the purpose of the research and their part in it – is of great importance.

Call-back

A second or subsequent attempt to contact someone chosen for interview.

Census

A collection of information from everyone within a population, as distinct from a sample.

Chi (or χ)-squared

A statistical test for comparing distributions of numbers. In market and audience research it is most often used to help us know whether a comparison we make of data from a random survey or surveys is significant or not. There are other statistical tests that can be used but chi-squared is the most widespread. See further explanation and tables in Appendices.

Coding

Codes are assigned to answers in questionnaires in order that they may be entered into a computer for analysis. Each question or item of data being collected has a column number or numbers assigned to it into which the codes are entered. Coding is relatively straightforward except when dealing with open-ended questions when codes have to be worked out and assigned after the fieldwork is finished.

Computer Assisted Telephone Interviewing (CATI)

When interviewing is done over the telephone, there is no need to use pen and paper with printed questionnaires. All the questions and most of the possible responses can be displayed on a computer screen. The interviewer can read out the question and enter the responses of the person being interviewed as instructed on the screen.

Continuous Research

Research which is repeated at regular intervals, usually for the same clients. Good examples are many of the media surveys, including self-completion diaries described in this book. The RAJAR and BARB research in the UK for radio and television respectively are good examples of continuous research.

Demographics

The basic variables that we use to classify a lot of quantitative data – sex, age, education, social grade or class and marital status, usually make up the typical demographics used in analysis. There are others.

Face-to-Face Interviews

The term is used to describe interviewer-respondent encounters in a quantitative survey when a structured questionnaire is used and answers are recorded simultaneously.

Flow

A word used to describe audience movement between networks especially at the times when programmes change.

Focus Group or Discussion

A basic method of qualitative research used to explore attitudes and behaviour and relying on group dynamics and social relationships.

Hall Tests

A test of a product or service for which a hall is hired and people invited to come in, try the product or service and give their opinions of it.

Household

A very variable thing. But we need a definition that will work everywhere and is consistent. The usual definition of a household is a dwelling place, building or buildings (or boat, caravan etc.) in which one or more persons live together and where the costs of food and other normal everyday household expenses and requirements are managed together.

Joint Industry Committees

These often exist to co-operate in media research. For example, newspaper and magazine publishers, the advertising agencies and advertisers may come together in order jointly to fund and direct readership measurement, rather than each of them conducting their own separate surveys. Joint industry committees exist in several European as well as some Asian and a few African countries for radio, television and press readership research. In Zimbabwe and South Africa there is co-operation between all media and some consumer products also in those countries' *All Media and Products Surveys* – AMPS in South Africa and ZAMPS in Zimbabwe. There is also NAMPS in Namibia.

Kish Grid

A table of numbers to be used when selecting a member of a sampled household.

Life-Style

Sometimes this is used as a classification in market research to denote a way of life or sub-culture within a society, illustrated by tastes, fashions, interests and opinions, rather than the usual demographics of social class, age, sex etc. There are many life-styles than can be defined and they tend to vary greatly between cultures. Life-styles are likely to become ever more important in audience research as the number of radio and TV stations increase and become identified with and appeal to different social groups or groups with different life-styles. Life-style segmentation is often especially helpful when analysing and researching youth cultures.

Mean

The arithmetical average of a set of figures.

Median

The middle number in a set of figures, with half the remainder being larger and half smaller.

Mode

The most frequently recorded value in a set of figures or results.

Moderator

The trained professional researcher who leads a focus group.

Objectives

Any proposal for research requires clearly stated objectives which will usually emerge from a perceived problem(s) or issue(s) that requires answers in order for decisions or action to be taken.

Occupation

Often used to classify respondents into social grades or classes.

Omnibus Surveys

A survey in which different clients put questions relating to their different products and services. Many countries have regular media omnibuses collected data on different media for different clients. Sometimes there may be no clients prior to the survey but the agency organising the survey designs it in such a way as to cover different products and services and then offers the results for sale. These are usually referred to as Syndicated Surveys.

Overclaim

A tendency, more common in some societies and social groups than others, for respondents to say that they have done or achieved more than is actually the case.

Panels

A sample of people who are asked to take part in survey research on more than one occasion or continuously. Panels are often used for research using diaries, for example recording television and radio use.

Penetration

A figure, usually expressed as a percentage, which states the proportion of a population with a certain characteristic – eg. satellite dish or cable connection.

Pilot

The name given to a preliminary survey in which a questionnaire is tested or field workers trained.

Population

The whole target group from which a sample is taken in survey research. The word may refer to the whole population, the adult population or any defined group within it.

Postal or Mail Survey

Survey in which the questionnaire or diary is completed by the respondent and returned to the research agency by post.

Pre-Test

A test of something before it is put on to the market. It is frequently used for advertising and often also for radio and television programmes.

Probability

Word expressing the likelihood of something occurring. It is also used to describe sampling based on random principles.

Probe

A technique used in questioning, in both qualitative and quantitative research in which the field researcher uses verbal or other prompts to elucidate further an answer or answers that have been given.

Profile

Characteristics of people in terms of various chosen characteristics which might include demographics, behaviour, household equipment, tastes etc.

Quota Sample

A form of non-random sampling of a population in which the interviewer has quotas of different categories of people to select and interview. It is less complicated than any random method, costs less money and is widely used in market and opinion research. The quotas are constructed in such a way as to represent accurately the population being studied.

Random Sample

There are various types of random sample, described in the text. In each case each individual in the population has a more or less equal chance of being selected.

Ratings

Widely used in radio and television research to describe the audience for a network or programme, usually at a specific time. An audience rating is usually expressed as a percentage of people in a given population at a given time who are listening to station.

Reach

This measure is used to refer to the percentage of the population who listened to or watched at least some of a programme, or a network, or service or group of services during a day or week. There are three common uses: *Programme Reach, Daily Reach* and W*eekly Reach.*

Refusal Rate

The number of people, expressed as a percentage of those contacted, who refuse to take part in a survey.

Reliability

A measure of the extent to which a questionnaire or any other research method produces similar results on different occasions or when used by different people.

Sample

A selection made from a population usually for the purpose of a representative quantitative survey.

Sample Size

The number of units in a sample.

Sampling Error

Any estimate taken from a survey is likely to be different from the true value for the population as a whole. The term *standard error* is often used to refer to this. There are ways of calculating the likely range of error within the rules of probability theory.

Sampling Frame

A construct of some kind enabling us to take a sample in a consistent way. Electoral lists, telephone directories, members' registers, attendance registers, street maps or census enumeration area lists could all be used as sampling frames or the basis for creating such frames. The frame should be used in such a way as to give each member of the population being sampled an equal or near-equal chance of selection.

Share

The proportion of a market accounted for by a particular product or service within a certain category. In television and radio it is calculated by adding up the amount of time spent listening or viewing the different channels and expressing figures for each channel as a percentage of all listening or viewing.

Show Card

Often used when dealing with list questions in which a respondent is asked to select an answer from a pre-written list. The list may be out to the respondent, or the interviewer shows a card for the respondent to read from.

Social Grade or Class

It is difficult to devise a scheme for socio-economic classification that can be used everywhere. The system used in Britain and some other countries is as follows: Something like it is probably required in most countries, but is often difficult to achieve. The social grade of any respondent in most surveys is based on the occupation or former occupation of the head of the household. (In some cultures this may not be the most appropriate way to classify the status of the entire household.)

Social Grade	Social Status	Occupation
A	Upper class	Higher managerial / administrative / professional
B	Middle class	Intermediate managerial / administrative / professional
C1	Lower middle class	Supervisory or clerical and junior managerial / administrative / professional
C2	Skilled working class	Skilled manual workers
D	Working class	Semi and unskilled workers
E	Those at lowest levels	State pensioners and widows with no other income, casual workers, long term unemployed

As this book went to press, the classification system in Britain was being changed.

Structured

Describes a questionnaire and it means that the wording and order of questions is set out precisely – in a structured way.

Universe

See Population.

Validity

The degree to which a chosen method will ensure that what is measured or described reflects reality.

Weighting

A process that is used to alter data sets so that under-representation or over-representation of certain sub-groups in a sample is corrected by applying numerical weights. The purpose is to ensure that each population sub-group has the appropriate numerical size in relation to others. Post-weighting – that is weighting at the analysis stage – is very commonly used in market and audience research to correct any imbalances in the demographic profile of a sample. For example, if we found that we had achieved a sample with 45% of it female and the population as a whole was 50% female, we might weight all female respondents by a factor of 1.11 and all male respondents by a factor of 0.91. In practice weights are more complex involving combinations of corrections for combinations of age, sex, social grade and education.

References

1 Radio is now growing rather more slowly than it was. Later we will look at data from some of the poorer areas of the world which show that there seems to be a large number of very poor people who do not appear to be moving into the modern world of the electronic media. The proportion of people out of touch with any modern means of communication may have stopped getting smaller.

2 Population Reference Bureau, *World Population Data Sheet*, New York: Populations Reference Bureau, 1998.

3 *World Radio and Television Receivers,* London: BBC World Service Marketing Information, 1997.

4 Sydney Head, *World Broadcasting Systems*, Belmont: Wadsworth, 1985.

5 Tom Lewis, *Empire of the Air*, New York: Harper, 1991; Sydney Head, and Christopher Sterling, *Broadcasting in America*, (6th Edition), Boston: Houghton Mifflin, 1990.

6 Matthew Chappell and CE Hooper, *Radio Audience Measurement*, New York: Stephen Daye, 1944, p2.

7 Quoted in Peter Menneer, Broadcasting Research: Necessity or Nicety? *Intermedia*: May 1984, Vol.12, No.3.

8 Robert Silvey, *Who's Listening?* London: George Allen and Unwin, 1974, p14.

9 See later section on sampling and statistics, pp32-36.

10 http://www.meadev.gov.in/map/indmap.html

11 WG Blyth and LJ Marchant, 'A Self-Weighting Random Sampling Technique', *Journal of the Market Research Society*, Volume 15, No.3, 1973, pp157-162.

12 Graham Mytton, *Listening, Looking and Learning*, Lusaka: University of Zambia, 1974.

13 Jonathan Lynn and Antony Jay, *The Complete Yes Prime Minister*, London: BBC Books, 1989, pp106-107.

14 Rajeshwar Dyal, *Cable Television: Glitter or Doom*, New Delhi: Indian Institute of Mass Communication, 1992

15 For more on pilot testing, see section 3.3.

16 Namibia All Media and Products Survey questionnaire, 1996.

17 Ibid.

18 Maurice Duverger, *Introduction to the Social Sciences*, London: George Allen and Unwin, 1961, pp148-149.

19 For a fuller examination of the audience measurement problem see Peter Menneer, 'Towards a Radio 'BARB' – Some Issues of Measurement', *ADMAP*, February 1989, pp42-5.

20 DJ Casley and DA Lury, *Data Collection in Developing Countries*, Oxford: Clarendon Press, 1981, p95.

21 Ghana Broadcasting Corporation, Audience Research Department internal memorandum.

22 Computer programmes can be used to facilitate this process. With computer-assisted telephone interviewing, it is automatic.

23 Chappell and Hooper, *op.cit.* pp.219-220. The word 'flow' is used to describe how audiences move between programmes and networks. It is usually expressed as a measure of where the audience came from and where it goes after each programme or daypart. See the *Glossary of Terms* in the Appendices.

24 The meters are under development as this book goes to press. There are three rival companies developing rather different technical solutions to the problem of measuring what the person carrying the device hears. The technologies should, if successful, be able to measure not only radio listening but television also, provided that the TV sound is audible. See Graham Mytton, 'Turn on, tune in and get measured by your watch', *Research* (the monthly journal of the Market Research Society, London), June 1998, pp32-33.

25 Toby Syfret, 'Worldwide Round-up of National Peoplemeter Systems' in Television Business International Yearbook 98, London: Financial Times, 1997, pp540-542.

26 Hugh Malcolm Beville Jr., *Audience Ratings*, New Jersey: Lawrence Erlbaum, 1988, p88.

27 Ibid. pp98-98.

28 For details of how most countries in Europe measure radio and television audiences see ESOMAR *1995 Report on Radio and Television Audience Measurement in Europe* and *Report on Radio Audience Measurement in Europe 1997.* Amsterdam: ESOMAR 1995 and 1997.

29 Robert Silvey, *op. cit.* p64.

30 Ibid. p65.

31 Ibid. *op.cit.* p92.

32 Ibid.

33 Ibid. p97.

34 The word 'omnibus' is often used in commercial market research to refer to regular quantitative surveys for which there may be several clients. One questionnaire carrying questions for these different clients is used. Media omnibuses, which carry questions solely about the media and for media clients are sometimes used. See *Glossary of Terms*.

35 Dennis List, *Radio Survey Cookbook*, Adelaide: Australian Broadcasting Corporation, Audience Research Department, 1990. The reputation of this excellent training manual, produced specifically for local Australian radio stations, soon

spread and the ABC received requests from many countries around the world. Dennis List decided therefore to produce an international edition, designed mainly for use in developing countries. Realising that telephone interviews were not suitable in many countries, he focuses attention in the new edition on other simple and low-cost methods. Readers of my book are strongly recommended to obtain a copy of the new version. It covers much of the same ground as this manual, but I find that using more than one source always helps learning. Dennis List also deals with many practical issues and problems, some of which I have neither the space nor the experience to cover here. The international edition is Dennis List, *Audience Survey Cookbook Simple Audience Survey Techniques for Broadcasters and Others, International Edition*, Adelaide: Australian Broadcasting Corporation, 1997. Copies can be obtained for 30 Australian dollars (about 20 US dollars). It can be ordered from ABC Audience Research, GPO Box 9994, Adelaide, South Australia 5001. Dennis List runs an Internet website http://www.tou.com/host/andres

[36] BK Khurana, 'Mechanism of Feedback for Rural Television', *Communicator*, April 1984, pp26-40, and personal communication from BS Chandrasekhar, July 1998.

[37] This is why great caution should be exercised when referring to any audience or media data produced about India. Many sources about TV and radio audiences in India are derived from research conducted only in the towns. See for example Julia Petersen and Tanuka Roy, 'The Indian Dilemma. A Volcano Waiting to Erupt', *Electronic Media and Measurement Trends – on a Collision Course?* ESOMAR/ARF Worldwide Electronic and Broadcast Audience Research Symposium, Vienna 26-28 April 1998. Amsterdam: ESOMAR, 1998, pp83-99.

[38] You may note that when some major sporting event like the World Cup or the Olympics are being televised globally, announcers will sometimes speak of one or even two billion viewers, or similarly very large figures. These are obviously impossibly high estimates and arise largely from exaggerated projections made from very limited data from developed and industrialised urban areas where some TV research is done to rural areas where almost always it is not.

[39] Robert Silvey, *op. cit*, p83.

[40] Peter Jenkins and Richard Windle, 'The New Listening Panel', in *Annual Review of BBC Broadcasting Research Findings* No.11, 1985, pp37-44.

[41] See Francis Buttle (ed) *Relationship Marketing*, London: Sage, 1996.

[42] Eila Romo, 'A Burmese Research Study – Over the Air', *Ricefields Journal*, Vol. III No1, March 1990, pp5-7.

[43] Pamela Reiss, 'Continuous Research for Television and Radio: The 1980s Approach', *Annual Review of BBC Broadcasting Research Findings*, No.8, 1981/2, pp13-26.

[44] Heloïse van den Berg and Henk van Zurksum, 'Now Listen and Pay Attention', Hilversum: NOS, no date.

[45] David L Morgan, *Focus Groups as Qualitative Research*, Thousand Oaks, London and New Delhi: Sage, 1997, pp1-13.

[46] P Lunt and S Livingstone, 'Rethinking Focus Groups in Media and Communication', *Journal of Communication*, 1996, No.46, pp79-98.

[47] There are codes of conduct to which all professional market researchers subscribe. ESOMAR's *International Code of Marketing and Social Research Practice* is probably the most widely used and is obtainable by post from ESOMAR, JJ Viottastraat 29, 1071 JP Amsterdam, The Netherlands. It is also available on the Internet at http://www.esomar.nl/codes_l.html There is a list of this and other guidelines in the bibliography.

[48] 'The BBC in Egypt: Social Context and Station Image' BBC World Service, International Broadcasting Audience Research, 1986. The remarkable thing about this and other similar studies in many parts of the world is that the BBC World Service has a very similar image and reputation virtually everywhere – reliable but with a tendency to being a bit dull or old-fashioned. It is something that the World Service is making a great effort to change, maintaining the reliability but at the same time trying to appear more interesting, lively and friendly.

[49] Anne Laking and Mick Rhodes, 'QED: Research for a Second Series', *Annual Review of BBC Broadcasting Research Findings*, No.9, 1983, pp118-120.

[50] Arthur Asa Berger, *Media Research Techniques*, Thousand Oaks, London and New Delhi: Sage, 1998, p107.

[51] David Silverman, *Interpreting Qualitative Data*, Thousand Oaks, London and New Delhi: Sage, 1993, p147.

[52] Jerome Kirk and Marc L Miller, *Reliability and Validity in Qualitative Research*, Thousand Oaks, London and New Delhi: Sage, 1986.

[53] BK Khurana 'Research in Doordarshan', *Communicator*, January 1987, pp6-17.

[54] If you want to do content analysis, there are relevant sections in the Berger, Duverger and Moser books listed in the bibliography. For more detail see K. Krippendorf, *Content Analysis*, Thousand Oaks, London and New Delhi: Sage, 1980.

[55] Neill McKee, *Social Mobilisation and Social Marketing in Developing Communities: Lessons for Communicators*, Penang: Southbound, 1992.

[56] See especially Joseph T Klapper, *The Effects of Mass Communication*, New York: Free Press, 1960. Klapper shows through his review of several studies, that the media seldom operate directly and alone. Their influences and effects are mitigated by intervening influences.

[57] Anne Wicks, 'Advertising Research' in Robin Birn, Paul Hague and Phyllis Vangelder, *A Handbook of Market Research Techniques*, London: Kogan Page, 1990, pp317-334.

[58] 'HEA AIDS Advertising: The effective use of mass media advertising to meet the challenge of AIDS' in The Institute of Practitioners in Advertising, *Advertising Works 8*, Henley on Thames: NTC Publications, 1994, pp51-79. *Advertising Works* is an annual publication of the IPA that publishes examples of research showing the effects of advertising, mainly in Britain.

[59] Ibid. p79.

[60] 'National Dairy Council: The riddle of Twin Peaks', in The Institute of Practitioners in Advertising, *Advertising Works 8*, Henley on Thames: NTC Publications, 1994, pp419-439.

[61] Ibid. p421.

[62] Ibid. p424.

[63] Ibid. p435.

[64] Godfrey Baseley, *The Archers: A Slice of My Life*, London: Sidgwick and Jackson, 1971.

[65] Peter W Vaughan, Everett M Rogers, Ramadhan MA Swahele and Verhan Bakari, 'Preliminary Findings of *Twende na Wakati* Effects on Family Planning Adoption and HIV/AIDS Prevention in Tanzania: 1993 to 1997', Paper presented at the Voice of America/United States Agency for International Development's Broadcasting for Child Survival Conference, Gallaudet University, Washington DC, April 1998.

[66] Two books are recommended for students wishing to understand media research from a wholly commercial and US perspective. Both have been produced for students of the subject. They are Hugh Malcolm Beville Jr, *Audience Ratings: Radio, Television, Cable*, Hillsdale, New Jersey, 1988, (Revised Student Edition); and Roger D Wimmer and Joseph R Dominick, *Mass Media Research: an Introduction*, Belmont, California: Wadsworth, 1991 (Third Edition).

[67] NB. Radio audience data are usually provided in three categories – weekdays and Saturdays and Sundays. In this hypothetical example, we have ratings for different hour periods or dayparts.

[68] Note that here and elsewhere I have used only one decimal point. In my view to use more implies a level of accuracy which is rarely, if ever, justified.

[69] Timeshift refers to programmes that are video-recorded at the time of transmission and viewed later. Peoplemeters are able to measure this and will report if the programme(s) recorded are actually viewed.

[70] BARB, *This Week's Viewing Summary*, Week Ending 26 April 1998. This chart and the following one include what is referred to as 'timeshift' viewing. People who use their video-recorder to record a programme in order to watch later are included in the audience figures for that programme provided that the programme is actually viewed within a certain period of time. The TV meters are designed to measure and record this behaviour.

[71] Graham Mytton, 'How Well Does Radio Reach the Poor?', Broadcasting for Child Survival: Conference Papers, Washington: Voice of America, 1998.

[72] *Trends in Radio Listening Quarter 1 1998*, BBC internal document. Classic FM, Talk Radio, Virgin Radio and Atlantic 252 are all commercial radio stations audible nationally in the UK. But the most popular commercial radio stations are the local ones, here grouped together as 'Any Local Commercial Radio'.

[73] Eleanor Cowie, 'Trends in Radio Listening 1991' in BBC Broadcasting Research Department, *Annual Review No 18*, London: John Libbey, 1992, pp9-15.

[74] Michael Brown, 'Media Research', in Robin Birn, Paul Hague and Phyllis Vangelder, *A Handbook of Market Research Techniques*, London: Kogan Page, 1990, pp334-345.

[75] For details of how readership is measured in Europe see *Readership Measurement in Europe: 1996 Report on Newspaper and Magazine Readership in Europe*, Amsterdam: ESOMAR, 1996.

[76] T Scarlett Epstein, *A Manual for Culturally Adapted Research (CMR) in the Development Process*, Bexhill-on-Sea: RWAL Publications, 1988, p27. See also T Scarlett Epstein, Janet Gruber and Graham Mytton, *A Training Manual for Development Market Research (DMR) Investigators*, London: BBC World Service, 1991.

[77] Rosemary Whewell, Former Research Director, National Radio, Wellington, personal communication, 1992.

[78] Nora Rizza, 'Television Images', RAI, no date.

[79] GBC Audience Research Department: Internal Memorandum, no date.

[80] GBC has had an audience research department for several years, and from long before it lost its broadcasting monopoly. Until the establishment of similar departments in the state broadcasting systems of Zambia, Namibia, Malawi, Zimbabwe, Senegal and a few others, GBC had the distinction of being the only broadcaster in sub-Saharan Africa with an audience research department, outside South Africa.

[81] Jaroslav Kostál, Audience Research Director, Czech Radio, personal communication, 1992.

[82] BK Khurana, Former Director of Audience Research, Doordarshan, New Delhi, personal communication, 1992.

[83] *Cable and Satellite Europe*, January 1996, p19

[84] BBC World Service surveys commissioned by audience research department between 1995 and 1998.

Appendices

[85] J Murdoch and JA Barnes, *Statistical Tables*, London: Macmillan, 1986 (Third Edition).

[86] PG Moore, *Principles of Statistical Techniques*, London: Cambridge University Press, 1969 (Second edition), p204.

[87] This table was provided by Continental Research, a major media and market research agency in the UK.

[88] This table was provided by MORI, a major market research agency in the UK.

191